W9-DHI-396

The Politics of Language in the Spanish-Speaking World

'Clare Mar-Molinero's work is readable, informative and thought provoking . . .
[It] should be of interest to language educators and planners, historians, and
political scientists as well as to linguists, Hispanists, and Latin Americanists
of many stripes.'

Jonathan Holmquist, Temple University, Philadelphia, USA

'A well-organised, readable account of complex and important issues.'

Ralph Penny, Queen Mary and Westfield College, London

Spanish is now the third most widely spoken language in the world after
English and Chinese. This book traces how and why Spanish has arrived at
this position, examining its role in the diverse societies where it is spoken
from Europe to the Americas.

Providing a comprehensive survey of language issues in the Spanish-speaking
world, the book outlines the historical roots of the emergence of Spanish or
Castilian as the dominant language, analyses the situation of minority
language groups, and traces the role of Spanish and its colonial heritage in
Latin America.

Throughout the book Clare Mar-Molinero asks probing questions such as:
How does language relate to power? What is its link with identity? What
is the role of language in nation-building? Who decides how language is
taught?

Clare Mar-Molinero is head of Spanish Studies at Southampton University.
An experienced author, Clare Mar-Molinero's previous publications include
The Spanish-Speaking World (Routledge) and the BBC course *Paso Doble*.

The Politics of Language
Series editors: Tony Crowley,
University of Manchester
Talbot J. Taylor,
College of William and Mary, Williamsburg, Virginia

In the lives of individuals and societies, language is a factor of greater importance than any other. For the study of language to remain solely the business of a handful of specialists would be a quite unacceptable state of affairs.

Saussure

The Politics of Language series covers the field of language and cultural theory and publishes radical and innovative texts in this area. In recent years the developments and advances in the study of language and cultural criticism have brought to the fore a new set of questions. The shift from purely formal, analytical approaches has created an interest in the role of language in the social, political and ideological realms and the series will seek to address these problems with a clear and informed approach. The intention is to gain recognition for the central role of language in individual and public life.

Other books in the series include:

Broken English
Dialects and the Politics of Language in Renaissance Writings
Paula Blank

Verbal Hygiene
Deborah Cameron

Linguistic Ecology
Language Change and Linguistic Imperialism in the Pacific Region
Peter Mühlhäusler

Language in History
Theories and Texts
Tony Crowley

Linguistic Culture and Language Policy
Harold F. Schiffman

English and the Discourses of Colonialism
Alastair Pennycook

The Politics of Language in Ireland 1366–1922: A sourcebook
Tony Crowley

The Politics of Language in the Spanish-Speaking World

From colonisation to globalisation

Clare Mar-Molinero

London and New York

First published 2000
by Routledge
2 Park Square, Milton Park, Abingdon, Oxon, OX14 4RN

Simultaneously published in the USA and Canada
by Routledge
270 Madison Ave, New York NY 10016

Routledge is an imprint of the Taylor & Francis Group

Transferred to Digital Printing 2005

© 2000 Clare Mar-Molinero

Typeset in Garamond by
BC Typesetting, Bristol

All rights reserved. No part of this book may be reprinted or
reproduced or utilised in any form or by any electronic, mechanical,
or other means, now known or hereafter invented, including
photocopying and recording, or in any information storage or
retrieval system, without permission in writing from the
publishers.

British Library Cataloguing in Publication Data
A catalogue record for this book is available from the British Library

Library of Congress Cataloging-in-Publication Data
Mar-Molinero, Clare, 1948–
    The politics of language in the Spanish-speaking world/Clare Mar-Molinero.
        p.   cm. — (The politics of language)
    Includes bibliographical references and index.
    1. Language and languages — Political aspects.   2. Spanish language — Political aspects.
    3. Language and education.   4. Language planning.   5. Nationalism.
    I. Title.   II. Series.
    P119.3.M36 2000
    460′.9′0904–dc21   99-058473

ISBN 0–415–15655–6 (pbk)
ISBN 0–415–15654–8 (hbk)

Contents

Acknowledgements

Many friends and colleagues have contributed to my writing this book. I cannot possibly list all of them, many of whom are fellow members of the School of Modern Languages at Southampton University. I would like to mention a few in particular. I am especially conscious of the extra burden I placed on my colleagues in the Spanish section during the period of study leave I was generously given. I am very grateful to Bill Brooks, Alan Freeland, Romay Garcia, Florence Myles, Alison Piper and Vicky Wright for their moral support and cheerfulness when needed, and their astonishing belief that I would see this to completion. I am particularly appreciative of the encouragement and support from Patrick Stevenson and Henry Ettinghausen, who read parts of the draft manuscript. I would also like to express my thanks to Professor Ralph Penny and the two anonymous reviewers of the book for their constructive and positive suggestions. Finally, I must record my thanks to my family, my husband, children and brother, for their interest in the project and their patience and help in achieving it. My three children Daniel, Kevin and Vanessa are living examples of the complexities of the politics of language in the Spanish-speaking world!

Introduction

California decides to abandon its programme of bilingual education for children of Spanish-speaking immigrants; the front-runners in the US presidential campaign, George Bush jnr and Al Gore, seek to outdo each other with the use of Spanish in their election speeches; the King of Spain opens the 1992 Olympics with a welcome in Catalan; Spanish-speaking Argentina is invited to send representatives to the annual Welsh Eisteddfod; *Granma*, the newspaper of the Cuban Communist Party, is published in English; the European Union agrees not to abolish the ñ from its official documents. What all these events have in common is that they represent in some way the inter-relationship between issues of language and those of politics and society. All are taken from situations in parts of the Spanish-speaking world; many more could be drawn from any other speech community in any other part of the world.

This book is about the political role of language and languages, in particular in the vast area of the Spanish-speaking world. This area is defined as those places where Spanish is either an official language, as in Spain and many countries of Latin America, or a language of a significant-sized speech community, as with the case of the *Latinos* in the US.[1]

Throughout I shall seek to answer a series of interconnecting questions regarding the political role of language in society. These range from:

- How is language linked to power?
- What is its link with identity and, in particular, with national identity?
- What part does language play – consciously or unconsciously – in nation-building?
- To what extent is language a tool in nationalists' agendas?

through to the ensuing questions such as:

- How does language affect a community's everyday life and behaviour?
- How is language taught and learnt?
- Who decides the above questions?

- What language or language-related policies exist?
- What resources are available to use, or learn, or promote languages?

These and many other questions provide the framework for the discussions of the political role of language in societies where Spanish is spoken sometimes as the only language, sometimes alongside other mother tongues, often as the dominant language, but occasionally in a minority situation.

Along with many other terms and concepts discussed in the book, the term 'language' is of course not unproblematic. Most would agree that when we use the word 'language' we are referring to a means of communication to transmit thoughts, ideas and information. Where we might be less in agreement is over what these forms might take. They may range from the verbal or written, to many other visual and non-verbal modes of communication. In the discussion of the role of language in education in Part III these issues will be further explored.

Of more immediate interest here is what we mean by '*a* language' and how we classify these – e.g. Spanish, Catalan, English, Welsh, etc. These too, it can be argued, are largely political constructs if, for example, we are trying to distinguish a 'language' from a 'dialect'. Common factors used to make this distinction usually include the size of the speech community who use a particular form, and the degree of mutual comprehensibility. However, working from the first criterion many would find it difficult to justify the division into languages of, for example, Norwegian, Swedish and Danish. Whilst using the definition of 'mutual comprehensibility' as a means of defining dialects of the same language it is hard to support the term 'dialect' being used to cover the range of forms of Chinese usually referred to in this way.

We must look for other factors that determine the choice of terms. So often these factors reflect political and social attitudes and pressures. They also reflect the contemporary interpretation of political maps. In this way forms of speech identified as characteristic of a particular nation often become national 'languages' marked off by political national borders, whereas differences *within* states are frequently seen simply as 'dialects'.[2] The Romance language continuum is an excellent example of this, as we shall see in later chapters where we explore the terminology used to describe, for example, Castilian or Catalan, Galician or Portuguese.

The book has been divided into four parts which move from the broad issues of identity and language to the specific outcomes of policies and educational practices. Throughout, the discussion is illustrated by examples from the Spanish-speaking world, as well as detailed case studies of specific countries. However, the introductory chapter in the first three parts – i.e. Chapters 1, 4 and 6 – serves to set the theoretical framework for the themes of the section, and therefore focuses very little on examples from the Spanish-speaking world.

Part I examines the important relationship between language and nationalism. Chapter 1 synthesises the work of some of the major writers on the study of nationalism, highlighting in particular the importance of the nationalist movements in the late eighteenth and the nineteenth centuries. Many of these writers specifically discuss the role of language in nation-building and in the construction of national identity. This will help form the basis from which to explore this role in the Spanish-speaking world.

Chapter 2 traces the origins and spread of Spanish as the result of imperial and colonialist designs, while Chapter 3 contrasts the dominance of Spanish with the competing and conflicting speech communities coexisting with it.

Part I shows how nation-building in the Spanish-speaking world is indeed closely related to attitudes to and the use of Spanish, or Castilian – even the issue of what to call this language is relevant to the overall argument. This section will focus somewhat predominantly on Spanish in the Iberian Peninsula, although by no means exclusively. This is unavoidable given that it is the birthplace of the Spanish language and because the political explanations for the later spread of the language must be traced from here. This should not be interpreted as a eurocentric bias, rather as an acceptance and understanding that many of the issues of the book have developed and influenced policies in the way they have precisely because so often dominant groups are indeed eurocentric in their outlook and their behaviour.

In Part II those general principles about rights and political organisation which are introduced with the idea of nation-building and colonial expansion are further explored specifically through an examination of models of Language Planning and particularly language policies in the Spanish-speaking world.

Again we move from the general to the specific cases of Language Planning in Spain and Latin America. In Chapter 4 we look at the issues raised by an understanding of linguistic rights, such as the conflict between collective and individual rights and how this affects language policies and language use. The link with territory in this equation is clearly important. Chapter 5 examines the post-Franco 1978 Constitution and ensuing legislation in Spain in detail for an understanding of language policies and linguistic rights. It then discusses how far the situation of linguistic rights and linguistic empowerment has improved in Latin America since the post-Independence period of monocultural nation-building.

Part III recognises that education is the single most important element in Language Planning and language policies, as well as a fundamental element in national identity forming. Chapter 6, therefore, outlines how language and education are linked by discussing issues of bilingual education and empowerment through access to language education. As an example of the link between language, identity and nationhood this section focuses also on adult education and literacy programmes amongst minority groups. Chapters 7, and 8, examine examples from Latin America and Spain.

In the concluding section, Part IV, we will speculate on the future of Spanish, both in terms of its vitality as a language in national contexts, and as a world language of international importance. Chapter 9 will therefore examine a part of the Spanish-speaking world that has not yet been discussed but which is in fact an area where the Spanish-speaking population is increasing at a significant rate, the case of the Spanish-speakers, or *Latinos*, in the US. Linked to this discussion, although clearly having much in common with other Central American and Caribbean countries, is Puerto Rico because of its special US status. In the case of the US we will be particularly interested to observe the situation of Spanish when, unusually, it is the minority, marginalised language of an underprivileged community. In the case of Puerto Rico, of particular interest is the phenomenon of the 'returning migrant', that circular condition of immigration and return that Puerto Rico's unusual relationship with the US has created. With improved high technology travel and an increasing breaking down of national frontiers at the start of the twenty-first century, the likelihood of more regular movements, including returning immigrants, seems a real possibility across the world. The stresses and challenges that this presents to people's sense of identity may well become an issue of far wider relevance than just the case of Puerto Ricans.

In Chapter 10, the concluding chapter, the role of language in society, and, in particular, in the Spanish-speaking world, is examined in this post-modern world of globalisation and high technology. Supra-national organisations may now be challenging the traditional nation-state, and, with this, notions of national identity. What will the role of Spanish in a supra-national Europe be? How does Spanish as a world language stand alongside English and other major global languages? Is there a 'Latin American' identity comparable to the emerging 'European' one? Is Spanish challenged in the places where it is spoken by other competing supra-national lingusitic and ethnic groupings, such as a Quechua-speaking community? Is there, in fact, any real meaning to the term 'the Spanish-speaking world'? These are questions we try to address in the concluding chapter.

It is important to stress that the focus throughout is on the *politics of language* and the way these operate in the Spanish-speaking world. Grillo (1989: 7–21) gives an excellent summary of current definitions of the field of the politics of language. Of his three main categories, which range from the macro to the micro observation of 'the political in language and the linguistic in politics' (Grillo, 1989: 21), this book will focus almost exclusively on the most macro — what Grillo terms 'language as political object'. He defines this as,

> the study of the relationship between language and social differentiation in the formation of national systems. The political is defined by reference to large-scale inter- and intra-national relationships, predominantly those pivoting on the nation-state, and the politics of language are about ways in which the domains of language use are defined by the forces which determine those relationships.

(Grillo, 1989: 8)

In no way, then, does this book claim to be a comprehensive sociolinguistic review of language in all the countries which are broadly included in the Spanish-speaking world. There is no attempt to do a country-by-country breakdown, and examples are taken for their intrinsic interest or as a generalised model. I hope to plug gaps and offer directions for further research through the bibliographical references.

I am only too aware of the dangers of using unanalytically defined existing categories which are themselves products of particular ways of interpreting the very issues discussed here. For this reason, I use the term 'Latin America' for convenience but with unease. I am, of course, only referring here to the Spanish-speaking areas of America. It is as a geographical area with a shared colonial history that I use this term. In the same way the name 'Spanish' or 'Castilian' has to be challenged and defined. Importantly, we need to realise that these terms hold different meanings for different speakers of the (more or less) same language. The matter is further complicated by the different nuances and understandings these terms have in English as opposed to Spanish. However, one of my principal aims in this book is to encourage and create a sensitivity to the issues of definition when working in the area of the politics of language. Many questions will be raised and I do not claim to answer them all.

Some readers may also feel that Spain looms disproportionally large in this discussion of the Spanish-speaking world. It is certainly true that Spain is often the focus, but I defend this on the grounds that Spain is still perceived in much of the Spanish-speaking world as the *madre patria*, hated or loved though she may be. It is hard, if not impossible, therefore, not to find Spain assuming a central role in much of the explanation and contextualisation of the configuration of the contemporary society, culture and politics of this Spanish-speaking world.

Part I

Spanish as national language

Conflict and hegemony

1 Language and nationalism

One of the principal reasons why language plays a part in the political life of most societies derives from another defining aspect of language not mentioned in the Introduction. Not only does language have an instrumental role as a means of communication, it also has an extremely important symbolic role as marker of identity. How else can we explain the fact that although humans communicate through language, they have allowed the creation of endless barriers by sustaining thousands of mutually incomprehensible modes of communication? Why has one *lingua franca* not emerged as the only normal way that humankind communicates? The answer must lie in an innate need and desire to protect difference across groups and communities. In this way language is inextricably bound up with defining this difference.

Such communities are described in many different ways – ethnic groups, tribes, regions, nations, states, etc. – but, over the past two hundred years at least, the most common unit into which the globe is divided is that of 'nation', 'state' or 'nation-state'. The formation and construction of these is often the result or object of nationalism. It is hardly surprising, then, that the relationship between language, on the one hand, and nationalism and the construction of national identity, on the other, is so important.

Theories of nationalism

This chapter, therefore, will seek to establish some definitions for the many terms and concepts surrounding the discussion of language and nationalism. Nationalism as a subject for debate has been significant since the late eighteenth century, but it has taken on a flurry of academic and media interest in recent years. Besides the very weighty literature on the subject,[1] specialist journals, conferences, TV documentaries, media interviews, and other such outlets discuss, examine and argue what nationalism is and what its effects are on our daily lives. In this relatively short discussion below, I can only hope to synthesise some of the main arguments in these debates and to find a path through the complex discussions which leads above all to a useful starting point for the focus on the role of language, and, ultimately, how this can be observed in the Spanish-speaking world.

One such debate concerning nationalism is over whether we are talking about a relatively recent phenomenon of some two hundred or so years, or whether in fact its roots lie in the depths of time.[2] To some extent which viewpoint we take depends on how we define nationalism. I would suggest that most definitions of nationalism agree that it must involve a sense of community based on self-conscious shared characteristics and with some form of political aspiration. It seems reasonable to agree with those who contend that nationalism is an age-old phenomenon, that communities have probably always bonded together aware of those things they have in common, and prepared to protect themselves against those from the outside who are different. This community can then be defined as a 'nation'. However, it is in the level of importance attached to political aspirations where the more modern concept of nationalism is relevant. This political aspiration may often (but not always) involve the creation of a 'state'. For many commentators the modern state, and nationalist movements who help create them, are the result of modernisation and industrialisation, with the loss of the old order, the rise of capitalism, the introduction of vernacular languages and the regionalisation of elites.

Gellner (1983) defines nationalism as 'primarily a political principle, which holds that the political and the national unit should be congruent' (1983: 1), and then goes on to say:

> Two men are of the same nation if and only if they share the same culture, where culture in turn means a system of ideas and signs and associations and ways of behaving and communicating . . . A mere category of person (say, occupant of a given territory, or speakers of a given language, for example) becomes a nation if and when the members of the category firmly recognize certain mutual rights and duties to each other in virtue of their shared membership of it.
>
> (Gellner, 1983: 7)

Alter (1991) writes:

> Nationalism exists whenever individuals feel they belong primarily in the nation and whenever affective attachment and loyalty to that nation override all other attachments and loyalties . . . Individuals perceive themselves . . . as members of a particular nation [and] they identify with its historical and cultural heritage and with the form of its political life.
>
> (Smith, 1991: 9)

Kedourie (3rd edn 1993) describes nationalism as a doctrine which,

> holds that humanity is naturally divided into nations, that nations are known by certain characteristics which can be ascertained, and that the

only legitimate type of government is national self-government.

(Kedourie, 1993: 1)

Smith (1991) defines nationalism as,

> An ideological movement for attaining and maintaining autonomy, unity and identity on behalf of a population deemed by some of its members to constitute an actual or potential 'nation'.

(Smith, 1991: 73)

In all these definitions the 'nation', or shared community, is recognised as having certain common characteristics. These may, but need not necessarily, include some or all of the following: a common language, race, religion, cultural traditions, history, body of laws, and territory.

A state on the other hand is better defined as a political construct, marked out by borders which can be artificially drawn. Maps are man-made artefacts frequently decided as the result of power struggles, often wars. Elements associated with states are institutional, such as governments and legal systems, armies and administration. Alter (1991: 11) paraphrases Max Weber's definition of a state as the body that imposes boundaries with the ultimate right to defend and control them.

Confusion can arise in the relationship between these two – nation and state. In the vast majority of cases states are not congruent with nations. Nations often straddle political state boundaries (such as in the case of the Catalans or the Basques in Spain and France, or the Aymara nation in the Andes). Or they may be enclaves within states, such as the Welsh in Britain. The history of nation-building however is so often that of the triumph of the majority or the most powerful who have swept minority communities to one side in order to create a monocultural society for their state. Sometimes this has been done unconsciously and, even with benevolent intentions. Assimilation to the majority norm was considered a way of being inclusive and of empowering everyone. This, indeed, was the philosophy of post-revolutionary France in the early stages of national identity building there. In other instances the obliteration of minorities has been deliberate and oppressive, or at the very least suppressive through neglect. There are many examples in the last two centuries of such attempts to construct national identities at the expense of the weak or marginalised, not least in both Spain and Latin America. This type of nationalism which sought to make the state homogeneous with one set of national characteristics leads to the creation of the nation-state, which is such a common phenomenon in the Western world, and partly responsible for the emergence of many nationalist separatist movements in the latter part of the twentieth century.

Nationalism, then, can be said to be a feeling, a consciousness, an ideology, forming a movement to harness these sentiments and to attain greater self-determination or even independence. What emerges from the literature on the subject, as can be seen in some of the quotations above, is that different emphases exist in terms of the nature of these objectives. This difference is often (somewhat crudely) divided into the categories of 'political' nationalism and 'cultural' nationalism (Alter, 1991; Fishman, 1972) or 'subjective' and 'objective' nationalism (Alter, 1991). The nation conceived of in political nationalism is sometimes referred to as the 'civic' nation (which far more closely resembles a 'state'), whilst cultural nationalism is associated with an 'ethnic' nation. The former, too, fits better with the modern/instrumentalist view of nation-building, whilst the 'ethnic' nation is seen as that community with roots in a far-off historic past built on myths and shared memories. These binary definitions of the nation and nationalism are inevitably over-simplified and in fact many of their elements overlap, which has, rightly, led many to question these dichotomies.[3] Nonetheless, these categories are commonly used and are useful for observing the different goals and ideologies of diverse nationalist movements.

Alter describing political/subjective nationalism explains how:

> A process of domestic political transformation generated the nation as a community for politically aware citizens equal before the law irrespective of their social and economic status, ethnic origins and religious beliefs. . . . [T]he unifying whole is formed by a uniform language, a uniform judicial and administrative system, a central government and shared political ideals. The sovereignty of the people is the foundation of state power.
>
> (Alter, 1991: 15)

This type of nationalism is usually associated particularly with the writing of Rousseau and in the aftermath of the French Revolution.[4] The ideals enshrined are considered liberal-democratic, and essentially political. Nationalism here consciously sets out to create a nation based on democratic principles of full participation and consent of the people. The defining characteristics promoted as part of the national identity are consciously (and subjectively) chosen and cherished. The French language, therefore, was deemed *the* national language of France, even though less than half the French population spoke it as a mother tongue. A similar constructed form of nation-building can be seen in many other parts of the world in the nine-teenth century, not least in Latin America after the wars of independence there.

Cultural nationalism, on the other hand, is identified by external markers which may include language, territory, race or common history and heritage. These are objectively seen, of a deterministic nature, and can be irrational and undemocratic. Membership of communities who perceive their sense of nation from this viewpoint can be highly exclusive, sometimes racist, but not necessarily politically aggressive. Often cultural nationalism involves a movement keen to promote cultural awareness and to protect its cultural differences, but not always with the intention of creating a separate political unit.

It is this second kind of nationalism, with its emphasis on different localised cultures, that characterised much of the nationalism associated with the nineteenth century Romantic movement in literature, music, architecture, art, etc. (Llobera, 1994: 171–4). Romanticism stresses the exotic, the local, and nostalgia for a glorious past which legitimises a community's uniqueness in the present. Whilst essentially a European movement, romanticism was also transported to the Americas and plays an important part in a certain type of national awareness in parts of Latin America in the nineteenth and early twentieth centuries. The link between romanticism and *indigenismo*, which will be commented on in later chapters, is one example of this.

The role of language in cultural nationalism has always been seen as central, following the work of the father of cultural nationalism, the German Johann Gottfried Herder. His work has certainly been of crucial importance in understanding modern nationalism. Although Herder and his ideas on language are mainly associated with cultural nationalism, as I will argue in the next section, language is frequently as important in the construction of national identity to movements of a political nationalist nature.

Language and national identity

Herder (1744–1803)[5] was writing at a time when a German state as such did not exist, and from a position of a German angered by the low prestige of his language, and its people (the *Volk*). His writings are therefore inspired by a sense of patriotism and by frustration as a result of this denial. Nonetheless, it is important to stress that, unlike many of Herder's followers, he should not be seen as xenophobic nor racist (at least in the modern sense). He disliked the French and much of what they stood for, and he was proud of German and the German people. But his writings stress the existence and importance of diversity. The important point is that this diversity, in his view, should not be mixed, diluted and devalued.

As Barnard explains:

> Herder approaches the problem of language in terms of . . . three dominant conceptual categories . . .: the principle of interaction, the concept of self-consciousness, and the doctrine of diversity.
>
> (Barnard, 1969: 57)

We have seen already how important all three of these concepts are to issues of language and nationalism. Language, we have argued, is about interaction, but it also represents self-consciousness and identity-awareness, as well as the maintenance of diversity. Nationalism, we have seen, is a self-conscious movement which seeks to protect its difference. It is hardly surprising, then, that Herder relates his views on language to the idea of the nation, views which have rightly earned him a place in the literature as one of the foremost early thinkers on the idea of the nation and nationalism.

Herder's prize-winning essay of 1772 *Ueber den Ursprung der Sprache* ('*Treatise upon the Origins of Language*') is often cited as the seminal work for the origins of linguistic nationalism. Its contemporary impact was perhaps most radically felt in his denial of the doctrine of the divine origin of language (Barnard, 1969). However, today we are more likely to consider the significance of this essay lying in his contention that 'reason and language are coterminous' (Barnard, 1969: 56). From this Herder claims,

> Each nation speaks in the manner it thinks and thinks in the manner it speaks . . . We cannot think without words.
>
> (cited in Barnard, 1969: 56)

A language for Herder is the means by which human beings grow to understand themselves and then to understand and share with those who speak the same mother tongue. This common language both unites them and allows them to differentiate themselves from other linguistic communities. He sees this diversity of languages as completely natural and unhierarchical. For Herder, language is the most important defining factor in the make-up of humans and in their communal grouping, the nation. It is also the means of linking with the past and ensuring the future for any one linguistic group.

> In this way language embodies the living manifestation of historical growth and the psychological matrix in which man's awareness of his distinctive social heritage is aroused and deepened. Those sharing a particular historical tradition grounded in language Herder identifies with a *Volk* or nationality, and it is in this essentially spiritual quality that he sees the most natural and organic basis for political association.
>
> (Barnard, 1969: 57)

In Germany the most prominent contemporary writers of Herder who followed his seminal ideas were Von Humboldt (1767–1835) and Fichte (1762–1814) (Edwards, 1985), who, however, focused Herder's theories in a far more xenophobic, and specifically anti-French, way. Fichte's claims for German superiority based on the superiority of the German language and the purity of the German race did not allow for the tolerance of diversity advocated in Herder's writings and can be seen to set the stage for more radical and politically-disastrous sentiments of racism which culminated in Nazism. In other parts of Europe Herder's ideas were immediately influential, and, as we will see in later chapters, his writings were central in nineteenth century Catalan nationalism.

The role of language as a link with the past, thereby giving legitimacy and authenticity to the sense of the nation, is a theme taken up by others, and is especially important in the writings on language and nationalism of Joshua Fishman, a particularly influential figure writing in this field in the twentieth century (e.g. Fishman, 1972).

Other recent writers on nationalism also comment on the role of language in nationalism. It is revealing to see how for so many of these writers language is an important factor whose signficance must be mentioned and discussed. What is interesting, though, is the often quite different role that language is given by these commentators in the development of nationalism. We have seen how Herder places language so utterly at the core of identity that we must categorise his type of nationalism as cultural/objective. He writes in 1783:

> Has a nationality anything dearer than the speech of its fathers? In its speech resides its whole thought domain, its tradition, history, religion and basis of life, all its heart and soul. To deprive a people of its speech is to deprive it of its one eternal good . . . With language is created the heart of a people.
>
> (cited in Fishman, 1989: 105)

Fishman seems to agree with this approach. He writes:

> History consists of names and dates and places but the essence of a nationality is something which is merely implied or adumbrated by such details. The essence exists over and above dynasties and centuries and boundaries, this essence is that which constitutes the heart of the nationality in its spirit, its individuality, its soul. This soul is not only reflected and protected by the mother tongue, but, in a sense, *the mother tongue is itself an aspect of the soul*, a part of the soul. . . .
>
> (Fishman, 1989: 277, original emphasis)

In Fishman's discussion on language and nationalism he defends Herder's position that the link between language and nationality is unquestionable and that they are 'inextricably and naturally linked' (Fishman, 1989: 278). And with the expansion of nineteenth century mass nationalism Fishman argues that this is no longer simply 'a natural link, [. . . but] also a cause, a goal and an obligation' (Fishman 1989: 279). Fishman stresses how in this age of nationalism the self-awareness of nations was articulated through what he calls the vernaculars, and he stresses how vernacular literature was an important vehicle in creating an awareness of national identity. He writes:

> The interaction between mother tongue and experiences of beauty, devo-tion, and righteousness — in short, the tie between the mother tongue

and collective 'peak' experiences – does not depend on abstract ideologies concerning the 'ethnic soul' or the 'national spirit'. Such experiences are more directly and formatively provided via the oral and written literature in the vernacular that both anticipate and accompany mass nationalism.

(Fishman, 1989: 281–2)

This idea that vernacular literature has played a role in representing to national communities their 'linguistic *differentiation* and literary *uniqueness*' (Fishman 1989: 284, original italics) is one that is fully explored and expanded in Benedict Anderson's excellent book on nationalism *Imagined Communities: Reflections on the Origins and Spread of Nationalism*, which will be discussed below.

Another modern commentator on nationalism who explores the ideas of Herder, and especially the importance of language to these, is Elie Kedourie. Kedourie emphasises that when discussing linguistic nationalism, he does not see that a distinction can be made (as some writers have done) between this and racial nationalism. He argues that language and race are inextricably linked. Referring to the legacy of Herder he states:

Originally the doctrine [of linguistic nationalism] emphasized language as the test of nationality, because language was the outward sign of a group's peculiar identity and a significant means of ensuring its continuity. But a nation's language was peculiar to that nation only because such a nation constituted a racial stock distinct from that of other nations.

(Kedourie, 1993: 66)

Kedourie highlights the emphasis in Herder's writings, and even more so that of Fichte, of keeping the language 'pure' by preventing borrowings or other influences from other languages. This notion of the total congruence between people and their language has major implications, as Kedourie says:

Two conclusions may be drawn: first, that people who speak an original language are nations, and second, that nations must speak an original language.

(Kedourie, 1993: 61)

Kedourie thus draws our attention to the political consequences of Herder's cultural nationalism, thereby reminding us of how impossible it is to keep these categories apart.

As Kedourie says:

The test, then, by which a nation is known to exist is that of language. A group speaking the same language is known as a nation, and a nation ought to constitute a state. It is not merely that a group of people speaking a certain language may claim the right to preserve its language, rather, such a group, which is a nation, will cease to be one if it is not constituted into a state . . . Again, if a nation is a group of people speaking the same language, then if political frontiers separate the members of such a group, these frontiers are arbitrary, unnatural, unique.

(Kedourie, 1993: 62)

This expectation that there is a congruence between the nation and the state, seen both here in an interpretation of Herderian thought, and equally apparent in the political nationalism of Rousseau and his followers is clearly at odds with the reality around us. Whilst it led to the justification for the creation (or defence) of nation-states, few if any politically marked-out states are naturally monocultural. The nationalist ideology of the nineteenth century by choosing to ignore this, has laid the seeds of many explosive separatist movements of the twentieth century amongst substate-level nationalist groups.

Various modern commentators on nationalism have recognised that whilst language is one of the most significant characteristics in nationalist movements far from simply serving as a culturally-identifying marker, it is also potentially a highly-charged political tool. Whilst Fichte, and to a lesser extent Herder, recognised that some intervention in the natural path of linguistic development might be necessary to keep the language as 'pure' or 'original' (as they saw it), free of external foreign influences, which is certainly a form of deliberate Language Planning,[6] others realise that this deliberate use and manipulation of language is even more overt and far-reaching.

Hobsbawm (1990) writes:

Linguistic nationalism essentially requires control of a state or at least the winning of official recognition for the language. . . . Problems of power, status, politics and ideology and not of communication or even culture lie at the heart of the nationalism of language.

(Hobsbawm, 1990: 110)

In stark contrast to the Herderian view of language and nationalism, Hobsbawm believes:

Contrary to nationalist myth, a people's language is not the basis of national consciousness, but, in the phrase of Einar Haugen, a 'cultural artefact'.

(Hobsbawm, 1990: 111)

Hobsbawm claims that the activities of Language Planning from standardisation and codification to what he describes as 'the virtual invention of new [languages]' (1990: 111), with the revival of nearly-extinct languages or the promotion and elaboration of selected dialects, create these constructed national languages.

Hobsbawm also argues that what he calls 'dialect literature' which was such an important aspect of the Romantic movement of the nineteenth century, whilst doing much to revive minority languages and bring them to the attention of their communities, did not in fact create linguistic nationalism. He believes that:

> Such languages or literatures could see themselves and be seen quite consciously as supplementing rather than competing with some hegemonic language of general culture and communication.
>
> (Hobsbawm, 1990: 111)

Many would argue with Hobsbawm's use of the term 'dialect' here to describe, for example, literature written in Catalan or Galician, Breton or Corsican. As we have seen Fishman preferred the term 'vernacular' which is also used by Anderson in a broader sense. In the situations described here by Hobsbawm it would seem, as so often is the case, that much depends on whether nationalist movements are being defined as only those forging the nation-building of a nation-state. The shaping of the nineteenth century French, or German, or Italian, or Spanish nation-states certainly indentified French, German, Italian and Spanish respectively as their hegemonic national language, despite literature and other cultural activities taking place in minority languages within their borders. But nationalism, surely, is also about aspirations from substate level 'national' communities, whose cultural awakening and revived self-consciousness Hobsbawm is in danger of dismissing in his view that they were happy to simply 'supplement' the overarching national-state identity.

As mentioned previously the distinction between 'dialect' and 'language' can be a difficult one. It takes on great significance in any discussion of nationalism if we agree with such commentators as Billig (1995) that this is an important political decision. He writes:

> Differences between dialect and language . . . become hotly contested political issues. . . . If it seems obvious to us that there are different languages, it is by no means obvious how the distinctions between languages are to be made.
>
> (Billig, 1995: 32)

And he continues:

> More is at stake in drawing the boundary of a language than linguistics. The battle for hegemony, which accompanies the creation of states, is reflected in the power to define language.
>
> (Billig, 1995: 32)

When Hobsbawm in the earlier quotation refers to 'dialect literature', he is (consciously or otherwise) placing this literature in a linguistic hierarchy where the 'national', i.e. 'state', language is higher than others spoken within this state, whether these are linguistically closely related and mutually comprehensible or not.

But as Billig argues:

> Nationalists, in attempting to create a separate nation, often will create a language as a distinct language, although they might claim to be creating the nation on the basis of the language, as if the latter was an ancient 'natural' fact.

> (Billig, 1995: 32)

In other words, nation-state builders may choose to term minority languages as 'dialects' in order to downgrade their status and importance, whilst minority linguistic communities may wish to promote their variety (or dialect) as a separate 'language' to enhance their community's sense of nation.

Billig points out that one of the ways in which 'dialects' might be converted into fully-fledged 'languages' is by writing them down, and thereby standardising them. This is a central theme in the work of Benedict Anderson whose writing on nationalism gives a very prominent role to language and in particular to written, and above all, print language. In his *Imagined Communities: Reflections on the Origins and Spread of Nationalism* (1983, 1992) Anderson argues that a significant cause of the emergence of separate national communities in Europe was the result of the increased use of the vernacular (as opposed to Latin) in public life, and especially the spread of the print-word. With modernisation, industrialisation and urbanisation came the rise of the use of the vernacular as the language of power in an increasingly secularised society (Anderson, 1992). The rise of the role of the vernacular was strengthened by the spread of the written word, even in societies with a restricted level of literacy as in eighteenth and nineteenth century Europe.

Anderson (1992: 44–6) identifies three important roles for the print-word in shaping modern nationalism and national identities. In the first place, the print word required standardisation of a selected linguistic variety, ensuring that a 'norm' emerged which enabled communication across the nation in a way that Latin previously had done. Secondly, the choice of one variety over others and the creation of a norm meant a reduction in diversity which both 'fixed' language across space and territory, but also across time providing a link with the past. This newly-found concept of time, both chronologically emerging from a shared past, and simultaneously with a shared present community is, as we have seen, an essential ingredient to a sense of nationhood (Anderson 1992; Williams, 1984).

A third important aspect of the standardisation of the vernacular, according to Anderson, is that it helped create linguistic hierarchies, establishing new power relationships with the chosen dialect, and those closest to this, dominating the more 'deviant' varieties. This is the same point made by Billig and Hobsbawm as to the highly political nature of identifying languages from dialects and selecting the official or national norm. In turn this status of the norm gives prestige to the print-word and the desire by minority communities to establish literacy in their languages.

The most influential idea to emerge from Anderson's book is his concept of the 'imagined community'. Anderson's famous definition of the nation is as 'an imagined political community – and imagined as inherently limited and sovereign' (Anderson, 1992: 6). He expands on this definition by saying that these communities are *imagined* because the members of even the smallest nation will never know most of their fellow-members, meet them, or even hear of them, yet in the minds of each lives the image of their communion' (1992: 6). At the same time members of these communities can imagine a space which is finite and bounded, thus reinforcing the sense of 'them' and 'us' so crucial in nationalist ideology. For Anderson, it is above all language, and especially print-language, which provides this 'image' of the community.

With the writing down of language, print-language produces 'blueprints' which create models and spread ideas. Writing about the period of wars of independence in Latin America, Anderson says:

> The independence movements in the Americas, became, as soon as they were printed about, 'concepts', 'models' and indeed 'blueprints'. . . . Out of the American welter came these imagined realities: nation-states, republican institutions, common citizenship, popular sovereignty, national flags and anthems, and the liquidation of their conceptual opposites. . . . In effect, by the second decade of the nineteenth century, if not earlier, a 'model' of 'the' independent national state was available for pirating.
>
> (Anderson, 1992: 81)

In this way we can see that Anderson regards the role of language in the creation of nations and for nationalist movements to be overtly political, as a carrier of political ideologies (in the case of Latin American nationalist movements specifically informed by the model of the French Revolution).

As we have seen earlier Billig too sees language as being manipulated for nationalist purposes, and he also develops Anderson's 'imagined' concept when he suggests that:

> Nations may be imagined communities, but the pattern of the imaginings cannot be explained in terms of differences of languages, for languages themselves have to be imagined as distinct entities. . . . At other times people did not hold the notions of language and dialect, let alone those of territory and sovereignty, which are so commonplace today and which seem so materially real to 'us'. So strongly are such

notions embedded in contemporary common sense that it is easy to forget that they are invented permanencies.

(Billig, 1995: 35–6)

The idea that the naming and categorising of languages as badges of identity is, according to Billig, a modern need. This is an important claim, and one that reminds us that whilst it may well be that a sense of community and shared identity has always been present amongst human groupings, much of the terminology and the political structuring we take for granted today is indeed modern and by no means as inherently 'natural' as we believe it to be. We will need to be reminded of this when looking at the Spanish-speaking world, where, it seems reasonable to say, the so-called 'renaissances' amongst the linguistic minorities in Spain of the nineteenth century do indeed display a new awareness and desire to name and codify their languages.

Anderson makes a similar point to Billig's when he argues that this sensitivity to classifying languages and then to writing them down is not only central to modern nationalism, but is the direct result of the rise of a bourgeois class in the newly-industrialising and modernising Europe of the nineteenth century. Developing his argument that communities only know each other by imagining themselves, Anderson claims that the radical difference between a pre-nationalist world ruled by small elites of intermarrying nobility who did know one another, is that this was superseded by new bourgeoisies whose only way of visualising and thereby believing in their community was through print-language. He explains how the rapidly increasing levels of literacy amongst this class made this possible, adding:

> But in a nineteenth century Europe, in which Latin had been defeated by vernacular print-capitalism for something like two centuries, these solidarities had an outermost stretch limited by vernacular legibilities.
>
> (Anderson, 1992: 77)

This key role that literacy gives language is indirectly strengthened in general by the place of education systems in the planning of nationalist movements and the creation of nations and nation-states.[7] The prominent writer on nationalism Ernest Gellner makes this an important part of his discussion of the construction of nations and national identity. Whilst his emphasis is on education and literacy, rather than language specifically, he in fact makes the same point as many other commentators we have already discussed (e.g. Herder, Fishman, Anderson) in stressing the link between the past and the present sense of community given by a sense of authenticity and shared history passed down and offered in written texts.[8] Gellner writes:

> A very important stratum in literate agrarian society are the clerks, those who can read and transmit literacy. . . . It is not just writing, but what is written that counts. . . . So the writers and readers are specialists and yet

more than specialists; they are both part of a society, and claim to be the voice of the whole of it.

(Gellner, 1983: 31)

Elsewhere Gellner has written that 'the minimal requirement for full citizenship is literacy' (in Hutchinson and Smith, 1994: 55). In this sense he agrees with Anderson in giving such importance to print-language in the creation of national identity. Gellner also argues that this full literacy can only be provided by a 'nation-size' education system, as he believes only this can have the sufficient resources. Gellner also goes on to emphasise the obvious fact that this national education and literacy must be in a selected language, and that this then both enables people to interact and communicate and share in the workings of their community, and, significantly, limits them to the (national) boundaries of this linguistic community. Once again, language is viewed as a marker of national frontiers, although Gellner's version of this is as a practical, enabling means of constructing the national community, rather than as a result of any given inherent quality of the national language. On the contrary, Gellner considers that for all those who resent membership of a state whose dominant language is not theirs and who therefore see themselves of another 'nation', there are as many who have willingly learnt a new language to gain entry to a 'nation' to which they are happy to adhere for reasons of other shared characteristics (such as religion, race, territory). He rather dismissively states:

Changing one's language is not the heart-breaking or soul-destroying business which it is claimed to be in romantic nationalist literature.

(in Hutchinson and Smith, 1994: 60)

As we have seen, many would profoundly disagree with Gellner on this. And, indeed, around this position will hang much of the later discussion as to the importance of language in the forming of national identities in the Spanish-speaking world. A crucial question to address will be to what extent communities have *willingly* learnt new languages in order to gain access to citizenship and nationhood.

Conclusion

In this brief discussion of the writings on nationalism and particularly of the role of language in nationalism and the construction of national identity I hope to have highlighted both the range of complexity in terms of the differing kinds of nationalism that are commonly identified and the contrasting interpretations given to these. I hope also to have made clear that there is in fact a good deal of agreement on the central issues, even when sometimes commentators have appeared not necessarily to acknowledge this agreement. Nationalism defies easy categorising and pigeon-holing; so many of its elements and characteristics overlap and interconnect. Thus the distinction between, for example, the cultural and political easily blur. It can, in fact, be argued that every nationalist movement must contain a sense of both. More difficult is to agree as to whether nationalism is above all inherent, unconscious and driven by 'objective' factors, or socially constructed and consciously directed. Similarly it is impossible to state categorically the nature of the political ideologies which nationalist movements promote. A simplistic attempt to say that all such movements are right-wing or left-wing ignores the enormous range of situations which inspire nationalism as we have already noted. Examples can be found ranging from elite groups wishing to maintain the *status quo* and their own position of power by imposing a state hegemony to construct a 'nation'; through like-minded people who, whilst recognising their differences, seek to agree through a democratic will, to identify ideals, structures, and characteristics which can be shared by all who inhabit a particular territory; to those leaders of minority communities who perceive themselves as oppressed by (sometimes authoritarian) majority regimes of states to which they politicaly belong. As we shall see, in the Spanish-speaking world there are examples of all these varying types of nationalist movements.

The role of language, as we have seen, is sometimes considered important merely by its very existence, as distinguishing one speech community from another. Or its significance is in the way it represents the character and feelings of a community and links this with its past and future. On the other hand others consider language as a manipulable tool of Language Planning, an essential ingredient in the deliberate construction of national identity markers.

What is clear from this is that those questions raised in the Introduction regarding the role of language in society are variously implicated in these different roles for language and its relationship with nationalism. Who speaks what language may define a nation; how it is taught or learnt may depend on national planning priorities. Whether there are resources and policies to select and promote a dialect or language could depend on whether it is viewed as an important part of a nationalist agenda. In short, from Herder to Gellner, in their very different ways, writing on nationalism has been interested in the way language affects human behaviour.

In what follows we will now set out to examine these issues by specifically focusing on the Spanish-speaking world. To what extent has language been a criterion in the make-up of nationalist movements in Spain or Latin America? How far will we want to define the countries of Spain and Latin America as 'nations' or 'states' or 'nation-states'? To what extent will these definitions depend on the role of language?

2 The 'Castilianisation' process

The emergence of Spanish as dominant language[1]

In this chapter we will investigate how the Spanish language developed from its early Latin origins in the Iberian Peninsula to a world language today. In doing this we will need to see how its status has always gone hand-in-hand with the status of the communities where the language is spoken. As we have seen in Chapter 1 the prestige and importance of a language mirrors the power and influence of its speakers. Throughout we will be asking how far the existence of Spanish defines separate identities, shaping their sense of nation and confirming the frontiers of their imagined communities. Or will the role of the Spanish language emerge less as an intrinsic value and more as a useful tool with which to construct national identity? Does Spanish perform a Herderian role in Spanish or Spanish-American national conscious- ness? Or, instead, will we see Spanish being deliberately selected, consciously created as an artificial construct, named and classified for political purposes as Hobsbawm, Billig and Gellner, amongst others, suggest is the role of language in nation-building?

Whatever interpretation we adopt of the creation and emergence of the 'Spanish-speaking world', that such a vast geographical and demographic entity exists is undeniable. By the end of the twentieth century it is forecast that at least 400 million people will speak Spanish, the vast majority as their mother tongue. Besides being spoken in Spain and Spanish-speaking America (including the US), Spanish is still spoken as a mother tongue or co-official language to a greater or lesser extent in Equatorial Guinea, parts of Morocco and in the Spanish enclaves of Ceuta and Melilla, in the Philippines, and in parts of North Africa and the Middle East where *Ladino* (Judeo-Spanish) can still be found.[2] These latter examples of Spanish-speaking communities are all ones where the use of Spanish is largely on the decline and even likely to become extinct altogether. The use of Spanish in Latin America, and particu- larly in the US, is, on the other hand, on the increase in regions and amongst communities where the birth rate is high. This coupled with the growing study of Spanish as a second language[3] is producing a vibrant and significant global Spanish-speaking population. For the purposes of this book I shall con- centrate only on Spain and the Americas, those areas where Spanish is buoyant and secure.

The origins of Spanish in the Iberian Peninsula[4]

I shall concentrate here on the emergence of Castilian as the dominant variety and on its development as 'Spanish'. Although I have argued that this development parallels the process of nation/state-building, I will not be offering a discussion of nation-building in Spain (or, in the later section, in Latin America) except insofar as this concerns the role of language.[5]

In terms of the history of the Spanish language, the periods prior to the Roman conquest of the Iberian Peninsula are of minor importance. Very little in the way of linguistic evidence from the Iberians, or the Celtic-speaking settlers can be found in today's language. The Basque language, which we will discuss in Chapter 3, does indeed pre-date the Roman settlement.

All the other languages and dialects that are found today in the Iberian Peninsula derive from Latin, and form part of the Romance language continuum that covers much of southwestern Europe (Crystal, 1987). The *Lingua Franca* of the Roman Empire was of course classical Latin, used in written texts and for legal and administrative purposes. However, the normal day-to-day form of communication was through so-called vulgar Latin. Inevitably the form of vulgar Latin spoken in different regions of the Iberian Peninsula began to take on separate characteristics, influenced by such factors as continuing pre-Roman linguistic habits, specific environmental features, characteristic trades and occupations of the region, etc. As a result new vernaculars developed which could no longer be easily understood as forms of Latin. By the eighth century, besides Basque, at least five distinct linguistic groups had emerged in the Iberian Peninsula (Diez *et al.*, 1977): Galaico-Portuguese, Asturian-Leonese, Castilian, Aragonese and Catalan. The Germanic-speaking Visigoths, who occupied the Peninsula after the Romans, had little impact on these developing vernaculars, partly because their long contact with the Romans meant that they were largely bilingual and able to continue the use of Latin in their administrative dealings. According to Penny (1991: 12), however, the establishment of Toledo, in Castile, as the Visigothic capital, and precursor to the early Spanish capital, is one way in which the Visigoths indirectly affected the future dominance of Castilian.

In 711 the Iberian Peninsula was invaded by Arabic speakers from North Africa. This Arab occupation lasted in one form or another for over seven centuries. Inevitably this occupation had a significant impact on the linguistic history of the Peninsula, also distinguishing it from the linguistic history of many other parts of western Europe. Not only did the Arab language itself leave traces (particularly of vocabulary) in modern Spanish (and to a lesser extent Portuguese), but the political reaction to the Arab invasion also played an important part in determining the future development of Iberian languages.

Not all the Peninsula was as strongly influenced by the Arab occupation. In particular, the northern parts were only occupied for short periods. For this reason, Basque was hardly affected by the use of Arabic. The Catalan-speaking areas too were only temporarily occupied with correspondingly less influence received from the Arabic language.

In a similar way the Galaico-Portuguese variety in the northwest had relatively insignificant contact with Arab speakers. Here, we see an example of the close relationship between nation-building and language-building. As Portugal became more clearly a separate entity, its linguistic variety became a confident national language. Galician, on the other hand, as we shall see in Chapter 3, declined under the influence of a stronger dominating speech community (the Castilian). The emerging Portuguese language was somewhat influenced by Arab-speakers as these two communities came into contact as a result of the Portuguese drive southwards.

At the time of the Arab invasion the Asturian-Leonese variety was probably the most dominant in the centre of the Peninsula (Diez *et al.*, 1977), but the role of Castile in the *Reconquista* is crucial in ousting the former from this position. The Christian opposition to the Arab invasion was increasingly directed from Castile. Particularly symbolic of this is the recapture of Toledo, as capital of Christian Spain in 1085. More and more the Castilian Crown was the dominant one in the loose federation of Iberian kingdoms fighting the Arabs. These distinct kingdoms were gradually brought together in the typical pattern of the Middle Ages throughout Europe – through conquest, joint military aims, and convenient marriages. The most significant of these marriages was that of Isabella of Castile to Ferdinand of Aragon (the so-called *Reyes Católicos* or Catholic Monarchs), thereby uniting in 1469 the power of Castile with the influence of Aragon and the Catalan-speaking regions. Many commentators see this as the beginnings of modern Spain. However, it is important to stress how loose such federations of kingdoms in that period really were, and how little they resemble the unity of modern-style states.

A further highly significant date linked with the origin of modern Spain is that of 1492. In this year the last of the occupying Arabs were defeated at Granada. This is also the year of the first of Christopher Columbus' voyages to the Americas, and therefore the beginning of the future vast American empire for Spain. From a linguistic point of view, too, this is an important year with the publication of the first Castilian grammar by Elio Antonio de Nebrija. His *Gramática de la Lengua Castellana* is the first grammar not only in Castilian (or Spanish) but also in a Romance vernacular language.

With Castile now dominating the Peninsula from a political and military point of view it was inevitable that the form of speech that had emerged as the dominant one was that of Castilian. This is symbolised in a sense by the fact that the first grammar book in Castilian is in fact written by an Andalusian. From this period onwards the blur between 'Spanish' and 'Castilian' begins.

The fact that it is Castilian powers that support and promote the colonisation of the Americas from this period, further serves to confirm the Castilian language above other languages still actively used in the Peninsula. From now on the Castilian suppression of the regions on the periphery is also reflected in linguistic subordination. With Catalans and Galicians banned from trading with the American colonies, these two non-Castilian languages were also prevented from being exported, leaving Castilian to thrive alone.

With Castile established as the dominant power, the language of this power was used increasingly in situations of prestige and influence, such as the Court, the Church, in legal documents, and in the administration of the Spanish state and its empire. This is reflected too in what must now be termed the Spanish *Siglo de Oro*, which saw a prolific output of literary and artistic creation, including such writers as Lope de Vega, Calderón, Garcilaso, Quevedo and Cervantes.

Nonetheless (as we shall see in Chapter 3) the non-Castilian languages did not all die out completely, and during this period there was still quite considerable tolerance towards them in the informal and local spheres of daily life. As we saw in Chapter 1, for many commentators, the requisites for nation-building are not in existence in these earlier historical periods. Whilst a sense of local consciousness is undoubtedly present, the idea of the nation is not. This is apparent, too, in the language behaviour of this time, with Castilian spoken by the elites and in the areas from where it most directly originated, but hardly known or used on the margins of the Peninsula.

Siguan usefully reminds us:

> It is . . . exaggerated to say that the Catholic Monarchs aimed at achieving the unity of Spain as a nation. . . . Other contemporary monarchies in Europe were following the same process that leads to nation-states. Rather than stating that these states were the result of a nationalist idea, it would be fairer to say that the idea of 'nationality' emerged in the process whereby modern states were created as an ideological justification and as its representation in terms of collective consciousness.
>
> (Siguan, 1993: 20)

One of the first signs of the conscious realisation that a Spanish nation needed to be 'created', through the imposition of a Castilian hegemony, is shown in 1624 by the Conde Duque de Olivares in his (secret) memorandum to Philip IV. In recognising the need for political and administrative centralisation he writes:

> The most important thing in Your Majesty's Monarchy is for you to become king of Spain, by this I mean, Sir, that Your Majesty should not be content with being king of Portugal, of Aragon, of Valencia,

and count of Barcelona, but should secretly plan and work to reduce these kingdoms of which Spain is composed to the style and laws of Castile, with no difference whatsoever.

(quoted in Linz, 1973: 43)

This is a major step forward in the path to the emergence of a modern state. However, in terms of the definitions of 'state' and 'nation' established in Chapter 1 such deliberate moves to construct 'Spanish' identity are far from reflecting a true 'nation'. It is clear from this memorandum that at this point at least the Aragonese still considered themselves 'Aragonese', the Valencians, still 'Valencians', and the Portuguese of course shortly after, in 1640, broke totally from the Spanish Crown to become forever 'Portuguese'. If a Spanish 'nation' is a legitimate term, then we cannot yet apply this in the early seventeenth century.

Not surprisingly, then, linguistic unity and conformity are no more (and no less) consolidated at this point than political unity. That is to say that whilst Castilian is now dominant, particularly in the highly productive world of letters, it is not yet the only language of Spain. It might be argued that until a conscious awareness of the need to promote Castilian as the only language of the state takes hold, then even nation-building of a political sort (as discussed in the previous chapter) does not take place.

However, it is certainly at this time that the increasing awareness of the importance of Spanish as the language of prestige and dominance is taking hold in most quarters. Diez *et al.* (1977) in fact argue that during the fifteenth century and into the early sixteenth century Castilian does indeed reach the category of 'national' language. They state:

> El dialecto leonés se usaba únicamente en el habla rústica. El aragonés, muy influído por el castellano, desapareció muy pronto de la literatura. La importancia de los grandes escritores de la lengua castellana coincide con el descenso y el desplazamiento de la literatura catalana. Incluso autores de otras regiones, lingüísticamente distintas, usarán el castellano como vehículo de expresión literaria. . . . Ya podemos hablar con toda propiedad de lengua española.
>
> (Diez *et al.*, 1977: 199)[6]

This significance of the language in a cultural sense was shortly to be confirmed in the political sense.

It is, however, not really until the eighteenth century that hard language policies establish the hegemony of Castilian in parallel with the now highly centralised Spanish state. The beginning of that century saw a highly significant power struggle for the Spanish throne that left many of the peripheral regions, notably Catalonia, Valencia and Mallorca, on the losing side. The consequence was the arrival in Spain of the Bourbon royal family, who installed the centralised state-building which was also then taking place in France. Alongside this went, of course, the repression of the regions and the residual rights of these communities (with the exception of the Basques and Navarra). As Siguan explains, this is the point from which we can see a conscious awareness of language in the construction of the Spanish state, and the goal of creating a Spanish nation:

> If until this moment, the progressive loss of importance of languages other than Castilian had been a secondary consequence of the policy of unification, as from that moment linguistic uniformity will be a directly sought objective, and this uniformity will be considered to be a rational step, but also the expression of national unity.
>
> (Siguan, 1993: 25)

As the first such deliberate move to install Castilian as the national language throughout Spain we can point to the creation of the Spanish Royal Academy, the *Real Academia de la Lengua Española* (the RAE), which was set up in 1713 on the instructions of Philip V in imitation of the French equivalent. The Academy's motto is '*Limpia, fija y da esplendor*'.[7] With this we can see the beginnings of the standardising, fixing and creating of norms of the language which, as we have seen, is an essential part of the process of linguistic nationalism. Following Anderson's model (1992: 44–6), we can see that with the work of the Academy, Castilian can now become the print language to draw together the Spanish 'imagined' community, simultaneously confirming its role in the linguistic hierarchy of the state.

Between 1726 and 1739 the RAE produced its first authoritative dictionary. This was followed in 1741 by the *Ortografía* of spelling norms, and then in 1771 by the *Gramática castellana*. The role of this latter is highly influential in a further part of the nation-building project as the basis for the teaching of the language.

Indeed another highly important aspect of the now deliberate planning of the national language again accords with the observations on language and nation-building discussed earlier. In 1768 Charles III decreed that 'throughout the kingdom the Castilian language be used in the administration and education' (quoted in Siguan 1993: 25). This is the first time that the use of Castilian in education is specifically singled out. As education became more available and more widespread this decree held greater significance, particularly, of course, in those areas, such as Catalonia, where some education had already been begun in Catalan. Most importantly, perhaps, is the fact that language is never taught and learnt in a vacuum. Now not only was the language of instruction Castilian, but the culture, ideas, values being transmitted through this language were Castilian. In this way Castilian culture was disseminated across the Spanish territory becoming what we recognise as 'Spanish' culture.

Two other national institutions also helped spread the use of the Castilian language and with it the sense of Castilian identity as representing Spanish identity. These are the Church and the army. The former, always highly influential in the lives of ordinary Spanish people, was rapidly Castilianised in the higher ranks of its organisation, and so, whilst the local village priest might still be from non-Castilian speaking regions and continue to use their vernacular, the heart of the Spanish Church (including of course its educational institutions) was Castilian-speaking. With Latin still used in the actual mass, there was very little left to be transmitted through the local languages.

The army contributed to extending the use of Castilian with the introduction of mass conscription. Despite a conscript's origins, and therefore his mother tongue, on being called up to the army, he would have to use and understand Castilian. Clearly this had a greater impact on the male population, but in that period wives of conscripts would often accompany their husbands.

Although the nineteenth century began in Spain with occupation by the French and the subsequent opposition to this, this is a rare moment of patriotic 'nationalist' unity bringing together Spaniards across the entire territory possibly for the first time. Deep ideological and social divisions are more characteristic of this century.

As regards language during this period, education continues to be a major force in ensuring the dominance of Castilian. By now education, and therefore the widespread knowledge and use of Castilian, has permeated down to the lower classes and is no more simply the property of the elites. Whilst this century does in fact see an important revival of some of the minority languages (see Chapter 3), Castilian is now indisputably the national language. Those speaking a relatively standard variety of it as their mother tongue are now in the majority. By now it seems reasonable to say that Castilian, or, rather, Spanish, is identified by many as one of their badges of national identity.

In fact it is strange to note that there is arguably more uniformity and acceptance of this national marker than many others, with constant political struggles challenging the continuing efforts to create a sense of Spanish nationhood which might be shared by all. The language question is surprisingly underplayed in these struggles. Liberals, Federalists and, later, Anarchists show little interest in Spain's linguistic diversity, even though in the case of the latter two, many prominent figures were in fact mother tongue Catalan speakers. In a similar way to the French, it would seem that the common view (if view there was at all) was that one unifying national language was an essential ingredient to democratic participation and empowerment. On the other hand, the traditionalists (and specifically the Carlists) reacting against the modernising and democratising aims of these groups also held no interest in the language question, despite the fact that much of their power base was in rural areas where non-Castilian languages were still widely-used. The view of society held by such traditionalist groups in many senses compares with the ideas held by such writers as

Herder and his followers, with an emphasis on the importance of the historical heritage and the purity of separate communities. Nonetheless the role of language as marker of this legacy is rarely important (with the marked exception, in a somewhat different context, of the later Catalan and Galician revivals, discussed in the next chapter).

Not only at a political level did nineteenth-century Spain struggle to secure a sense of national identity and patriotic pride. At the end of the century Spain also experienced a crisis which at a more symbolic and emotional level challenged belief in a shared community of common values and objectives. The humiliating loss of the last Spanish colonies, the end of the once great empire, in 1898, had a profound effect on attitudes to the Spanish nation. A group of intellectuals, usually linked together under the name of the '98 Generation, were prominent in their questioning of the fate of Spain, critical of her inability to throw off the failings of the past, and anxious to see a strong united Spain join the modern world around her.[8] For many of these commentators the future lay in a revival of belief in the greatness of Castile and all that this region stood for. Many of these writers were intolerant of any writing in non-Castilian Peninsular languages, which was beginning to flourish at this time. Some such as Baroja and Unamuno were in fact Basque themselves, but nonetheless wrote in Castilian and particularly in the case of the latter focused their praises on the glories of Castile and the Castilian language. Miguel de Unamuno, the highly influential writer and philosopher, was well aware of the growing interest in the non-Castilian regions in their languages and in a renewed literature in these. His contact and letters exchanged with the Catalan poet Joan Maragall are famous. Unamuno, however, was convinced that Castilian was *the* Spanish language and that it stood above any other Peninsular language in defining national identity. In his *En torno al casticismo*, a collection of essays written between 1894 and 1911, he writes:

> La lengua es el receptáculo de la experiencia de un pueblo y el sedimento de su pensar, en los hondos repliegues de sus metáforas . . . ha ido dejando sus huellas al espíritu colectivo del pueblo . . .
>
> (Unamuno, 1957: 42)[9]

Unamuno was aware of Herderian thought indirectly through the work of Hegel (Serrano, 1998: 353–6) as is clear in this quotation, and he emphasises the role of language in the national psyche, at the same time developing Rousseau's belief that the people (for Unamuno 'el pueblo') are 'the nation'. This *pueblo* for Unamuno is led by Castile as represented by the Castilian language.

> Hay otro hecho y es de que la lengua oficial de España sea la castellana, que está lleno de significación viva. Porque del latín brotó en España más de un romance, pero uno entre ellos, el *castellano*, se ha hecho

lengua nacional e internacional además, y camina a ser verdadera lengua española que va formándose sobre el núcleo castellano.

(Unamuno, 1957: 43)[10]

For Unamuno, and many others of this group of writers, the dominance of Castile was indisputable.

As we shall see in the next chapter, even Rosalía de Castro, one of the most important figures of Galician letters, chose in her later years only to write in Castilian. These intellectuals have had a profound impact on debates concerning the question of Spanish national identity. The emphasis on the role of Castile was highlighted by such influential writers as Ortega y Gasset and Menéndez Pidal. Both are quoted in López García:

> Castilla ha hecho a España y Castilla la ha deshecho. Núcleo inicial de la incorporación ibérica, Castilla acertó superar su propio particularismo e invitó a los demás pueblos peninsulares para que colaborasen en un gigantesco proyecto de la vida en común.
> (Ortega y Gasset *España invertebrada*, cited in López García, 1985: 63)[11]

> Castilla es hegemónica entre los pueblos peninsulares hermanos, porque en la individualista España, Castilla abriga en su masa popular un más eficiente individualismo.
> (Menéndez Pidal *Los españoles en la historia*, cited in López García, 1985: 63–4)[12]

At the start of the twentieth century Spain found herself isolated from the rest of Europe in terms of her lack of industrialisation and modernisation, and of her political processes. Although the state bureaucracy was highly centralised in Madrid, the more successful economies of the peripheries, such as in Catalonia and the Basque Country, were presenting major tensions in terms of national identity. The beginnings of industrialisation were giving rise to substantial social instability.

The period of the First World War allowed for some economic progress as Spain, a neutral bystander, acted as provider to the warring sides. This was followed, however, by a time of major recession, mirrored in politics by the dictatorship of Primo de Rivera (1923–31). As so often in Spain's history, this dictatorship was characterised by forces of centralism and oppression of the minority communities and their languages.

In 1931 the king was forced into exile, which led to the proclamation of the Second Republic, a period of hectic radical policies and incipient reforms, in such areas as land reform, education, the establishment of a secular state, autonomy statutes for Catalonia, the Basque Country and Galicia. All of this, however, was cut short by the outbreak of the Civil War, the result of the inability of the country to sustain the conflicting challenges of these reforms. As I have commented elsewhere:

These attempted reforms reflect the cleavages that cut through Spanish society in the nineteenth century – religious splits, cultural-regional splits, social-political splits – and which, it is essential to stress, do not necessarily correspond. The fact that, for example, the cultural aspirations of the Catalan bourgeoisie were not the same as the anti-Catholic anarchist working class movement also active in Catalonia, has a lot to do with why the success of the peripheral nationalisms was not greater. The 1936–39 Civil War was, amongst other things, a bloody manifestation of Spain's multiple identity crises.

(Mar-Molinero, in press)

One feature of the Republic's desire to reform the Spanish state was its recognition of a need to de-centralise, and to underline this in greater support for the non-Castilian languages. As we will see later, Catalan in particular benefited from this greater tolerance and encouragement.

In Chapter 5 we will discuss the role of language in the nationalist agenda of the Franco regime which followed the Civil War, and which once again sought to create a Spanish nation from a highly centralised Castilian focus in Madrid.

Although Castilian's importance has grown over the centuries on the Iberian Peninsula, it nonetheless can be seen to closely reflect the successes or weaknesses of the project of a Spanish nation. Ironically perhaps, the strength of Castilian beyond its place of origin may seem stronger and often less ambiguous than in Spain itself. However, as we shall see in the following section, the Castilianisation process in Spanish-speaking America once again runs side by side with the nation-building process.

Spanish in the Americas[13]

Precisely at the moment that Castilian can be said to have consolidated its position in the Iberian Peninsula, it was given a further boost to its prestige and development with the birth of Spain's American Empire. As we have noted, Spanish has been exported to other areas of the world, but by far the most important and vital region beyond Europe for the use of Spanish is in Spanish-speaking America. It is essential, in fact, to remember that the proportion of the global Spanish-speaking population found in Europe is a small minority compared with Spanish-speaking America. A legitimate question, therefore, must be whether the centre now of the Spanish-speaking world and the focus for an analysis of the language is in fact America and no longer Spain, despite being the birthplace of the Spanish language.

In this section I shall trace the arrival of Spanish in the Americas and discuss the language policies followed there in the colonial period. I shall then look at the pattern of language use in the region in the period since independence. There will not be space to discuss each country individually, but instead we will look for the trends and note any differences.[14]

As we have already seen, in 1492 Christopher Columbus made the first voyage to the Americas on behalf of the Spanish Crown. From then over the next three centuries, Spain expanded its settlement and colonisation of much of Central and Southern America. As a result today Spanish is used as the official language in eighteen independent states: in the Caribbean, Cuba and the Dominican Republic; in Central America, Mexico, Guatemala, Honduras, El Salvador, Costa Rica, Nicaragua and Panama; and in South America, in Colombia, Venezuela, Ecuador, Peru, Chile, Bolivia, Paraguay, Uruguay and Argentina. As we have noted earlier, it is the mother tongue of a significant-sized population in parts of the US, and is the co-official language in the US 'protectorate' of Puerto Rico.

The colonising enterprise was twofold: political-economic and religious. The former helped extend global Spanish influence in a time of the great European empires, as well as providing Spain with abundant wealth in terms of natural resources and, later, in the lucrative trade routes of this region. The latter was an ideological justification for the imposition of Spanish control and ownership on the region. This twofold enterprise is reflected too in the twin bodies affecting the settlement of the region, and, ultimately, its linguistic configuration; that is, the Spanish Crown (and its administration) and the Church (and its clergy).

The colonial period is characterised by the gradual but inexorable move from multilingualism – the coexistence of native preconquest languages with Spanish – to a Castilianisation process leaving Castilian as the dominant linguistic variety throughout the colonies. When the early colonisers arrived, the continent was home to many hundreds of Amerindian languages, amongst which existed some that performed the role of *lingua franca*, or dominant linguistic variety in vast empires, such as the case of Quechua in the Incan empire of the Andean region, or Nahuatl of the Aztec empire through parts of Mexico. Other major indigenous languages being used at the time of the conquest, often as a means of communication in areas where many other mother tongues were spoken, are Mayan with its centre in the Yucatan Peninsula, Guarani in present-day Paraguay, and Mapuche or Araucano in Chile.

Inevitably the language of the conquerors began to be imposed in important areas of daily life, such as administration, trading, and legal transactions. As we have commented already, the language of dominant powers is the language that will normally become the most prestigious and widely used. This soon occurred with Spanish in the American colonies. This process was helped too by the existence of the written form of Spanish in linguistic contexts where conventional European-style writing did not exist. We can describe this process as an early form of Anderson's concept of an 'imagined community' in that it served to bring together both in reality and psychologically what was a vast inaccessible geographical area. We are not yet talking of a 'nation' as was to emerge in later centuries through the bonding by print-language, but a Spanish-speaking community was securely reinforced by the existence of written government documents, chronicles, the exchange of letters and of course religious texts.

In the early colonial period, through to the seventeenth century, the language policy of the Spanish Crown – and therefore the Church – encouraged the use of the native languages. This was partly the consequence of the practical reality that not enough of the conquered population knew Spanish, and so an early objective was to teach Spanish to the native nobility in order that they might help in the local administration and liaise with the populace (Von Gleich, 1994: 84). But another reason was the belief at this time that the most efficient way of Christianising the indigenous population was through the use of their native mother tongues. At first this was achieved by using bilingual (native) interpreters, but gradually the religious orders considered that it would be more successful for them to learn the native languages. However, on the whole many of the Spanish clergy were reluctant and unenthusiastic about learning indigenous languages and still relied heavily on interpreters.

However, Cerrón-Palomino (1989) argues that right from the start of the colonial period there were pressures to move away from the use of the indigenous languages and to impose Castilian. He identifies three types of pressure: political, cultural-religious and linguistic (Cerrón-Palomino, 1989: 21). The first is in line with the desire throughout the Spanish empire for tight unity and for centralisation (as we have already seen was developing in Spain itself). The Spanish American empire was not divided into the many separate countries that we find on the map today, but for administrative purposes, into four large 'Viceroyalties', all dependent on the Spanish Crown. Spanish was one vehicle through which to achieve this centralising process.

Secondly, it was argued that as long as the native population continued to operate only in their mother tongues, even for religious purposes, they would continue to remain outside the values and principles of Christian ways of living. The third point is closely related to this last as it was claimed that the non-Castilian mother tongues were not suitable, linguistically-speaking, to convey the ideas and values of Christianity. They were seen as inferior languages lacking the grammatical and semantic richness to deal with the sophisticated complexities of Christian thought.[15]

As a result of these pressures the Spanish Crown began to declare decrees and policies which eventually represented a clear and unambiguous policy of Castilianisation. For example, in 1634, Von Gleich (1994: 86) explains that 'Philip IV issued an order to archbishops and bishops commanding priests to use "the gentlest possible means" to teach all Indians Spanish'.

However, the real move to total Castilianisation coincides with the occurrence of the same process in Spain itself. The decree of Charles III directing the use of Castilian in administration and education was to be applied in the American colonies too. From now onwards the Church's work was to be through Spanish only. Whilst most Spanish priests and clergy were not unhappy with or actively welcomed this decree, the Jesuits had always been firmly committed to learning and working through the indigenous languages.

Their expulsion from Latin America in 1767 paved the way for little opposition to the new policy. The Crown did in fact stipulate that as part of this policy the teaching of Spanish should be made available to the indigenous population. However, this was largely ignored, on the one hand because of the lack of resources to deliver such full-scale education, and on the other, because of a deliberate lack of commitment from the Spanish-speaking landowners. For the Spanish-speaking elites it was more comfortable to have labour from a population who were ignorant and disenfranchised by their lack of mastery of Castilian.

Clearly the characteristics of the Spanish introduced into the Americas at the time of the conquests and colonisation is relevant to any discussion of this variety, or rather varieties, today. In order to identify the features of Latin American Spanish (or Spanishes), it is helpful to note what influenced the varieties spoken at the time of the major settlements.

It is commonly argued that American Spanish is heavily influenced by the Andalusian form of Spanish, with which it appears to have much in common. Reasons for this are given as being the fact that Andalusia, and especially Seville, was the place of departure for most of the colonising voyages. It has been claimed that the majority of the early settlers were Andalusian. We have already seen that the minority (non-Castilian) communities were initially prevented from being involved in this colonisation process, and that this was directed from Castile. In fact most of the early 'conquistadores' were Castilian or Extremaduran. The dialect of the latter group is significantly similar to Andalusian Spanish. Nonetheless, as Lipski (1994: 36–9) argues, there is not sufficient evidence to be categorical about this claim for Andalusian. As he explains, it would seem that Andalusian immigration, if it is the majority group, is only marginally so. He also argues that some of the features which are claimed to be held in common are not restricted to the Andalusian variety of Spanish. Also significant in the populating of the Americas was the role of immigration from the Canary Islands, which were a stopping point for the ships en route to the Americas. Lipski also emphasises the fact which we have already seen in the previous section that this is a period when the languages of the Peninsula are still in relatively early stages of their development, and Castilian and its Andalusian dialect had only recently emerged as the modern forms we can recognise today. The Spanish language and dialects of both the Peninsula and the colonies were still very much in the early phases of the consolidation of their modern characteristics.

Lipski suggests that it is also interesting to note the social origins of the settlers and how, if at all, this might affect the language spoken:

> The sociolinguistic profile of Spanish settlers in the New World . . .
> departed significantly from the demographics of the Iberian Peninsula.
> Both peasants and landed gentry were severely underrepresented in the
> colonies, and the first waves of settlers were predominantly members of

skilled trades, small landowners, from marginal zones or areas beset by climatic disasters, and individuals who for whatever reason had not done well economically or socially in Europe.

(Lipski, 1994: 40)

He emphasises how in this period education was considerably less widespread and consequently literacy often not possessed even by the elites. He also stresses the different lifestyles in the colonies from that experienced in Spain – with fewer luxuries and more need for 'hands-on' work by all – which further reduced the differential between upper and lower classes in social and cultural norms including speech.

By the eighteenth century, as the opposition towards the Spanish Crown began to gather the steam that eventually led to the wars of independence and the birth of independent Latin American republics, Spanish was firmly established as the language of public and official life. The elites were monolingual in Spanish and increasingly the wider population was becoming functionally bilingual, in order to trade and survive. Nonetheless a vast proportion of the population was still largely monolingual in one of the mother tongue indigenous languages.

With the loss of the majority of the colonies from Spanish control in the early nineteenth century the region was fragmented into many diverse republics, eighteen of which as we have seen, were to be governed by Spanish-speaking elites. This division into independent republics was highly constructed and, in many senses, unnatural. In some cases geographical barriers created boundaries, but very often nothing so logical formed the frontiers. In particular the new states[16] paid no attention to preconquest 'nations' or indigenous peoples[17] who for social, cultural and linguistic reasons made up clearly coherent communities which now found themselves straddling political borders (such as the Mayans in Mexico and Guatemala, or the Aymara people in Peru and Bolivia, to name two amongst many examples). As a result, these highly-constructed new republics faced as an early challenge the urgent need to promote a sense of nationhood. We can see then that the kind of nation-building that took place in post-colonial Latin America was of a deliberate, overt, political kind. Spanish not only was not the language of the majority of Latin American populations, but it was also the language of the expelled colonial power. Nonetheless as part of the political nationalist agenda it was chosen as one of the tools to help unify and create the 'nation'.

It is no coincidence that many of the early leaders of independent Latin American republics were directly or indirectly influenced by the events and thinking of the French Revolution and its aftermath. Simon Bolivar (known as 'the Liberator'), one of the most influential thinkers and fighters for Latin American independence, had studied the great French writers of the eighteenth century and visited Spain, France and Italy at the beginning of the nineteenth century. Bolivar was particularly influenced by Rousseau and his vision of a nation based on political equality. All citizens, according to Rousseau and thus to Bolivar, should play a part in the new democratic state, and should therefore have access to a means of communication to allow this participation. In the same way that French was deliberatedly promoted as the language of the French nation and unifier of the French people, in many of the young Latin American republics, Spanish was consciously promoted as a national identity marker and as a passport to citizenship.

The nature of the nationalist drive in the many independent states of course varies, and so too does the role of language in the nation-building. In some situations the conscious Herderian link with nation = language = state equation is stronger than in others. This is the case in Mexico, where the language is deliberately elaborated to fit nationalist dogma:

> The process of decolonialisation, however incipient, is initiated in the nineteenth century with scientific studies of Amerindian languages . . . As a result the new leaders engaged in a reform of Peninsular Spanish, adopted everyday vocabulary from Indian languages, and began to delve deep into the national past.
>
> (Hidalgo, 1994: 191)

Hidalgo concludes:

> So strong was the ideological foundation of the nineteenth century that at the onset of the twentieth century one finds a major preoccupation with language and ethnic diversity. The nation-state is firmly consolidated and the Indian languages begin to dramatically decrease in the face of paradoxical efforts to preserve them.
>
> (Hidalgo, 1994: 192)

This combination of a desire to install European culture and values (through the language, the religion, literature, government, etc.) with an interest in the 'national' past and its indigenous peoples can be observed in various parts of Latin America. Often this represented a romantic movement inspired by Westernised intellectuals whose attitude towards the preconquest past has been criticised as being patronising and essentially assimiliationist (Díaz-Polanco, 1987, 1988). We will be looking in more detail at the role of the non-Spanish languages in the post-colonial nation-building period in Chapter 3.

The construction of nationhood in nineteenth-century Latin American republics is closely reflected in the many constitutions drawn up in these states. These documents set out the rights and duties of the members of the new nations, i.e. the citizens.[18] The tension lies in the definition of citizenhood, in deciding who could participate in the life of the nation-state. Alvar (1986: Chapter X) has undertaken a fascinating and detailed analysis of these constitutions and the many changes they underwent in establishing what constituted citizenship. He stresses the role of literacy and, in particular, therefore, literacy in Spanish as a frequent requirement in, at least, the early constitutions, thus effectively disenfranchising a large proportion of the (indigenous) populations in much of Latin America. Alvar charts how over the century in many states which had started with utopian visions of nationality and citizenship in the hope or expectation that all its inhabitants would learn to read and write in Spanish, gradually a pragmatic realism took over which recognised the lack of resources, training or even commitment to the large-scale education provision that this entailed. Without this provision, the early constitutions were documents of institutionalised inequality. As Alvar comments:

> El hombre que no sabe sus derechos y que no es libre para ejercerlos se queda en una triste condición en la que los derechos civiles serán para él como la inesperada limosna que le viene a la mano, los derechos políticos le están vedados y los derechos sociales no los logra, porque difícilmente alcanza este mínimo de economía que le permita vivir con la dignidad que el hombre debe exigir.
>
> (Alvar, 1986: 283–4)[19]

Constitutions were changed to make the literacy requirement less prescriptive, but at the same time recognise their governments' commitment to national education.

Once again, then, we see the important link between membership of a nation, language and education. For, if governments were serious in their desire to include all their inhabitants in their construction of the national identity by promoting the desirability of universal literacy, then it was obvious that they must also defend the right to education and support this with the necessary resources. In his survey of constitutional statements regarding governments' responsibilities in national education provision, Alvar writes:

> De una u otra manera, casi sin excepción, todos los gobiernos se han enfrentado con los mismos problemas y han tratado de darles solución. En tales casos hay que descender de las grandilocuencias olímpicas a la pobre realidad cotidiana, y la pobre realidad afecta al presupuesto nacional, a los docentes y a la lucha contra el analfabetismo.
>
> (Alvar, 1986: 280–81)[20]

We can see, then, that the Spanish language and a national education system were seen by the nineteenth-century nation-builders as important tools in their enterprise. Thus, the Castilianisation process was now underwritten by the constitutions, laws and centres of education throughout Latin America.[21] As Campos Carr comments:

> After Independence, education became the means for 'national integration' for each country, an attempt to unify a sometimes very diverse population under the allegiance of one flag. Education has remained, nevertheless, the product of the social class that has dominated each period.
>
> (Campos Carr, 1990: 51)

As part of this nineteenth-century Castilianisation process in Latin America, debates surfaced as to the unity of this language, as opposed to the potential fragmentation leading to significantly different dialects that the political and geographical diversity seemed to indicate. This debate has continued ever since.

On the one hand, the push to have everyone learn Spanish often meant that the providers of this language teaching were fiercely protective of the 'unified' language and determined to defend its norms, as laid down by the Spanish RAE. A highly significant moment in this defence of the essential unity of the Spanish language in Latin America was the publication of the Venezuelan linguist Andrés Bello's famous *Gramática de la lengua castellana destinada al uso de los americanos* in 1847 (Thompson, 1992: 55).

However, the tension existed between maintaining the norms and centralisation of the Spanish language as prescribed from Madrid, and recognising local features and their role in consolidating national identity, and so the new republics began setting up their own national language academies in the early part of the nineteenth century (Edwards, 1985).

Until well into the twentieth century, then, language and education policies in Latin America promoted monolingualism and a Westernised monocultural view of society. The obvious pluralism of the region and wealth of diversity and linguistic hetereogeneity were ignored or suppressed in the drive to create unified national identities. The link with Spain in this was ambiguous, as, on the one hand, the new republics wanted to throw off their dependence on and control by the imperial Crown, but, on the other, the values, culture and, of course, language were the legacy of and inspired by the European colonisers:

> La lengua ha sido testimonio de la opresión y del imperialismo: lo que a finales del siglo XV era una realidad histórica, por más que la humanidad se lastime, en el siglo XX sigue siendo instrumento de intervención y de extorsión de las conciencias.
>
> (Alvar, 1986: 335)[22]

We will discuss later on how far this is still a valid observation in Latin America today.

'Español' or 'Castellano'

Thus far I have referred to the spread of Spanish across the globe as the 'Castilianisation' process. It could of course be argued that a more correct term might be 'Spanish-isation'. However, I have tried to emphasise that this process has its roots firmly in the emergence of Castilian as the dominant variety in the Iberian Peninsula. It is reasonable to argue that the point at which 'Castilian' or 'Spanish' become interchangeable when discussing the language issue in Spain is around the eighteenth century. However, not eveyone agrees that these terms are indeed interchangeable. This controversy is particularly complicated in Spanish-speaking America. In this section we will briefly examine this controversy[23] to see if any clarity can be brought at least to the causes of the debate, if not the outcome. I would like to stress that our discussion is further complicated by my belief that the terms have a different nuance in English – where the subtleties of the distinction are largely unknown – from Spanish.

In the first section of this chapter we noted the progress of Castilian as the language of the most powerful group in the Iberian Peninsula, and how the dominance of Castile eventually led to the dominance of Castilian over other dialects and languages of the Peninsula. It is important to stress that this process saw Castilian influenced and shaped by its contact with the other dialects and languages, and during its development took on some of the forms, words and characteristic sounds of the other languages, as is always the case when languages come into contact. As the Castilian influence spread, and in particular with the growth of a foreign empire in Europe and the Americas, this dominating language became more and more distanced from its roots in Castile. Initially in fact Castilian was little more than a *lingua franca* and only later became the mother tongue of much of Spain, and then the elites of the Empire.

López García (1985) in fact argues very forcefully in an interesting and provocative book that the language which became Spanish or *español* is not in reality 'Castilian' but what he describes as a *koine*, the result of various dominant Peninsular dialects. He therefore arrives at the interesting conclusion that this led the Spanish *koine* to give rise to a community or 'nation' speaking a shared variety, rather than the reverse.

> Podríamos decir que el concepto comunitario español no surgió en un territorio que daba nombre a la lengua – como el francés –, ni en torno a una etnia que la bautizó igualmente – como el alemán –, sino que en la península es la lengua lo que crea la comunidad y justamente la lengua en calidad de instrumento de comunicación aprendido y por lo tanto libremente adoptado.
>
> (López García, 1985: 61–2)[24]

This is a somewhat unusual explanation of the birth of Spanish, but one worth considering. Even if we remain with the idea that 'Spanish' is principally a development of 'Castilian', this development certainly followed the pattern outlined by López García as it served as the prime means of communication across the loosely linked parts of the new kingdom, and to that extent we can support his argument that the language created the national community, and not the other way round.

Whether we accept that Spanish developed directly from the Castilian dialect, or whether we believe it was an amalgam of various Peninsular dialects, prominent in which was Castilian, it remains true that throughout the centuries people have continued to use both names 'Castilian' and 'Spanish' to refer to the same language. It is possible to find arguments as explanations for both nomenclatures, and impossible to claim that either one is the definitive name.

For example, in Spain preference is sometimes observed for 'Castilian' when the aim is to emphasise the dominance of this Peninsular community over any others, as we noted with the '98 Generation. Not surprisingly too, in order to counter this effect it is often those from areas other than Castile but where Spanish, rather than one of the other Peninsular languages, is the mother tongue, who are particularly quick to object to the use of 'Castilian' to describe 'Spanish' (such as the Andalusian linguist Gregorio Salvador who is a stern and frequent critic of this use, e.g. Salvador, 1987, 1992).

On the other hand, as we will discuss in detail in Chapter 5, the choice of 'Castilian' over 'Spanish' might in fact be a deliberate recognition that Spain possesses more 'Spanish' languages than just Castilian, such as Basque and Catalan. In both the constitutions of the Second Republic in 1931, and after the death of Franco in 1978, 'Castilian' rather than 'Spanish' was chosen to identify Spain's official language.

How we name our language is yet another mark of our identity, and therefore it is important in the messages it gives. This is as true in terms of how others see us as how we see ourselves. The comparison here with 'British' and 'English' or with 'England' and (for example) 'UK' and the terms 'Castile/Castilian' and 'Spain/Spanish' is interesting (see Williams, 1995). On going abroad, many UK citizens are familiar with the tendency to hear themselves referred to as 'English' and as coming from 'England', even when they are Scottish, Welsh or from Northern Ireland. On the other hand, the same is not true of Spaniards in the sense that no one associates them as coming from Castile.

The corollary of the focus on the place and nationality of all from the United Kingdom as being 'English' to foreigners is that there is no dispute as to the name of the language spoken by the majority there, i.e. English. Insofar as outside Spain, Castile is not recognised as significant, the use of 'Castilian' by foreigners to describe the language is rare, with the important exception of Latin Americans. Lynn Williams (1995) argues that the British Empire, with England clearly heading it, reached its height later than the

Castile-led Spanish Empire, and that England therefore has left her legacy more recently for those outside the UK identifying the culture, language, social norms, etc., of its people, whereas Castile is not associated on the outside as the focus of Spanish culture and language. Whilst within Spain people may express their identity as Castilian, Catalan, Basque, Aragonese, etc., outside everyone is perceived as 'Spanish'.

The issue of 'Spanish' versus 'Castilian' however is highlighted by the ambiguous attitudes to it in Latin America. It is hard to pinpoint which term rather than the other is used in Latin America. However, both are used in daily speech and in official documents. Alvar (1986) has examined this phenomenon in his survey of national constitutions, and finds that 'Spanish' predominates, but that there are quite a few places where 'Castilian' is used instead (e.g. Ecuador, Panama, Paraguay, El Salvador and Venezuela). Alvar notes how some countries have changed the name of their official language in later editions of their constitutions, and that this appears to be a continuing trend. It has been suggested (Thompson, 1992: 55) that 'Castilian' was preferred in many of the earlier constitutions because it was a political and ideological rejection of any legacy of the former colonial power. In a language attitude survey carried out by Alvar (1986: Chapter 3), in Guatemala, it emerged that 'Castilian' was more widely used than 'Spanish' and that the main reason seemed to be that the informants could associate 'Spanish' with 'Spain' (and therefore not with Guatemala) whilst 'Castilian' was not identified with anywhere in particular (despite its origins in Castile). Speakers are equally adamant about which term they use as to its validity and appropriateness. In Guatemala, and other parts of Latin America, the lack of awareness of Castile, leads to a preference for the use of 'Castilian', whereas in, for example, the US, Spanish-speakers dislike the term 'Castilian' precisely because it is linked to a region of Spain with which they feel no association whatsoever.

It is difficult to find easy categories or neat explanations for the choice of terms when describing this language, particularly in Latin America. Clearly, as is shown in the Guatemalan survey, the term used will reflect local and national usage. 'Castilian' is the usual term in Guatemala, and everyone uses it, and many when asked why, simply said because that was what it was called at school. But this issue does also seem to excite very personal reactions and attitudes defying easy classification and predictions for the future. A typical example of this highly subjective association with the name of, in this case, a Mexican's mother tongue, can be seen in a comment from the famous philosopher, writer and Nobel Prize winner Octavio Paz:

> Yo me siento ciudadano de la lengua española y no ciudadano mexicano; por eso me molesta mucho que se hable de lengua castellana, porque el castellano es de los castellanos y yo no lo soy; yo soy mexicano y como mexicano hablo español y no castellano.
>
> (cited in Salvador, 1987: 92)[25]

Conclusion

At the start of this chapter I suggested we would want to ask what the nature of the role of Spanish has been in the nation-building of Spain and Spanish America. In answering this it is necessary to decide to what extent either Spain or the Latin American republics in fact meet the criteria to be classified as 'nations' or 'states'. The role of language is closely related to this.

I would suggest that in neither case are we dealing entirely with discrete 'nations'. It must be clear that all of these Spanish-speaking countries are in fact multicultural and multiethnic and by the definitions offered in Chapter 1 containing within their political borders many nations, whether these be Catalan, Basque, Galician in Spain, or any of the many indigenous nations in Latin America.

The '98 Generation in particular tried to claim the existence of the Spanish 'nation' created naturally and inevitably from the historical process that saw the pre-eminence of Castile. Unamuno and others who shared his ideas write of the role of language in this concept of Spain in the same vein that Herder saw the link with language and national identity. They were writing of course at the height of cultural nationalism in Europe and many nationalists were expressing similar ideas. In fact, paradoxically, at exactly the same time, as we shall see in the next chapter, the Catalans (and to a lesser extent the Galicians) were promoting their own sense of a separate identity in terms of language, history, and culture. It is hard to find compatibility between these different views of the 'nation' in the Iberian Peninsula. Instead, the history of the development of Castilian and its role in public life in Spain is very much one that confirms the political nationalist approach. We have gradually seen an awareness of the conscious role of language in centralising the Spanish state and imposing one particular culture in the form of nationalist policies and the deliberate construction of a Spanish nation-state. In later chapters we will be arguing that this is still the case today.

In Latin America the first notable point (observed by e.g. Anderson, 1992: 47) is that in the opposition to the Spanish Crown and the beginnings of the formulation of new 'American' identities, language was not an issue. It could not be an issue as the European-origin elites spoke the same language as the colonial power. Language in Latin America played a different kind of role in the early stages of the independence movements, as we noted in Chapter 1, with the role of print-language providing the coherence and form of transmission of the ideas and models which were to support and legitimise the wars of independence. Once this independence had been won, the crude political divisions into numerous 'states' meant that the young Latin American republics needed to plan their nation-building in an entirely overt and deliberate way, where Spanish was frequently one important tool designed to achieve national unity and sense of identity.

Given the way, then, that Spanish has been so consciously directed and manipulated in the desire to create nations, it will not be surprising to find the conflict and antagonism this has frequently caused those non-Spanish language communities with whom Spanish came and comes into contact, as we will see in the next chapter.

3 Counter-nationalism and the other languages of the Spanish-speaking world

The conclusion arrived at in Chapter 2 was that the countries of the Spanish-speaking world do not fall easily into the category of 'nation' as understood in Chapter 1. That is to say that countries such as Spain, Mexico, Peru or Nicaragua, for example, cannot be described as communities with a totally shared sense of unity as the result of possessing a range of common characteristics seen as prerequesites for nationhood. In many of these cases the essential solidarity is too easily exposed as fragile with various social and cultural cleavages preventing it. This is hardly surprising when we remember how many ethnic groups are contained within the political boundaries of these countries. As we have seen, they have been built into states through alliances, wars, economic pressure, demographic trends, policies of centralisation, etc., and the result is plural societies made up of substate-level nations. The level of resistance from these stateless nations and their self-awareness and desire for autonomy is an important issue in evaluating the success of nation-building in Spain and Latin America, and one major factor in the course of language development.

It is true that patriotism can often be called on in relations with outside communities, and in these circumstances (ranging from wars to, for example, sporting events) people may well consider themselves 'Spanish' or 'Mexican' or 'Peruvian', etc. However, even this may be uncertain: the 1992 Olympic Games in Barcelona were certainly seen first and foremost by most Catalans as being *Catalan* rather than *Spanish*. Every effort was made to underline this, ranging from the use of Catalan before Spanish in all announcements, to the flying of the Catalan as well as the Spanish flag, and the advertising in major international media of the existence and importance of Catalonia. Equally, at the other end of the scale in terms of resources and self-confidence, many indigenous communities in Mexico or Peru may have no interest nor awareness of the role of Mexico or Peru in the global scene. A symbolic example of this is the easy way the indigenous (mainly Aymara) people cross daily over the 'international' bridge between Peru and Bolivia, completely unaware and unaffected by the legal and political details of passport and customs controls. The international bridge represents a line on a map; maps have no meaning to many illiterate and undereducated Aymaran people.

In this chapter we will examine the history of some of these communities in order to see the effect and influence this has had and, significantly, continues to have on Spanish and Latin American nationalisms and on the Castilianisation process.[1] In the first part I will examine the major non-Spanish linguistic communities in Spain – the Catalans, Basques and Galicians – and in the second part representative examples of indigenous linguistic communities in Latin America, such as the Quechua-speaking, the Nahuatl-speaking and the Guarani peoples. We will also briefly discuss the impact of other linguistic communities in Latin America. Underlying the discussion throughout in this chapter is of course the role of language in creating counter-nationalism and alternative imagined communities.

The linguistic minority communities in Spain

In Chapter 2 we saw how slowly the move from very loose federation to tight centralisation took place in the Peninsula, and how this affected the development of Castilian and its place as dominant language. Here we will examine how far some of the non-Castilian languages also continued to develop and what role they played within their linguistic communities. We will concentrate on those languages which still today are spoken by sizeable populations and have been recognised in recent Spanish constitutions as significant communities. Of the many separate kingdoms and regions which flourished up until the fifteenth century in the Peninsula, today only the Catalans, Basques, and Galicians are usually recognised as having discrete linguistic varieties which can be called 'language'. This is, however, disputed by some, reminding us of the difficulty of defining 'language' and 'dialect' and of the largely political criteria which are applied. We will see below how some are not convinced that, for example, Galician is in fact a separate independent language, and we will hear claims for other regions, such as Valencia, Asturias and Aragon, to have their language (and therefore, potentially, their 'national' identity) recognised. By choosing to concentrate on these particular three I am following common practice which recognises the special status normally granted them as '*comunidades históricas*', as well as acknowledging the size of their populations and the range of cultural and political features which allow them to stand out as coherent separate communities with different traditions and cultures from the central Castilian-Spanish one.

In the desire to recognise these three communities' differences from much of the so-called 'Spanish' norm and the need, therefore, to examine their frequent conflicts and tensions with the central state, there is a danger of linking all three together and ignoring their very significant differences from each other. It is certainly true that on many occasions these communities have found it useful to unite in their shared opposition to the Madrid government, but it is inaccurate and unhelpful to think that they are all three broadly similar. Their geographic situations, natural resources, demographic trends, economy and cultural legacies ensure three very different regions. Not surprisingly, the role of language and the linguistic characteristics of each region also vary importantly. Even the extent to which we can, using our earlier definitions, defend the use of the term 'nation' to describe these three communities is very different.

The Catalans[2]

When Castile was only beginning to assert its importance in the fight to oust the Arabs, the Catalans peopled a powerful and prestigious seaborne empire, which stretched from the Iberian Peninsula through parts of France and to enclaves in southern Italy, Greece and parts of North Africa. The Catalan language mirrored the prestige of this political power. Catalan emerged as a respected language and was considered on a cultural par to Italian and French in the post-Latin era of medieval Europe. Catalan was spoken in much of its territory, even beyond the Iberian Peninsula, and used as the language of public and official life and, increasingly, of written documents and literary life, as Latin was largely replaced. Only in Aragon did Catalan remain merely a spoken variety. An important output of literary and philosophical texts was produced in this period, particularly in the fifteenth century and expecially in Valencia. The existence of this important literary heritage is an essential part of Catalan's continuing status today, and one factor in its success and survival even in times of great persecution and oppression. Inevitably as Castile began to dominate the Peninsula, the importance of the *Països Catalans* (the Catalan Countries) diminished and parts were lost (like Roussillon to France) or separated from Catalonia. In the rest of this section I shall be referring to the region of Catalonia, a territory of nearly thirty-two thousand square kilometres in the northeastern point of the Iberian Peninsula, which does not include Valencia, the Balearic Islands, or any of the other regions which previously had been part of the Catalan Countries. However, the legacy of the Catalan language was left in these regions, and so I will briefly return to the issue of Catalan outside Catalonia later on.

The political and clerical hierarchy was increasingly Castilian-speaking, and, as we have already noted, the Castilian Crown introduced more and more centralising laws and policies. However, it is not until the beginning of the eighteenth century that Catalonia lost her last residual rights and laws. By then, however, the Catalan language had already become largely a spoken variety only. One of the consequences of the loss of the use of Catalan as a written language was a parallel loss of fixed norms and a resulting dialectisation and fragmentation (Valverdú, 1984). Catalan found itself then at the lowest ebb in its role as flagbearer of its community. Up until the nineteenth century, the Castilianisation process that we traced in Chapter 2 militated against the strength and vitality of Catalan.

As we have mentioned already, the nineteenth century saw an increased interest and awareness in regional communities with an idealised championing of their cultures, languages and traditions, led by the Romantic movement, which was itself very influenced by the writings of Herder. This phenomenon is also seen in Spain, most notably in Catalonia. The movement that is associated with this revival of Catalan culture and Catalan language is known as the *Renaixença*, and is certainly a rebirth of Catalan pride and confidence.

Initially the *Renaixença* was exclusively a cultural movement, and above all else a moment of major poetic output. Catalan poetry was not only vibrant at a literary level, but at a popular one too, with the (re-)introduction in 1859 of the medieval-style poetry festivals, the *Jocs Florals*. Conversi comments:

> The cultural movement of the *Renaixença* (Renaissance) provided an ideal basis for the subsequent spread of nationalism. Its beginnings as a literary movement during the 1830s and '40s were slow, and at the start it seemed no more than a local expression of regionalist pride. . . . Modern Catalan literature began to develop until its outstanding epic, lyric and dramatic poets became the vanguard of Spanish culture at the turn of the century. . . .
>
> In Catalonia, in contrast with the lethargy of other Spanish regions, a musical, artistic, literary and political wave of creativity swept every sector of society.
>
> (Conversi, 1997: 13–15)

Conversi also makes the point that much of this artistic and creative production was in fact a reaction against the modernisation and industrialisation which Catalonia was then experiencing. The cultural movement served as an escape into the past, and, according to Conversi (1997: 16) a 'historicist reconstruction of an idealised past focused especially on the Middle Ages'. As we have explained earlier, this ability to look back to the successes of things Catalan in an earlier era, are crucial to the self-confidence of Catalans today. This legacy, now revived and reconstructed by the nineteenth-century writers, provided the legitimacy for the sense of Catalan identity which was becoming increasingly important, not only culturally but also politically.

This revival in their own cultural awareness, and an increasing frustration with the perceived backwardness of the politically-corrupt and primarily agricultural central Spanish state, fuelled the Catalan people's awakening interest in political as well as cultural nationalist issues. The desire began to be felt for greater autonomy in organising their own affairs at a time of industrialisation and modernisation in Catalonia, not shared in the rest of Spain, and with a growing realisation and pride in their separate cultural identity, not least their language.

The specifically Catalan regionalist, and soon nationalist, movement to emerge was preceded by a Spain-wide federalist movement led by a Catalan, Francesc Pi i Margall. Pi i Margall and his followers were influenced both by the Romantic movement and, in political terms, by Proudhon. The federalist agenda which Pi i Margall expounds particularly in his book *Las*

Nacionalidades (1877) shows both anarchist and romantic tendencies. For example his definition of federalism,

> La federación es un sistema por el cual los diversos grupos humanos, sin perder su autonomía en lo que les es peculiar y propio, se asocian y subordinan al conjunto de los de su especie para todos los fines que les son comunes. Es aplicable . . . a todos los grupos y a todas las formas de gobierno. Establece la unidad sin destruir la variedad, y puede llegar a reunir en un cuerpo la humanidad toda sin que se menoscabe la independencia ni se altere el carácter de naciones, provincias, ni pueblos.
>
> (Pi i Margall, 1973: 187)[3]

Pi i Margall proposes federalism for the Iberian Peninsula (to include Portugal) precisely because he recognises its significant diversity, not least in its range of languages (Pi i Margall, 1973: 330). His importance as precursor for the Catalan (and later Basque) nationalists is not so much in his dream of a federal Spain, where he still firmly believes in a 'Spanish' nation and describes the other communities mainly as 'provinces', but in his clear and detailed criticism of the *'principio unitario'* which he believes has failed Spain.

For many commentators the founder of modern political Catalan nationalism is Valentí Almirall, who was influenced by Pi i Margall's ideas, but ready to apply and adapt them to a more specifically Catalan-oriented situation. As Conversi explains:

> Almirall was heir to the Republican tradition of Pi i Margall . . . [but] foresaw greater possibilities of carrying out a separate programme for Catalonia in which federalism would be anchored in local traditions, rather than relying on 'abstract' national and international principles.
>
> (Conversi, 1997: 19)

In 1886 Almirall published his influential book *Lo Catalanisme* where he examines the nature of Catalan identity, its race, national psychology, and personality. He identifies the Catalan language as the most prominent characteristic of being Catalan, which marks out the language as one of the principal 'core values' of Catalan nationalism (Conversi, 1990, 1997).

A pivotal year in the development of Catalan political nationalism is 1892. On the one hand, it sees the drawing up of a programme known as the *Bases de Manresa*, which was a manifesto of political demands for Catalonia agreed amongst various Catalanist groups (notably all middle class and representing the elites of Catalan society) in the town of Manresa. These demands included political autonomy, control of education and the local civil service and police force, and the declaring of Catalan as the only official language in Catalonia. Although this is hardly a text of wide popular participation, and of course, it was not negotiated with any central Spanish government, it is important as the first major political nationalist agenda in modern Catalonia.

Equally important is the publication in the same year of *La Nacionalitat Catalana* by Enric Prat de la Riba, who was to become the principal political figure in this period of Catalan nationalism. This can be considered the key text to an understanding of early Catalan nationalism, moving on from the work of Almirall, but still moderate in terms of not advocating total Catalan independence.

Prat de la Riba, like many Catalan writers in the nineteenth century, was clearly indebted to the ideas of German romanticism and to Herder, which he was acquainted with principally through the writings of the Catalan philosopher Llorens i Barba (Siguan, 1993: 37). *La Nactionalitat Catalana* is full of sections emphasising the national spirit of Catalonia and the role of language in this, in exactly the same terms outlined by Herder. For example, in the following[4]

> Si ser Patria, si ser Nación era tener una lengua, una concepción jurídica, un sentido del arte propio, si era tener espíritu, carácter, pensamiento nacionales, la existencia de la Nación o de la Patria era un hecho natural, como la existencia de un hombre, independiente de los derechos que le fuesen, de hecho, reconocidos. . . .
>
> Llegamos a la idea clara y neta de nacionalidad, a la concepción de esa unidad social, primaria, fundamental, destinada a ser en la sociedad mundial, en la humanidad, lo que es el hombre para la sociedad civil.
>
> (Prat de la Riba, 1982: 72–4)[5]

Prat gives much space and emphasis in his book to the role of language at the heart of the national spirit, and quotes directly from Herder to support this (Prat de la Riba, 1982: 99–100):

> Para conocer un pueblo hay que poseer su lengua, para apreciar su literatura hay que conocer la lengua en que está escrita. Cada nación piensa como habla y habla como piensa.
>
> (Prat de la Riba, 1982: 100)[6]

Finally, Prat places the role of the Catalan language squarely in the centre of his definition of Catalan identity. Its revival and self-assurance is part of Catalonia's realisation of her national identity and individuality. Prat describes the process of re-discovery of the language,

> La lengua materna no era un *patois* en descomposición. Al llegar la hora de despertar las viejas hablas populares, la lengua catalana se alzó, sincera, fuerte, plena de vida renovada y emprendió la larga reconquista de la cultura catalana. . . . La lengua catalana tenía gloriosa historia: la habían hablado y escrito reyes y conquistadores, sabios y apóstoles, poetas y legisladores.
>
> (Prat de la Riba, 1982: 138)[7]

Prat de la Riba pushed forward Catalan political nationalism with the establishment of the (Centre Right) nationalist party the *Lliga*. By 1907 Prat was elected president of the Barcelona local government, the *Diputació*, and in 1914 president of the newly-established *Mancomunitat*. The latter was a grouping of the four Catalan provinces of Barcelona, Tarragona, Girona and Lleida into one administrative unit and, as such, is a precursor of the *Generalitat*, the present government of Catalonia, first set up during the Second Republic, and then revived after the death of Franco. The *Mancomunitat* had fairly limited powers, and especially compared with the Catalan autonomy of today which we will discuss in Chapter 5, it was notably active in the area of promoting and standardising the Catalan language.

In 1907 Prat's administration set up the *Institut d'Estudis Catalans*. Under the auspices of this very influential organisation much work on the elaboration and standardisation of Catalan took place mirroring the growing unity and confidence of Catalan culture and political life generally. The major figure in this enterprise was the linguist Pompeu Fabra who between 1913 and 1932 directed the compilation and publication of definitive orthographic norms for Catalan, a Catalan grammar and a Catalan dictionary. The dialectising process that began with the decline of the written language from the sixteenth century onwards was effectively curtailed by this enormous codification activity. Once again we are reminded of Anderson's emphasis on the role of print-language in the expression of national identity (see Chapter 1).

The Primo de Rivera dictatorship of 1923 to 1930 put an abrupt stop to the flourishing Catalan cultural and political nationalism, and proved a foretaste of the later repression of the Franco regime. Catalan symbols were banned, including the use and teaching of the language. A highly centralised Castilian-speaking Spain was once more the objective of the regime.

The frustration felt with this supression of Catalan nationalism resulted in renewed activity and enthusiasm on the declaration of the Second Republic in 1931. Much of the legislation pursued under the new Statute of Autonomy granted Catalonia then has been taken up again and developed since the death of Franco, in the new democratic period, which we will discuss in Chapter 5. But all of this was brought to a complete and brutal halt first with the outbreak of the Civil War in 1936 and then during the long years of the Franco dictatorship.

Catalan nationalism can be seen to be a movement with wide popular support which whilst initially propelled by the Catalan upper classes, soon enjoyed the participation of the majority of the middle classes, and eventually, particularly during this century, by the working classes too. However, the arrival of many non-Catalan working class immigrants to the region has challenged this Catalan hegemony, and we shall return to examine this in later chapters. In contrast with other communities that we will be discussing in this chapter, the level of support from the middle and upper ranks of Catalan society is crucial in evaluating the success of the movement.

We have seen, too, that Catalan nationalism was both a cultural and political movement, and that the role of language is central to the sense of national identity. The confidence and strength of Catalan nationalism, its wide popular support, and the highly successful and visible badge of its identity in its language have meant that the region has frequently been a very acute thorn in the flesh of Spanish nation-building. As we will see later, this counter-nationalism to Madrid's efforts continues to be a major political issue today.

I have throughout this discussion of modern Catalan nationalism, dating from the nineteenth century, concentrated entirely on Catalonia. However, as we noted earlier, there remain other regions of Spain whose shared history mean that they also have characteristics which certainly make them different from the central Spanish state, and, to a greater or lesser extent, are shared with Catalonia.

The situation of Valencia and the Balearic Islands can be ambiguous. Today they are both autonomous communities and have felt themselves separate from Catalonia for many centuries. However, in both communities linguistic forms that most commentators describe as varieties of Catalan are spoken.

In Valencia — despite having produced some of the most famous writers of the Catalan Golden Age of letters — Catalan became the language of the rural lower classes and lost the prestige it managed to retain in Catalonia even in its most persecuted moments. Valencia in the nineteenth century was a predominantly agrarian society, and one of the least backward agricultural economies amidst the sluggish Spanish chaos. It was a relatively successful and confident society with, however, strong ties with Madrid, rather than Barcelona. There was, therefore, little support for the nationalist aspirations developing in Catalonia, although some interest in the cultural revival was shown amongst the literary elites in Valencia. This resulted in some awakening attention to the Valencian linguistic variety which led a tiny minority to claim a Valencian language other than Castilian or Catalan. This is a continuing issue today, which we will discuss later.

The Balearic Islands also paid some attention to the flourishing cultural activities in Catalonia, and some literary output in Catalan was produced in the Islands, but, like Valencia, this was not linked to any political movement in this very conservative and rural region. We will see when discussing the post-Franco period that today there is a renewed interest in the Catalan language and in an awareness of a Balearic identity.

The Basques[8]

Like the Catalan-speaking area, the Basque-speaking area also straddles the French border, bordering on the Bay of Biscay. The area forming a discrete Basque-speaking community became more and more compressed over the centuries of wars and conquests. We will once again be concentrating the discussion on the Basque Country as defined in political terms as being on the

Spanish side of the border. Obviously nationalist movements – both in the Basque case and the Catalan one – identify their homelands as potentially including all those who share such characteristics as language, race, cultural traditions and history, irrespective of modern political borders. Leaving aside the two Basque regions in France, we will examine the so-called Basque Country, usually now referred to as *Euskadi* (some seven thousand square kilometres), made up of the provinces of Alava, Vizcaya and Guipuzcoa, and, very briefly, the region (formerly kingdom) of Navarra. Although containing some Basque-speaking communities, the latter has always been separate from the Basque Country and has seldom shared in the Basque nationalist movement.

Because of their geography (inaccessible mountains and valleys; coastal towns best reached by sea) the Basques remained largely isolated from the main pattern of events in the Peninsula. Whilst the boundaries were eroded and their territory gradually shrank over the centuries, they remained surprisingly unaffected by the invaders, and those passing through between the Europe of the north (including for a time parts of the Spanish empire) and the powerful capital of Madrid in the south. This is also true in terms of influences on the Basque language. Basque is probably the oldest language in Europe; not only is it not a Romance language, but nor is it Indo-European, as are the vast majority of European languages. Its origins are barely known, and rest on certain archaeological evidence of placenames. However, the important point to stress is its total inaccessibility for Romance speakers – unlike the closeness of the other four major Peninsular languages (Castilian, Catalan, Portuguese and Galician).

Obviously this isolation and distinguishing features (which included other markers as well as language) gave the Basques a very clear sense of separate identity, and for many years this was also reflected in a high degree of political autonomy. In a general sense, the Basques cooperated earlier with the central Spanish Crown than the Catalans, and, significantly, unlike the Catalans, they backed the winning side in the War of Succession which brought the French Bourbon kings to the Spanish throne. In return they were allowed to maintain their special *fueros*, which were local laws and rights, whilst the Catalans lost any remaining ones in 1716.

Nonetheless, it would be wrong to think of the Basque Country as a tightly coherent region. In many ways it has always been more diverse than Catalonia, which partly explains the later emergence of Basque nationalism with its political rather than cultural emphasis. The Basques were divided in terms of geography – between valleys, between the interior and the coast, and between rural areas and cities – nor was there one focal centre to Basqueness, as Barcelona might be said to be for Catalanism. The language too was highly dialectised, both because of the geographical fragmentation, and because, unlike Catalan, there is no tradition of an early Basque written literature. The turbulent history of nineteenth century Spain was particularly acute in the Basque Country where it represented these deep divides in Basque society, between the traditionalists in the rural areas, and the modernists (pro-Madrid) population of the cities. A central part of the Carlist wars of the nineteenth century revolved round the issue of maintaining or removing the Basque *fueros*. To some extent it is the symbolism of the eventual loss of these which triggers the start of the Basque nationalist movement:

> The modern Basque Country was created by the defeat of Carlism and the victory of liberalism and it emerged deeply divided. Foral abolition meant the political alienation of the peasantry. It also meant the political, economic and cultural ascendancy of the expanding urban centres.
>
> (Heiberg, 1980: 49)

Like Catalonia – and unlike most of the rest of Spain – the Basque Country in the nineteenth century experienced rapid industrialisation and the success of its heavy industry. The urban bourgeoisie created by this, however, was very Castilianised and closely connected with Madrid, with very little interest in Basque culture or way of life.

Basque identity sprang from a reactive desire amongst the rural population to protect what they perceived as a dying culture. Whereas in Catalonia (and Galicia) a cultural nationalist movement preceded a political one, in the Basque Country, if anything the reverse was the case.

Basque nationalism is initially the political agenda of one individual: Sabino Arana (1865–1903). Arana was middle class and from the outskirts of Bilbao, but he was not part of the urban industrial oligarchy, and in fact came from a staunchly Carlist family. His political objectives were to promote Basque nationalism in order to prevent what he saw as the encroachment of all things Castilian, which were also, he felt, threatening traditional values and morals.

Far from emerging from a cultural movement, as in other parts, Arana single-handedly 'invented' many of the cultural symbols of Basque nationalism. He coined the name of the nation – Euskadi – created its flag and national anthem, and selected its 'national' day. Significantly, he was not a mother tongue Basque speaker, but having admired the strength of the Catalan language that he had observed when studying in Barcelona, he set out deliberately to perfect and use Basque and to produce a Basque grammar.

Unlike Catalan, Basque was not spoken by a large proportion of the Basque population. Partly because of its lack of a literary tradition, partly because of its inaccessibility in dealing with Castilian-speakers, and partly because it had become inextricably associated with backward peasantry, Basque was a low prestige language, barely heard outside the countryside. Arana's early enthusiasm for promoting the use of the Basque language was short-lived (Conversi, 1997: 57–8). Arana did not see language in a Herderian sense of representing the spirit of a nation, although he does see Euskera[9] as 'the support of our race and the buttress of the religiosity and the morality of our people' (cited in Heiberg, 1980: 54). At the most the language represented a marker of Basque distinctiveness for Arana, and he is quoted famously as saying:

> If we had to choose between a Vizcaya populated by *maketos*[10] who spoke only Euskera and a Vizcaya populated by *bizcainos*[11] who spoke only Spanish, without doubt we would select the latter. . . . The difference between languages is the means of preserving us from the contagion of Spaniards and avoiding the mixing of the two races. If our invaders learnt Euskera, we would have to abandon it . . . and dedicate outselves to speaking Russian, Norwegian or some other languages unknown to them.
>
> (cited in Heiberg, 1980: 54–5)

Arana organised his movement into the *Partido Nacionalista Vasco* (PNV) which was ideologically similar to Prat's *Lliga* but, significantly, Castilian-speaking. It was above all political activity that characterised the early Basque nationalism. However, Arana himself did collate 'new' Basque words in order to protect the language from Spanish borrowings, and a Basque language academy was set up. One major challenge for this was the various different – and often mutually incomprehensible – dialects which still existed in Euskera. Folk festivals ('floral games' modelled on the Catalan *Jocs Florals*) were held from 1879 to celebrate Basque poetry, sport and singing. But none of this activity matched the scale found in Catalonia.

Whereas we have argued that language was to be seen as the major plank in the Catalan national identity – and still is today – not only was language in early Basque nationalism of considerably less importance, but it was in fact race that was the core marker in identifying true Basqueness at least until well into the twentieth century when racial politics have been so discredited. For Arana a true Basque had to be able to prove at least two generations of Basque ancestry (by possessing four Basque surnames). The significance of this emphasis on race is that it makes Basque nationalism thoroughly exclusive; it is impossible to 'become' Basque. In contrast, Catalan nationalism has always been seen as far more inclusive, particularly as it is possible to learn and acquire the Catalan language.

We will see later that it is in fact with the radical terrorist stage of Basque nationalism and the enormous challenge the ETA organisation has given successive central Spanish governments that the emphasis on racial definition shifts, and other more inclusive markers, such as language, come more to the fore.

Basque nationalists have always considered Navarra as a part of the Basque homelands. However, Navarra's history is quite separate from the Basques. The kingdom of Navarra remained separate from the '*Señorio*' of Vizcaya. Navarra in fact was the last of the Peninsular kingdoms to come under the Castilian Crown in 1512, and this kingdom too had its own *fueros*. Unlike the Basque Country, Navarra hung on to its *fueros* under Franco, reflecting the very different political character of the two regions. It is true that in parts of Navarra, Basque has always been spoken, and therefore there is indeed some shared cultural and linguistic history, but in terms of fuelling any Basque nationalism, this has always been negligible.

The Galicians[12]

Galicia is situated in the northwestern tip of the Iberian Peninsula; its nearly thirty thousand square kilometres border Portugal to the south, and have a long coastline to the west and north. It is an isolated corner of the Peninsula and has always been an almost entirely agricultural region with high rates of poverty and low rates of literacy. Whereas both Catalonia and the Basque Country have seen their native populations diluted with the arrival of many immigrants which challenges their unique identities, the Galicians have experienced no immigration, but, instead, have themselves found the need to emigrate, to other parts of Spain and Europe, and to Latin America. The role of emigration to their sense of identity is important. The Galician abroad has a very strong belief – no doubt idealised and mythologised – of what constitutes Galicianhood and the Galician homeland.

As we have already noted, Galaico-Portuguese was one of the varieties to emerge from the Latin of the Roman Empire period. But, whereas Portugal went on to become an independent state with a fully-fledged independent language, Portuguese, Galicia remained subordinated first to the kingdom of Leon, and then eventually to Castile (Siguan, 1993: 122). This absence of any political power is reflected in the Galician language which through the centuries assumed the role of home language in a spoken form only, with Castilian increasingly used in all public and official life. However, before this loss in status took place completely, Galician did have a golden period, somewhat similar to that experienced by Catalan. Partly as a result of the importance of Santiago de Compostela as a major pilgrimage destination, Galician produced a signficant corpus of literature, above all lyric poetry, between the twelfth and fifteenth centuries. This poetry, at its peak, was carried throughout the Peninsula and into France by the itinerarant troubadours of that period.

In the main, however, Galician declined rapidly as a language of any prestige, particularly as not only the local administration, but also its highly-respected local clergy chose to use Castilian. The language's contact with Portugal was cut off, and Castilian soon dominated the region. However, Galician remained the mother tongue of native Galicians (as it still largely does today).

Any sort of revival in cultural pride in Galician took longer to arrive in Galicia than Catalonia, given the language's low status and the level of education of its population. However, the European Romantic movement did have some influence in the nineteenth century here too. Some Galician poetry began to be produced, but the beginnings of the movement which is known as Galicia's renaissance, the *Rexurdimento*, are not until the 1860s. In 1861 a poetry festival was held modelled on the Catalan ones and known as the *Xogos Florais*. This was followed in 1863 by the most influential publication of this period, the *Cantares Gallegos* by the well-known Galician poet Rosalía de Castro. The latter is a prominent figure in the revival of Galician literature, and yet towards the end of her life she decided to turn her back on Galician and write in Castilian. This ambiguous attitude to the Galician language, an insecurity and sense of inferiority, is always present in any discussion of Galician nationalism.

Unlike in Catalonia and the Basque Country, no political movement emerged in Galicia until well into the early twentieth century. Even then the incipient Galician political nationalism is timid in comparison to the other two Peninsular movements we have discussed. The movement which was eventually to become the political wing of Galician nationalism was born in 1916 as the *Irmandade da Fala*, that is a 'brotherhood' to protect and promote the Galician language (Henderson, 1996: 242; Siguan, 1993: 42). As in Catalonia, this period sees considerable codification and elaboration of the forms of the language, with the setting up of a Galician language academy and the production of grammars and dictionaries.

It must be stressed, however, that the basis of support for the Galician nationalist movement was very small, consisting mostly of middle-class intellectuals. There is no doubt that the Galician language is, like Catalan for Catalans, a major symbol of Galician nationalism. It is no coincidence that Galician nationalist politics emerged from a movement initially concerned with the protection, promotion and standardisation of the language. However, whilst the population all spoke Galician (unlike in the Basque Country), the prestige language which everyone aspired to learn was indisputedly Castilian. In Chapter 5 we will examine how much, if at all, this attitude has changed in post-Franco Galicia. We will also discuss how far the tug that Galicia always feels between the two major languages of Portuguese and Castilian has affected, and continues to affect, constructions of Galician identity.

Conclusion

In this section we have seen how, despite the powerful Castilianisation process that took place from the fifteenth century onwards, there remain in the Peninsula non-Castilian speaking linguistic communities whose mother tongue, particularly since the nineteenth century, is widely used. We have seen too how important these mother tongues are to the sense of identity of these communities. For the Catalans, and to a lesser extent, the Galicians, their language indeed is the symbol of their difference from others and their own shared personality and psyche; in other words, the mark of their 'nation'. This observation suggests that the nation-building process of the central Spanish state has not been completely successful. Certainly in terms of nineteenth century forms of cultural and political nationalism the creation of a confident unchallenged Spanish national identity has not been achieved. In the twentieth century, and especially since Franco's death as we will see later, this model of a monocultural nation-state has been challenged, and not only from the peripheral regions.

The 'other' languages of Latin America

We have seen in the first section how the survival and, at times, vitality, of the non-Castilian languages in Spain have been part of a struggle between the imposition of a Castilian hegemony to create 'Spanish' nationhood and the assertion and promotion of alternative nationalisms, particularly the Catalan. The two most successful counter-nationalisms in Spain have been the Catalan and the Basque, and it is no coincidence that these are also two regions with strong economies in relation to the rest of Spain. Moreover, in all three of the communities we examined, to a greater or lesser extent, the national identity of that community is shared and at times promoted by the elites and the middle classes. This, of course, is the profound difference from the situation we will examine in Latin America, and the principal explanation as to why ethnolinguistic communities here have been largely unsuccessful in challenging the Westernised (Castilian-language) national identity created since the wars of independence. The indigenous communities of Latin America are poor, underprivileged, and marginalised sectors of their state's society. With the partial exception of Paraguay, the middle classes are entirely monolingual in Spanish. This situation has inevitably produced a one-way road towards the assimilation of the indigenous communities to the economically and socially more advantageous Spanish-speaking way of life.

As we have already noted in the previous chapter, when the Spaniards arrived in the Americas they found a continent containing many hundreds, if not thousands, of languages, whose discreteness and mutual incomprehensibility was reinforced by the geographical isolation of so many of the communities, and the lack of communication between them. The following is a very general summary[13] of the major language groups in their geographical areas.

Nahuatl was spoken in much of present-day Mexico, but above all in central Mexico, focusing on Mexico City. Its influence was felt as far south as parts of Central America and as north as present-day New Mexico and Arizona, and we will discuss below the role of this language of the Aztec Empire. In the Yucatan Peninsula and parts of Central America *Mayan* was the main language and, as can still be seen today, was widely spoken in this area of Mexico and much of Guatemala.

In the Caribbean and parts of the facing coastal areas, such as the Venezuelan and Colombian coasts, the main languages were *Carib/Arawak*, *Taino*, and *Siboney*. These are amongst the first indigenous languages to disappear with the early decimation through wars and disease of the native populations of, particularly, the Spanish-colonised Caribbean islands.

From southern Costa Rica through to most of Colombia the *Chibcha* language was dominant. But as in all the areas we are tracing, other minor languages and dialects were also present. For example, one of the best known and still widely-spoken indigenous languages, *Quechua*, could, at the height of the Inca empire, be heard as far north as southern Colombia and as far south as northern Chile, but the further away from the centre of the empire in the Peruvian Andes, the more other languages and dialects coexisted in these regions. In particular, from southern Peru through much of Bolivia, parts of Chile and Paraguay *Aymara* was widely spoken, and remains a significant indigenous language today in parts of Peru and Bolivia.

In Chile *Mapuche/Araucano* was the main language. In the other southern-most countries, sometimes grouped together as the 'River Plate' states, of Argentina, Uruguay and Paraguay, there was, and still is, vast linguistic diversity, but the *Guarani* language is spoken by significant numbers. This language's special history in Paraguay will be discussed below.

Finally, in the Amazonian forest areas many hundreds of language varieties often spoken by a very small population have existed, and some continue to exist. Throughout Latin America, in the most inaccessible areas, pockets of numerically tiny linguistic communities have been found, their very 'discovery' by the outside world being likely to threaten the survival of their languages.

More scholarly and detailed research on the indigenous languages and their history, characteristics, spread or demise is, of course, available.[14] What interests us here is to select those areas where the strength of the language may indicate power and influence by its speakers in at least some stage in their history. In these communities at least we may expect to find some inter-action with the nation-building enterprises of Latin American states. Three such linguistic communities which have presented some kind of challenge to the construction of Castilian-dominated national identities over the centuries are those where Nahuatl, Quechua and Guarani are spoken. We shall, therefore, briefly examine these three communities below.

Before doing this, however, we should note that there exist other communities in Latin America which are not those of either the indigenous groups nor are Castilian speaking. Immigrant groups other than the Spaniards have created communities in Latin America which have to a small degree influenced the linguistic configuration and identity of the countries. For example, in Venezuela and Paraguay there are German-speaking communities which are the legacy of German missionaries. These are tightly-knit inward-looking communities who have had very little impact on the wider Spanish-speaking or indigenous communities. On the other hand the large Italian immigration to Argentina has had a marked influence on the Argentinian variety of Spanish, and is clearly identified by its speakers as a mark of their Argentinian identity. In Argentina, too, there is a community of

Welsh-speakers. Similarly some Galicians, Catalans and Basques have retained their mother tongues in ways that had they remained, respectively in the United Kingdom or Spain, might have been more difficult to do. Again, though, these communities have had little effect on the wider communities that they are part of.

Finally, the largest influx of outsiders other than Spaniards was of course the scores of slaves taken to the Americas. Whilst the effect of African languages in contact with European languages and the phenomenon of pidgin and creoles have been widely studied, the occurrence of Spanish-based creoles in Latin America is not wide, and mostly found in parts of the Caribbean. Whereas African culture has had an enormous influence in such areas as music, food, art, and even religion, there is very little evidence of linguistic impact.

In summary we can say that these non-Spanish immigrant communities have contributed (and with recent Asian immigration continue to contribute) to the melting pot of influences making up modern Latin American states, they have not had the strength or individuality to present any form of counter-nationalisms to the official national agenda.

Nahuatl: the legacy of the Aztec empire[15]

As we have noted, when the Spaniards arrived in Mexico between 1519 and 1521 they found a region with many different linguistic varieties, the most important of which were Nahuatl and Mayan. Not surprisingly the dominant language for much of the region, Nahuatl, was the language of the rulers of this empire, the Aztecs:

> Nahuatl was not only the native language of the Aztecs but the second language of their subjugated tribes. As the most powerful tribe of the Aztec alliance, the native speakers of Nahuatl extended their invasions to the north and south of the Valley of Mexico. Nahuatl was hence used and accepted as the standard language of politics, commerce, law, economics, science, art, education and literature.
>
> (Hidalgo, 1994: 186)

The process of Castilianisation which we outlined in Chapter 2 can be observed in what the Spanish colonisers referred to as 'New Spain', and Nahuatl along with all the other indigenous languages was gradually reduced to a marginalised and inferior status and role in the Spanish-dominated colonial society. However, it must be noted that the geographical and social extent of the use of Nahuatl was such that the Spaniards recognised this language as having certain features and properties which placed it in their eyes in a position of greater prestige than normally associated with the indigenous languages (Brice Heath, 1972; Hidalgo, 1994; Cifuentes, 1994). In his *Historia de México* (1780–81) the cleric Francisco Xavier

Clavijero develops this support for the richness of Nahuatl (Hidalgo, 1994; Cifuentes, 1994) following the theories of his time that certain languages possessed superior attributes, whilst others were inadequate in the fullest sense. Cifuentes describes Clavijero's verdict on Nahuatl which reminds us of the current thinking of his time towards the role of language and its reflection of its speakers' identity.

> Según lo determinaban las ideas filosóficas del Siglo de las Luces, sobre las cuales trabajaron Clavijero y sus contemporáneos, debía existir una coherencia entre el grado de cultura y las peculiaridades del idioma: a una mayor civilización correspondería una mayor abundancia en el léxico, un rico sistema numeral y la posibilidad de expresar los conceptos metafísicos necesarios para el desarrollo del pensamiento. Asimismo, un síntoma de civilización era la unidad en la lengua, unidad que era consecuencia de un control y atención sobre la forma del idioma por parte de sus hablantes, específicamente de sus gobiernos. A juicio de los especialistas, el idioma mexicano uno de las variedades del náhuatl – satisfacía los requísitos para ser considerado una lengua de civilización. . . .
>
> (Cifuentes, 1994: 213)[16]

This favourable attitude to Nahuatl, however, is not translated into governmental support or recognition by the independent Mexican republic. In the nineteenth century the push by the central government to make Spanish the national language leaves the Mexican indigenous languages abandoned. Whilst, as we have noted earlier, some interest in the languages is shown by linguists and anthropologists in terms of classifying and describing them, the necessary support for their use in public and official life is largely lacking. Some support for the use of indigenous languages in education, and for the belief that by learning through the mother tongue the indigenous population can more easily participate in the wider, Castilian-dominated society does emerge in the second part of the nineteenth century, particularly during Benito Juárez's government in the late 1850s (Brice Heath, 1972: 68–71). On the whole, however, although there was far greater interest in researching Indian cultures and languages during this period, this was principally as objects of academic or scientific interest, not as practical studies for their support and promotion.

The consequence of the post-independence drive to spread the 'national' language of Spanish is a huge drop in the numbers speaking indigenous languages in favour of those speaking Spanish. Cifuentes (1992: 9) states that at the beginning of the nineteenth century, and the early days of independence, 64 per cent of the Mexican population of 6,000,000 were indigenous; whereas by the beginning of the twentieth century only 13 per cent of the total population were indigenous. If we assume that these categories correspond broadly to those speaking indigenous languages and those speaking Spanish, this is an astonishing decline.

In 1995 out of Mexico's total population of nearly 94 million, over one million were speakers of Nahuatl (Baker and Prys Jones, 1998: 396). It is still the most widely spoken indigenous language in Mexico today, and its size ought to suggest some status and role in the life of the Mexican nation. This, however, is hard to support. During this century there have been far more initiatives in bilingual education, and, more recently, bilingual and bicultural education (discussed more fully in Chapter 8) which have improved the status of the indigenous languages and necessitated some work on their standardisation and codification. However, the methods, conditions and attitudes of those providing this education contribute in reality to gradual assimilation to the central state's norms. Hidalgo argues that this is an inevitable outcome in such a relatively new nation-state, where the central government is still constructing a sense of 'Mexicanness':

> Peripheral ethnicities are overshadowed by central ethnicity and tend to gravitate towards Mexicentrism lest they be condemned and stigmatized. In the Mexican multilingual mosaic, language is less important than ethnicity. . . .
>
> (Hidalgo, 1994: 201)

In this context it is significant that in many Nahuatl-speaking regions today, people refer to their language as 'Mexicano' rather than 'Nahuatl', and to Spanish as 'Castilla' (Hill and Hill, 1986). Once again we can see the importance attached to the name of a language. Here, the indigenous speakers are claiming the true national legacy – Mexicanness – for their language as opposed to the 'foreign' and non-Mexican Castile. There is a pride in their language and ethnicity, but there is also a recognition that in fact Spanish is the language of social mobility and public life.

Nahuatl is regarded by many Mexicans as a symbol of their national past rather than a vibrant culture of the present day. Those speaking the language have been too marginalised to present any real challenge to the state's construction of Mexican national identity over the past two centuries. Nahuatl is one of various non-Spanish languages spoken in Mexico, and, although in recent years more resources have been spent on teaching these, the policies and ideology of the Mexican state have been to use Spanish as a national unifier and to create institutions to protect this (such as the Mexican language academy), and the media to promote it.

In later chapters we will return to the current role of the indigenous communities in contemporary Mexico, and in particular discuss the recent events in the predominantly Indian region of Chiapas, to see whether cultural and linguistic diversity is more tolerated than it was during the earlier years of nation-building.

Quechua: from imperial lingua franca *to endangered language*[17]

When the Spanish *conquistadores* overran the Inca empire between 1527 and 1532 they found, as they had in Mexico, a region with a highly diverse linguistic configuration, but with one language dominating as *lingua franca* and for use in all official purposes – Quechua. Although there were very many languages spoken in the Inca empire, there was a clear and deliberate policy to use Quechua as the official language for purposes of administration and commerce. Cerrón-Palomino summarises the Incas' language policy as follows,

> . . . the state recognized Quechua, in the form of the 'Chinchay' southern variant, as the only official language; this language was compulsory for the local nobility, civil servants, members of the administrative system and traders; the official use of the language in the realm of government and administration did not preclude the use of the particular languages or dialects of the various ethnic groups in other situations; and, finally, the language learned through immersion by bringing future local governors to the capital.
>
> (Cerrón-Palomino, 1989: 17)

We can deduce from this (and other commentators, e.g. Von Gleich, 1994) that the Inca language policy was aimed at communication efficiency, and does not appear to have any aims in terms of nation building. Other languages were tolerated; the Incas were not concerned with imposing their culture, simply with dominating other ethnic communities for economic and political reasons.

As in all regions of the Spanish empire, the colonial period saw the process of Castilianisation, which, however, began with a short period when the indigenous languages were promoted, particularly by the Church. The use and promotion of Quechua only began to decline from the seventeenth century. From then on, however, it was a steady, inevitable decline from a prestigious language of power to a marginalised speech of low status, despite retaining to this day a large population of speakers.

The newly-emerged Peruvian republic, in much the same way as the Mexican republic, sought to stamp Westernised Spanish-speaking values and norms on its national identity – what Cerrón-Palomino (1989: 24) calls a 'unilingual Christian Peruvian identity'. However, as he stresses, this was challenged during the nineteenth century and early twentieth century both by defeat in a war with Chile, and by the increasing unrest of the majority indigenous population. From the latter develops what is referred to as the indigenist movement, which expressed itself in social, political and artistic defence of the rights of the indigenous population. The results were largely tokenistic and with very little effect. One of the most militant advocates of the need to redefine the role of the Indian in Peruvian society was the famous writer and politician José Carlos Mariátegui. In his major publication where he discusses contemporary Peruvian society *Siete ensayos de interpretación de la realidad peruana* Mariátegui argues that the Indian 'problem' is not, as so many commentators have suggested, one of different ethnicity and lack of education, but above all one of land. The Indians' dispossession of their lands underpins their exclusion from economic success and erodes a stable base for their sense of community – a necessary factor in creating any national belonging. As Cerrón-Palomino says:

> Going beyond the official indigenism and the paternalistic and exotic sermon, Mariátegui drew on the indigenous movement in his consistent role of stirring the Indians' historic consciousness.
>
> (Cerrón-Palomino 1989: 24)

Mariátegui himself suggests that the indigenous people cannot participate in national life because they are forced to limit their protests and experiences to restricted local areas. Deliberately or not, the descendants of the vast Incan empire have been fragmented and divided, and not yet included in the new Peruvian enterprise:

> A los indios les falta vinculación nacional. Sus protestas han sido siempre regionales. Esto ha contribuido, en gran parte, a su abatimiento. Un pueblo de cuatro millones de hombres,[18] consciente de su número, no desespera nunca de su porvenir. Los mismos cuatro millones de hombres mientras no son sino una masa orgánica, una muchedumbre dispersa, son incapaces de decidir su rumbo histórico.[19]
>
> (Mariátegui, 1973: 49)

Whilst the role and status of the Indian figures significantly in Mariátegui's writing, the issue of language is rarely mentioned. As with the Mexican indigenous communities' role in modern national societies, language when it is discussed at all, is seen as being something that should be respected and taught in order to facilitate entry into the Spanish-speaking world.

In the twentieth century more bilingual education has been available, but still seen largely as a transitional support. Respect for Quechua (and to a lesser extent Aymara) in its own right has occurred during certain moments, notably the military regime of 1968 to 1975. In later chapters we will discuss the significance of this brief moment in modern Peruvian history when Quechua was declared an official language in the constitution.

Guarani: a national language[20]

The case of Guarani is a fascinating example of the exception to the rule. Whereas, as we have noted, in all the former Spanish empire of Latin America indigenous languages and cultures have been marginalised, and in some cases have become extinct, Guarani in Paraguay has survived, and is an official language alongside Spanish. Of the present population of five million 90 per cent speak some Guarani. Two million consider themselves bilingual and over one and a half million are monolingual Guarani speakers (Baker and Prys Jones, 1998: 459). Equally significant is the fact that Guarani is normally used as the *lingua franca* by other indigenous groups, such as those who live in the Chaco region. As Fasold (1984: 15) explains 'Guarani . . . is a prerequisite for status as a genuine Paraguayan.'

Why has this situation arisen in Paraguay and not in any other former Spanish colony? The three main reasons seem to be the degree of Guarani hegemony already present when the Spaniards arrived; the role of the Jesuits in Paraguay; and the country's political and geographical isolation over the years.

We could certainly argue that the first reason alone would have been unlikely to be sufficient, given that a similar dominance of Nahuatl and Quechua were found in the Aztec and Inca empires respectively. The pre-eminence of Guarani on the arrival of the Spaniards certainly meant that they continued to use this as a language to communicate across the area, in the way the original colonisers used Nahuatl and Quechua, but the difference lies in the fact that unlike in the latter two cases, as we have outlined, the Castilianisation process that followed the earlier colonisation practices did not exclude and downgrade Guarani in the same way. This must be accounted for to a considerable extent by the role of the Jesuits in Paraguay.

The Jesuits were particularly determined to use the indigenous languages of the peoples they wished to Christianise, and to understand and build on their native cultures and ways of life. In Paraguay, which was the headquarters of the Jesuits in the Americas, they organised the indigenous peoples into communities known as *reducciones*. The language used was Guarani and religious texts were translated into this indigenous language by the Jesuits.

> The controversial Jesuit enterprise drew together more than 100,000 Indians in what may have been the largest indigenous cooperative experiment in the history of Latin America.
>
> (Lipski, 1994: 304)

When the Jesuits were expelled from Latin America in 1767 they left in Paraguay an indigenous community with a greater sense of dignity and prestige in terms of their social organisation and their language than anywhere else in the colonies.

To this must be added the fact that Paraguay is a very geographically isolated and inaccessible country. The Spanish settlers there experienced greater hardship and lack of communications with Europe than most colonisers. It made sense, therefore, that they should integrate with the local population and share their customs and language to a degree not known elsewhere.

In particular there was a great deal of intermarrying, which also had the result of encouraging bilingualism in Guarani and Spanish.

This geographical isolation was compounded by political isolation after independence, as Paraguay has experienced since the early nineteenth century an almost constant stream of authoritarian dictatorships who did not encourage contact and relations with other parts of Latin America. In fact, Paraguay suffered devastating wars with its neighbours instead, and was completely cut off from the cultural and political sophistication of the cosmopolitan world (of Buenos Aires, for example).

It is important to stress that even in Paraguay the two official languages did not perform equal roles. This is mainly explained by the fact that Guarani has been standardised and developed only recently as a language of literacy. Moreover, although it is true that the vast majority of the population spoke it, and many only spoke Guarani, attitudes towards it were not always entirely favourable and it did suffer some stigma as an 'Indian' language. This is reflected in the way Spanish has been the principal language used in administration, law and, importantly, education.

In this century, however, this has been changing (Rona, 1975). The acceptance that Guarani is the most widely spoken language in Paraguay has been coupled with a pride in this and a perception that this is an essential mark of Paraguayan identity. As Rona (1975: 286) remarks, 'All Paraguayans realise that the Guarani language is the most genuine manifestation of their being an independent nation.' Recently there has been work on the standardisation of Guarani and it has been introduced into the education system. To many commentators it appears a successful and vibrant language, protected and assured by its role as identity marker for the vast majority of Paraguayans.

However, we should not forget that not everyone in Paraguay speaks Guarani (nor necessarily Spanish). There are other indigenous groups speaking different languages, as well as small and tightly-knit immigrant communities, who include German and Japanese speakers. The neglect and marginalisation that these linguistic communities have experienced shows that the success of bilingualism and the prestige of one indigenous language does not automatically lead to greater tolerance and respect for all languages. The fact that Guarani plays an important political and social part in creating Paraguayness and these other languages do not, may go some way to explaining the difference.

Conclusion

In the overwhelming majority of cases the indigenous communities, their languages and cultures, have been marginalised in Latin America by the Spanish colonisation process and its legacy of Spanish-speaking elites who replaced the Spaniards after independence. The symbolic role of these languages has not had any real outlet either in the specific case of consolidating localised feelings of 'nationhood' amongst the indigenous communities because of their fragmentation, powerlessness and lack of communications. Nor have the non-Castilian languages played any real role in the forging of new 'national' identities in the post-colonial republics, although sometimes they are part of a sense of an exotic national past.

In terms of the definitions we offered in Chapter 1 the independent countries of Latin America are states, or nation-states, but far from being homogeneous nations. The different indigenous communities might indeed claim that they are 'nations', but until recently, at least, the necessary self-awareness and with it the 'imagining' of national boundaries and demarcation has not taken place. And even when, such as with the indigenism movement, some awakening of this consciousness may have taken place, language did not play a major role. Later on we will discuss whether this continues to be the case with late twentieth century indigenous movements and struggles, such as the Zapatista movement of Chiapas in Mexico.

The triumph of Spanish

In this chapter we have examined the successes and failures of the non-Castilian languages in the Spanish-speaking world. By discussing specific examples we have seen where these languages are closely linked to particular communities and underpin their sense of identity. We have traced how the languages and communities come into contact with the central states and governments of which they are part and to what extent this has led to conflict, coexistence, and even cooperation. To a very large extent conflict has ensued, frequently leading to the marginalisation or total obliteration of the non-Castilian speaking group. This is even the case, as in Latin America, where the community is not necessarily the numerical minority, but where they have clearly been disenfranchised from power. Only a few communities – notably the Catalans – have managed to retain their strong sense of a separate identity and advance this alongside the state hegemony (and sometimes at the latter's expense). Whilst Guarani is clearly a success story in terms of the survival of a preconquest language, its role in Paraguayan nation-building is that it has come to represent the majority central state's identity. There is not a Guarani nation and a Spanish-speaking nation, but only a Paraguayan one. This model is of course the one that the Spanish state has long aspired to with a total fusion of the medieval kingdoms and cultures. Unlike in the Paraguayan case, we would argue that this fusion has not happened. Nor, despite the claims, has such a fusion taken place in the multiethnic communities that coexist uneasily in most Latin American states. *Mestizaje* – the mixing of races – has obviously happened, but many ethnic groups are not integrated, nor even assimilated, and the claims for 'Mexicanness' or 'Peruvianness' are very tenuous.

Nonetheless, if the sense of nation is still elusive in these many countries we have examined, it is impossible to deny the fact that the Spanish language has triumphed in its overwhelming domination in all these societies. The other languages may skirmish at its edges, but Spanish is undisputedly the language of public life, of the media, of status and social advancement. The Castilianisation process has been unstoppable, but in the late twentieth century we are perhaps beginning to see a greater readiness to tolerate and support a more pluralistic vision, albeit from a position of immense superiority on the part of the Spanish language.

Part II

Legislation and the realities of linguistic diversity

4 Language rights, language policies and Language Planning

In Part I we explored the role that language can play in nation-building and in the perception of national identity. We saw how, in particular in the emergence of nation-states in the nineteenth century, political, economic and, sometimes cultural, criteria normally led to a drive for monolingualism (and monoculturalism). Spanish clearly dominates in the countries we have examined, but equally clear is that it has not eradicated other languages. In Part II, then, we will seek to explore the realities of this multilingualism. Faced with the existence of linguistic pluralism, how have politicians proceeded? To what extent does the Spanish-speaking world recognise the rights of different communities to protect their mother tongues? How far are resources concentrated on supporting the majority language of Spanish only? So far we have traced the history of this multilingual picture; in this section we will discuss how governments and other organisations are approaching linguistic issues in the Spanish-speaking world today.

Firstly, in this chapter, we need to examine the theoretical issues and models which provide a framework for the linguistic organisation of the Spanish-speaking countries. There are three, interconnected, areas to discuss: the notion of linguistic rights, language policies and legislation, and the academic discipline of Language Planning.

Linguistic rights

The concept of (and support for) 'human rights' has been examined for some time now. The writers of the Enlightenment discussed them; the opponents of slavery invoked them. In this century concrete declarations have been agreed by international agencies, such as the League of Nations and the United Nations.[1] The *Universal Declaration of Human Rights* was published in 1948, and various charters and international convenants have been produced since.[2] Skutnabb-Kangas and Phillipson describe the three different stages – or 'generations' as they are known – in identifying universal human rights this century:

The *first generation* related to personal freedoms, civil and political rights. These were extended in the decolonisation phase from the rights of individuals to the right of oppressed peoples to self-determination. The *second generation* related to economic, social and cultural rights. The *third generation* covers 'solidarity' rights (peace, development and unspoilt environment).

> (Skutnabb-Kangas and Phillipson, 1994b: 73)

They also explain that these three 'generations' constitute nonetheless a 'coherent whole'. However, all commentators stress the fact that in these formulations of human rights, linguistic rights have seldom been mentioned, and that the conception of linguistic rights has emerged later and is still being defined. Significant progress has been made recently in this area with the drawing up of a new charter, *the Universal Declaration of Linguistic Rights*, under the auspices of UNESCO. This was originally endorsed at a meeting of the International PEN Club and CIEMEN (the Centre Internacional Escarré per les Minorías Etniques i les Nacions) along with various NGOs in Barcelona in June 1996. The Declaration identifies individual rights such as the right to be recognised as a member of a linguistic community, the right to use one's language in private and public, and the right to maintain and develop one's own culture, as well as collective rights, such as the right to education in one's own language, the right to cultural and media services in one's own language, and the use of one's own language in official and administrative domains (Puig i Pla, 1997: 5).

Skutnabb-Kangas and Phillipson suggest in a similar vein what linguistic rights entail at both an individual and collective level.

> At an *individual* . . . level everyone can identify positively with their mother tongue, and have that identification respected by others . . . It means the right to learn the mother tongue . . . and the right to use it. . . . It means the right to learn at least one of the official languages in one's country of residence.
>
> At a *collective* level [it implies] the right of minority groups to exist (i.e. the right to be 'different' . . .). It implies the right to enjoy and develop their language and the right for minorities to establish and maintain schools. . . . It also involves guarantees of representation in the political affairs of the state, and the granting of autonomy to administer matters internal to the groups. . . .
>
> (Skutnabb-Kangas and Phillipson, 1994a: 2)

This reference to autonomy has proved to be a very controversial right to enforce in the centralised nation-states which we observed had emerged during the nineteenth century. It is however a political form that is being increasingly used in various parts of the Spanish-speaking world, as we will discuss in the next chapter. Hamel (1997a: 7) sees autonomy as a 'modern form of self-determination within pluralistic nation states' which also avoids segregation and ghettoisation.

Chen offers a related definition of linguistic rights which clearly identifies the role of the state in the recognition and protection of these:

> Language rights are the rights of individuals and collective linguistic groups to non-interference by the State, or to assistance by the State, in the use of their own language, in perpetuating the use of the language and ensuring its future survival, in receiving information and State-provided services in their own languages, and ensuring that other lawful rights . . . will not be handicapped or subject to discrimination for linguistic reasons.
>
> (Chen, 1998: 49)

The obligations such a definition put on the state require legislation and Language Planning, as we will discuss below.[3] It will be useful to remember this definition of linguistic rights when we examine the legal initiatives taken by governments in the Spanish-speaking world in the following chapter.

Already to emerge in the two definitions offered so far is the dual aspect of linguistic (and human) rights in terms of the individual and the collectivity. Hamel (1997a) explains how in the history of human rights there has been a trend from initially identifying these as basic individual rights towards more social, and therefore more collective, rights. These are much more difficult to express and guarantee within legal frameworks.

> Collective rights, a fairly recent concern, are controversial as such in ethical, philosophical, and judicial terms . . . since they may always conflict with individual rights. And their implementation can become critical because in many parts of the world they question deep-rooted power structures.
>
> (Hamel, 1997a: 3)

It is crucial to be aware of this issue insofar as it is also clear in the literature that commentators believe that the concept of linguistic rights only becomes important when talking about linguistic minorities (e.g. Chen, 1998; Hamel, 1997a; Paulston, 1997; Skutnabb-Kangas and Phillipson 1994a, 1994b).[4] That is to say that dominant majority linguistic groups enjoy linguistic rights automatically by virtue of their position of dominance and power. It can be reasonably argued that minorities can only be protected and supported by viewing them as a collective whole rather than as individual members. As Hamel argues:

> Perhaps language, as a means of communication and the reproduction of collective identity, highlights more than other cultural traits the

impossibility of enjoying minority rights defined individually, hence the necessity to recognize collective rights.

(Hamel, 1997a: 8)

In response to the recognition of linguistic rights two (contrasting) principles have been developed as ways of protecting these. The principles of territoriality and personality also reflect the two concepts of collective and individual rights respectively. The *personality principle* recognises an individual's right to use his or her mother tongue in any public interaction wherever they might be within a state's jurisdiction; the *territoriality principle* applies to a community's right to have its mother tongue used and recognised in public life anywhere within a specified particular territory (Mar-Molinero and Stevenson, 1991; Nelde, 1991; Watts, 1991; Nelde, Labrie and Williams, 1992). The territoriality principle does seem to favour linguistic minorities by guaranteeing them certain rights within their own space in the face of dominance and encroachment from majority linguistic groups, and has therefore been the model adopted in various European contexts as well as Canada. However, there are those who also believe that the emphasis on linguistic rights exclusively bound to one territory runs the risk of forming marginalised, monolingual enclaves.[5] Frequently the application of the territoriality principle has led to the substitution of one kind of (majority) monolingualism by another (minority) one, and, with it, potentially, reversed intolerance and discrimination (see Myhill, 1999). However, critics of the personality principle will argue that when two or more languages come into contact, if one is more dominant, more widely-known, with greater prestige, it is unrealistic to imagine that speakers of this latter language will learn the less prestigious language and that the right of the individual to use their mother tongue will fail on practical and pragmatic grounds. Hamel (1997a: 11) argues for the need 'to protect a language by means of . . . collective nontransportable rights'. More recently examples of a mixture of the two principles being applied in legal frameworks can be seen, and we will discuss how far this is the case and whether it is successful in the Spanish-speaking world in the following chapter.

Another dichotomy to emerge in the definition of linguistic rights is between their 'expressive function' and their 'communicative function' (Hamel 1997a: 4). This dualism reflects what we have already noted as being fundamental to the nature of language – its symbolic and instrumentalist characteristics. These set up dualisms in just about everything that then interplays with language – for example the Herderian view that leads to cultural nationalism, as opposed to the instrumentalist analysis which drives states to construct national languages. At one level there is, or should be, the right to freedom of speech and expression in the language associated with an individual's or community's identity. At another level it is a matter of communicative facility which allows for easier and fairer access to information and participation. An abnegation of these rights, then, can be said to be both a moral as well as a political wrong (Chen 1998).

Moreover, De Witte (1985, 1993) warns that not only the nature of but also the objectives too of linguistic rights can be twofold, and that these will have very different consequences. He distinguishes between 'rights to freedom' and 'rights to equality' (De Witte, 1993: 303). De Witte explains that the right to freedom to use one's mother tongue may often be seen as a largely 'negative' right, as he sees it, as it simply implies that the state need do nothing, including not preventing its use. In this situation people are at liberty to use their mother tongue, but, in practical terms, may well not be able to do so as the public authorities do not have the corresponding duty to know the minority language.

De Witte argues forcefully for the recognition and application of linguistic equality. It is important, however, to understand that this does not necessarily mean making everyone the same. As De Witte warns,

> Throughout the nineteenth century, and even now to a very large extent, the main thrust of the principle of equality has been to eliminate all those 'arbitrary' distinctions between persons which were the legacy of the *ancien régime*.
>
> (De Witte, 1993: 303)

As he convincingly argues, equality for minorities is often achieved by allowing them to be different.

> Equality . . . can be invoked for claiming a treatment which is at the same time identical in substance but differentiated in (linguistic) form.
>
> (De Witte, 1993: 304)

The egalitarian idea of making everyone the same has been the justification of policies of assimilation and even oppression during the period of nation-building up until at least the middle of the twentieth century. Only recently in fact has the notion of protecting difference, and therefore diversity, which must lead to pluralism, begun to underlie concepts of linguistic rights.

This is a complicated issue. Proponents of linguistic rights are almost always defenders of minorities, as we have noted, and usually also defenders of linguistic diversity. The 'rightness' of diversity is an unquestioned principle implicit in all documents concerning language rights. We have commented throughout that linguistic diversity and multilingualism are certainly normal throughout the world, and that monolingualism is a constructed political decision in most cases. However, there are those who do not support the basic premise that diversity is normal and to be protected, but hold a position that, we could argue, has been supported as early as from the writings of Herder. For these every community has one language only, the soul of its identity, and wishes to guard its language separate from any other community. Any seepage by other languages is a dilution of national identity. And for others, the existence of multilingualism is recognised but considered an expensive luxury.

As we have already mentioned, individual and collective rights do quite often conflict, and the need to decide how to prioritise becomes a delicate, and usually political, decision. Who and how to decide on whether linguistic rights should take precedence over, for example, housing rights in the allocation of resources, or freedom of movement, can become hugely controversial. Brookes and Brice Heath (1997: 197–207) in an excellent review of one of the pioneering volumes on linguistic rights, *Linguistic Human Rights: Overcoming Linguistic Discrimination* edited by Tove Skutnabb-Kangas and Robert Phillipson (1994), caution against any naivety in believing that the granting of linguistic rights to minorities is always done by a state in that minority's best interests. They write:

> For example, economic rights and land-tenure issues, as well as mineral and oil rights, may lead nations to grant linguistic rights and even encourage education in minority languages in order to ensure lack of access to information and legal rights by particular groups.
>
> (Brookes and Brice Heath, 1997: 199)

Fishman warns in a similar kind of way that democratic principles can lead to a conflict of rights, where the more powerful usually control the outcome:

> Just where and when the limits of democratic rights should be drawn, be they linguistic or more general, can well be viewed as a dilemma within the democratic ethos itself. Limits can be set in self-serving ways and those who wield greater power are particularly likely to have a disproportionate say in the establishment of such limits.
>
> (Fishman, 1994: 51)

It is a mistake too to imagine that all communities value their mother tongue highly. This is also related to the extent to which their language is held as a central marker of their identity. If the mother tongue is not a core value to a community's identity, or if its prestige is so low as to lead to rejection, then the linguistic rights sought by such a community are more likely to concern access and assimilation to the dominant language, with little interest in the preservation of their mother tongue (Brookes and Brice Heath, 1997; Paulston, 1997). As Brookes and Brice Heath importantly argue there is a need to understand that more than one position regarding multilingualism does exist. On the one hand there exists 'the belief that linguistic diversity rather than homogeneity is universally desirable' and that this is supported by 'the claim that diversity will reduce conflict and produce better group relations'. On the other hand, those supporting monolingualism claim that a 'common' language has participatory and economic benefits. This is a familiar debate but one that must be understood when examining the objectives of language policies and Language Planning. Fishman usefully reminds us that even when the concept of diversity and multilingualism is considered the acceptable and more democratic one to underline language rights, there still remains the dilemma of economic and social realities:

> Languages may very well all be equally valid and precious markers of cultural belonging, behavior and identity, while nevertheless being far from equally valuable or viable as vehicles of either intergroup or econo-technical communication. Whether, where, when and how to draw the line between the two, i.e. between ethnolinguistic democracy, on the one hand, and ethnolinguistic equality, on the other, is often a matter frought with tension, guilt and outright conflict as well.
>
> (Fishman, 1994: 51)

Language policies

So far we have been discussing in very general terms the issues at a philosophical or moral level concerning language rights. Issues of equality, freedom of speech, respect, tolerance and the like are universal values, which have indeed been recognised as such by international bodies such as the United Nations. On the whole, however, the necessary legislation that makes rights into realities has to be enacted at the level of national governments. Certain rights can be enshrined by international law, and with lengthy legal processes upheld, but the day to day structuring of communal life is normally only affected by laws and their administration at the level of sovereign states. It is true – and this is a theme that we will return to at the end of this book – that we find ourselves increasingly in a world whose economies, societies and even politics are so interlinked that the notion of state sovereignty is being strongly challenged. This is no less true in the case of the protection and formulation of human (and linguistic) rights. The tensions between the European Union and its member states is a case in point. In Chapter 10 we will examine the extent to which language policy is now conducted from the centre of the EU rather than from the member states, or whether any supranational organisations in Latin America have a greater influence on language issues than the individual countries of the region. However, here we will concentrate on what still remains the most important focus for the enactment or denial of language rights, that is the most powerful global political unit, the nation-state.[6]

Paulston suggests the kind of *areas* where the state can develop language policies and draw up legislation which may include,

> matters such as choice of official language, language requirements for naturalization or citizenship, use of official or native language in court

as well as interpreters, the right of access to, that is, facilitation of access to, the dominant language by instruction in schools, in the army . . . , in the workplace, by religious bodies, etc. . . . Finally, we have the policies that aim to help or hinder language maintenance or shift.

(Paulston, 1997: 190)

Above all, government policies will directly apply to official and public use of language(s), but indirectly these will also have an effect on non-official and private use. In some extreme cases governments have proscribed the use of minority languages in any form including within the home and family. The latter could be seen in the very early days of the Franco regime in Spain and its repression of any use of Catalan, Galician or Basque.

Turi (1995: 112–13) categorises language legislation as having four different *functions*: official, institutionalising, standardising or liberal. His first category, of course, refers to the legislation produced to grant languages official status, either in the entire state and/or in certain specified territories. 'Official' here usually applies to the language to be used in all governmental, administrative, legal, educational and, in general, public discourse, written or oral.

Turi describes 'institutionalising language legislation' as:

Legislation which seeks to make one or more designated languages the normal, usual or common language in the unofficial domains of labour, communication, culture, commerce and business.

(Turi, 1995: 112)

The standardising category refers to legislation governing the actual form and corpus of the official language(s) in certain public domains. Turi uses 'liberal' to describe that legislation which enshrines those language rights we have outlined above.

The literature discussing language policy as a discrete activity is very sparse. Almost always commentators have discussed language policy and Language Planning together.[7] I have chosen to distinguish between *language policy* and *Language Planning* as combining them seems to me to run the risk of confusing decision-making and implementation. The *policy* reflects decisions and choices which to be understood must be set in the ideological and political context in which they are taken and by whom. Whereas the *planning* which we will discuss in detail in the next section involves the means by which policy makers hope and expect to put policies into practice. This distinction was made early on by one of the original writers on Language Planning, Joan Rubin, when she warned that 'policy-making is not planning' and went on to say:

Often, when evaluating the process of language *planning*, people say that language *planning* has failed. Upon closer examination, it turns out that there was little clear indication of the means of implementing the *policy* and little consideration of alternative means to achieve the goals. If the *policy*-maker does not have proper background information and does not recognise that the *plan* must be co-ordinated with other socio-cultural processes, it is more than likely to remain just a *policy*.

(Rubin, 1977: 285; my emphases)

Another commentator to consider this separation of the two concepts as useful is Schiffman. He offers the following definitions taken from Bugarski (1992) to distinguish between the two:

The term *language policy* here refers, briefly, to the policy of a society in the area of linguistic communication – that is, the set of positions, principles and decisions reflecting that community's relationships to its verbal repertoire and communicative potential. *Language planning* is understood as a set of concrete measures taken within language policy to act on linguistic communication in a community, typically by directing the development of the languages.

(Schiffman 1996: 3–7)

As we have seen, the state may enact legislation of either a favourable, promotive nature to support languages, vote them resources and enshrine certain rights for their speakers. Or, the policies may be restrictive leading to repression and intolerance. National language policy is not necessarily overt and obvious. Sometimes linguistic objectives emerge as a consequence of related governmental policies. For example, in the United Kingdom there is no formal legislation to say that English is the official language; nonetheless, the status of English as such becomes entirely evident through such things as the national education curriculum, or the language used in legal documentation. Language Planning, on the other hand, is always explicit and overt.

As we have seen in the comment from Rubin and in the implication of the previous paragraph, language policy is part of overall governmental policy and must be understood as being closely inter-related with other social and political objectives and decision-making. This was a point we have noted already in the writing of some of the commentators on language rights and is very fully developed by such writers as Blommaert (1996), Breton (1996), O Riagáin (1997), Ozolins (1996), Schiffman (1996) and Williams (1992).

Blommaert (1997) and Glyn Williams (1992: Chapter 5), in excellent and provocative critiques of Language Planning, both make insightful comments on the area that I have identified as 'language policy'. Both warn of the naivety of not seeing the highly political and ideological way governments can construct language policy.

For Williams language policies and the consequent Language Planning is always eurocentric as it is predicated on beliefs that originate from the nineteenth century views of modernity. At that time the perception was that 'successful' nation-states with a unifying single national language were examples of modernisation, whereas multilingual states tended to harbour traditional communities which would, therefore, prevent progress and efficiency. This was certainly the prevailing view in the post-independent Latin American republics. But as Williams claims:

> The dichotomous referents of modern/traditional, advanced/traditional and even rural/urban are merely ideological supports for the modernisation thesis and, as such, have to be discarded, together with the associated typological constructs. This is as true of language as of any other societal feature – languages are not in need of modernisation any more than difference can be conceptualised in terms of modern/non-modern.
>
> (Williams, 1992: 127)

Williams then goes on to comment on policy making in particular:

> It is also important to realise that policy is the product of social and political factors, even though the orthodox philosophy views policy in action on behalf of, rather than in the interest of, the public body or society. Thus it is evident that policy involves policing on the one hand and politics on the other. . . . It is also clear that planning and policy relate to the state while having a direct influence on civil society. This, in turn, leads to an awareness of political power, function, interests and social change and to ignore these factors is tantamount to treating a lack of policy as policy.
>
> (Williams, 1992: 129)

Blommaert (1996) also stresses the heavily ideological basis to language policies and the need to understand this. In a critical overview of the discipline of Language Planning over the past few decades he arrives at a conclusion which can well encompass our observations on the debates on language rights and the role of language policies in reflecting these. He writes of Language Planning, which he conceives of in a broader sense than will be used here:

> Summarizing, language planning was almost invariably aimed at reducing the sociolinguistic complexity of a country, and motivated by assumptions of efficiency and national integration. In doing so, it involved an implicit model, based on an idealization of the European nation-state, and including an organic view of language and society. . . .
>
> (Blommaert, 1996: 212)

Once again we see the constantly recurring tension of 'efficiency' and 'national integration' which seems to be tied to monolingualism (or at least to as few tolerated languages as possible) as opposed to the acceptance of diversity and multilingalism. If as Blommaert and Williams argue language policies are essentially eurocentric, inspired by the ideas of nineteenth century nation-building, then it will be interesting to examine how far this is the case in the Spanish-speaking world.

Language Planning[8]

From the discussion in the previous section I would emphasise that it is possible, even common, to have language policies without having Language Planning. That is to say, an objective may be formulated, usually but not uniquely, at state-level, but for a variety of reasons, not least resources, the implementation to achieve this is not carried out. We have already noted, for example, that many of the Latin American countries made bold claims regarding citizenship in their constitutions, but without the necessary education, the linguistic requirements could not be achieved. Sometimes, of course, a language policy may only refer to a relatively localised area – the use of gender-free language in the workplace, for example – where, again, the actual implementation may depend both on resources and on supportive attitudes to the policy. I would argue that Language Planning cannot take place without the existence of a language policy, although this policy may be implicit or covert.[9]

Language Planning, like language policies, has existed for centuries in some form. The work of the language academies from the seventeenth century is one example of this, as is the compilation and publication of grammars and dictionaries. Education systems have also been throughout history a central part of the implementation of any language policies. However, the academic discipline of Language Planning (LP) is usually dated to the 1960s and associated with writers who were products of the recently developed areas of sociolinguistics and the sociology of language. The principal trigger for this particular timing was the widespread need in many parts of the developing world to plan and construct post-colonial states and their own national identities. For this reason, much of the early work on LP is very clearly oriented towards these kinds of societies. Their needs are very specific and to a great extent different from language issues in developed countries, like Spain, or parts of the world where the colonial experience was more distant, like Latin America.

Cooper (1989: Chapter 2) in an excellent review of the literature on Language Planning identifies twelve different (if related) definitions that have been offered to describe Language Planning since writers began seriously to differentiate this discipline in the 1960s. Cooper then goes on to offer his own, thirteenth, definition!

> Language Planning refers to deliberate efforts to influence the behaviour of others with respect to the acquisition, structure or functional allocation of their language codes.
>
> (Cooper, 1989: 45)

To this I would want to add that this language behaviour is normally that of a community or society as a whole, even if the changes may sometimes begin at a very individual level.

As explained in the previous section, I have attempted to separate 'language policy' from LP, although so often in the literature this is not the case. The various models that emerged to give a framework to LP over the years usually, therefore, include policy in their first stage, i.e. selection. The selection or choice of, for example, official or national language(s) and how to promote this is, however, quite clearly a decision, taken by governments at state, or occasionally local, level. The other stages that are identified by these models, however, are part of the implementation process and therefore form the basis of LP. A synthesis of the models offered by Haugen (1966) – who is usually credited with being the first to coin and define the field – Rubin (1977) and Cooper (1983) identifies the following stages to be followed in LP after the selection process: norm codification, or standard-isation (of the grammar, lexicon, pronunciation, etc.) often across regional and social variation; functional implementation; and functional elaboration (especially where new functions are deemed necessary for the chosen code).

It is generally accepted that the stages are implemented through three broad categories: corpus planning, status planning and acquisition planning (Kloss, 1969; Cooper, 1989). *Corpus planning* refers to the form of the language or languages. This may include development or choice of the writing systems (e.g. the adaptation of Amerindian languages to a Latin alphabet), and to standardised spelling norms. The latter, as we will see later, has been very important in the case of Galician and Quechua.

Corpus planning is also the focus for the standardisation processes which have so often taken place on selecting and promoting official languages. Where varieties and dialects have existed, planners have prescribed the stan-dard norms in grammar, phonology and the lexicon. This is of course by no means as technical and value-free as is sometimes claimed, and is one of the instances when covert policy decisions may in fact be taken by the language planners rather than the government.

In many countries a major on-going part of the work of corpus planners has been in the elaboration of new terminologies and vocabularies to respond to the expanding domains for which the language or code is being used. In this sense, corpus planning is very closely linked with status planning, which, amongst other things, is involved in identifying and promoting these new domains.

Status planning is involved in promoting the status of the language by encouraging its use, as we have noted, in wider areas and in particular by public authorities, such as government and the judiciary. Status planning also seeks to improve attitudes towards the language to facilitate its accept-ance through campaigns as well as the increased use by public figures. As with other categories of LP, status planning supports and promotes new language behaviour by providing more resources for it, from financial support to training and materials.

Acquisition Planning (Cooper, 1989) is a more recent category of LP which develops aspects of status planning by focusing on how the language can be learnt and acquired. If status planning improves people's attitudes to the use of the language, acquisition planning helps them to learn it through education and use in the media, for example.

It may be argued that the usefulness of dividing LP into such categories lies in the fact that we can then identify the likely bodies or individuals responsible for carrying out these different objectives. A programme of corpus planning will necessitate the participation and leadership of language experts. Whereas status planning is more likely to be led by administrators in close contact with politicians, if not actually politicians, acquisition planning is of course the domain of educators above all. The role of other groups, such as the media, the business world, or religious bodies, is also of great importance especially in the development of status planning, but this is usually done in conjunction with government officials, linguists or teachers. We have implied throughout this discussion that LP is an activity that is carried out by governments, to which we could also add supranational official organisations (such as UNESCO or the EU). The latter, however, as with the case of non-governmental groups (folk societies, pressure groups, religious organisations, etc.) if they are to be entirely successful will ultimately need the support, and probably the resources of the government. On the one hand, the directives of international, supranational level groups are often not binding on sovereign governments; on the other, activities at a subnational level may lack sufficient resources or public awareness and therefore support. We will return to an examination of these different levels of LP in Chapter 5 when we see how it has been conducted in the Spanish-speaking world, and in Chapter 10 when we speculate on the increasing importance of supranational agencies.

We have implied in the above discussion that these categories of LP are discrete, separate areas. This is a mistake, as it soon becomes very obvious that the different forms of LP are in fact highly inter-related. Teaching materials (acquisition planning) require the outcome of standardisation and codification work (corpus planning). Writing systems and expanded terminologies (corpus planning) feed into the new domains and functions promoted by status planning.

Glyn Williams (1992) in particular is at pains to emphasise the inter-relationship between status and corpus planning, which he notes are both ultimately directed by political objectives. He points out that whereas status planning is about the relative status of different languages (whether official, tolerated, minoritised, etc.), corpus planning through its standardisation activities is concerned with the relative status of different varieties within the language (Williams, 1992: 147). He continues:

Whenever the minority language enters into new domains it has repercussions for its corpus, not necessarily because of any 'deficiency' in
that language but because of its social reconstitution. One feature of
minority languages is that they tend to be systematically separated
from those domains which are crucial for social reproduction, domains
such as work, administration, etc.

> (Williams, 1992: 147)

Williams also argues the important point that with official and expanded
status, minority languages tend to develop a wider variety of social, i.e.
class, varieties. At this stage they cease to display only geographical variation
but also have social variation, leading to the need for corpus planning of their
standardisation (Williams, G., 1992: 147).

To some extent it is this understanding of the total congruence between the
classic distinction of corpus and status (and also acquisition) planning that has
led to the emergence of another category, and one that is particularly important in Spain, that is *normalisation planning*. We will discuss the linguistic
normalisation programmes of the Spanish autonomous communities in
detail in the next chapter. For the moment a useful definition of this category
would be:

> Normalization consists of . . . three tasks . . . a) to empower minority lan-
> guages in order to make it possible for [them] to satisfy the communica-
> tive needs of a modern society; b) to increase the number of speakers/users
> and increase the communicative competence of current users, and c)
> expand the geographic scope of the language within a given area.
>
> (Cobarrubias, 1987: 60)

In this definition we could say that (a) is a strong form of status planning, that
(b) is a form of acquisition planning, and that (c), to which we could add
'social' scope, is also a form of status planning. Those commentators who
developed this concept (in particular the Catalan sociolinguists Aracil,
Ninyoles and Valverdú) stress that normalisation will only follow standardisation (i.e. the corpus planning aspect). But in the development and promotion of minority languages they see the need for this entirely integrated
approach where a language is to be placed (or returned, perhaps in the case
of Catalan) to a 'normal' level of equality vis-à-vis other (majority) languages.
This is a concept which is widely accepted in Spain but less known in other
areas; however Cobarrubias suggests that:

> Even though linguistic normalization may be branded differently in dif-
> ferent communities, it captures very well the general aspirations of many
> minority speech communities for linguistic equality and raising the
> status of their language in a meaningful way.
>
> (Cobarrubias, 1987: 57)

Whilst status and corpus planning activities are of course extremely important, I would argue that by far the most crucial ingredient in any implementation of language policies is that of acquisiton planning, or the education system. The policies followed and the successes and failures of these in terms of languages used and languages taught, as well as societal attitudes to them, encapsulates that society's, or at least, its government's commitment or rejection of the kind of language rights mentioned earlier. The education system is also, as we have seen, an important focus for the creation, construction and consciousness-raising of national identity, marked as it may be by language identity. For this reason, we will dedicate the whole of Part III to a discussion of language and education, and make less reference here and in the following chapter to what is often termed language-in-education planning.

Language and power

What should have become apparent in this brief discussion of the issues of language rights, policies and planning is that all take place in a political arena where the focus is on relationships – usually between dominant and dominated groups or majority and minority groups – and, above all, on power (see, e.g. Fairclough, 1989; Kaplan and Baldauf, 1997: Chapter 7; Tollefson, 1991, 1995). That is to say, in all these areas we are referring to such things as the power to decide who speaks which language(s), who learns or teaches which language(s); who controls resources and, even, access to the so-called democratic processes. Since we have seen that language is both about identity and about communication, then these issues also reflect the power to decide how to construct a community's identity, and what access to information groups may be permitted. This power of course will normally lie with the centralised state, and as Tollefson claims:

> State language policies, although often associated with a rhetoric of 'equality' and 'opportunity', frequently serve to channel migrants and other linguistic minorities into low-paying jobs in the peripheral economy.
>
> (Tollefson, 1995: 3)

Language is so closely linked to other social and political issues, as we have seen, that language debates and tensions often reflect other social changes or conflicts. Language policies will therefore normally mirror other social policies. It is no surprise, then, that these policies have frequently been one of two tendencies, the tendency towards assimilation, homogenisation and, therefore, dominant monolingualism, the justification being for unity and for efficiency. Or, the recognition of minority groups and their rights has led to attempts at pluralist models and the promotion of diversity. Colin Williams (1991) is one of a growing group of commentators to argue that language's role in society should be analysed in ecological terms (see, also, e.g. Mühlhäusler, 1996). He argues that insofar as language behaviour is an integral part of social change, this change should be analysed in terms of 'several key concepts sharpened by the ecological revolution'.

> This would focus on the interdependence of humans and nature, and that between constituent cultures of a territory. . . . It would alert us to the fact that diversity is strength, and that cultural pluralism within a harmonious system is a rich endowment. It would suggest that the previous decades' relative neglect of lesser-used languages was a thinly veiled championing of powerful, centralist forces, whose practice was often disguised behind technical and pseudo-scientific methodologies designed to integrate populations into new collectivities.
>
> (Williams, 1991: 73)

Williams believes that language policies can play an important part in recognising this 'strength in diversity' and promoting potentially endangered languages, so long as there is a holistic social and political approach to language planning. In the following chapter we will see which of these models, of linguistic diversity or lingusitic hegemony, are more common in the Spanish-speaking world. We will ask, for example in the Latin American context, if there are endangered languages, along the analogy of endangered species, and whether these are being and should be protected by language and social policies. Above all, however, we will be identifying who controls power in relations between linguistic communities in the Spanish-speaking world and what the politics of language of these regions therefore will be.

5 The state and language policies in the contemporary Spanish-speaking world

In Part I we saw that there are very few countries in the Spanish-speaking world where only Spanish is spoken. Spanish is certainly the official language in all. It is also the dominant language in all. It is the language of public life and of the governing classes. It is, therefore, the language of power. In this chapter, then, we will see how far those in power and therefore in control of policy-making set out to identify and respect the linguistic rights of all the communities living within their jurisdiction. Are these rights repressed or promoted through government policies? What kind of Language Planning, if any, is pursued as a result of language policies? Do attitudes towards language rights in this century in any way differ from those we examined in the earlier history of the Castilianisation process? In much of this history, decisions affecting language were the consequence of other policies of national integration; in this century we will observe examples of where the politics of language actually shape other social policies.

Spain: from dictatorship to the *estado de las autonomías*

In this part we will examine three areas: the issue of language rights under the Franco regime, the language policy and legislation of the post-Franco 1978 Constitution, and the Language Planning of the present autonomous communities.

The denial of language rights in the Franco years

We noted in Chapter 2 how over the centuries Spanish governments became more aware of the need to use language, and particularly the promotion of Castilian, as part of the project of nation-building. One of the most clear and overt examples of this is the attitude of the Franco regime which followed the 1936–39 Civil War. As this is also a relatively recent period in Spanish history, it is essential to realise how the Franco dictatorship is still a key point of reference in any understanding of contemporary Spanish politics and society. The post-1975 *Transición* and present democratic system must be discussed against the background of the previous regime. This is particularly true in the case of language politics.

The Franco period (1939–75) is a time of state-led policies that are the very embodiment of the denial of linguistic rights as identified in the previous chapter. Franco had of course led the winning side in the Civil War who were known as the 'Nationalists', a highly significant label that underlined his regime's project to define Spain and Spanishness throughout the thirty-six year dictatorship. This project was characterised by its principal supporters: the right-wing quasi-fascist *Falange* movement (whose influence in fact declined during the regime), the Catholic Church, the army, and those conservative forces and traditionalists who had supported the Nationalists throughout the war.[1] The result was a highly centralised, conservative, right-wing regime. It was also for much of the time a very insular regime which for many years was ostracised by the international community, and, in response, reinforced its defences against the outside world, strengthening the sense of 'them' and 'us' and repelling many cultural and social influences.

Absolutely crucial to the regime's definition of Spain was the exclusion of those who threatened the sense of there being one single, unchallenged 'Spanish' identity. The regions on the periphery, the linguistic minorities, were not part of the idea of a powerful, unified, central Spain. The rhetoric of the regime emphasising '*la patria*' and its imperial past glories focused on the legacy of the Castilianisation process and would not tolerate any deviation from this.

Inevitably, then, language was recognised by the regime as a major symbol of identity, both with the Spanish language in the centralising process, and with the need to repress any alternative languages. Those aspects of linguistic rights which we identified in the previous chapters – such as linguistic equality, access to mother tongue teaching, use of the mother tongue in public discourse, respect for linguistic difference, etc. – all were explicitly or implicitly denied. This conscious rejection of linguistic rights was achieved both through the overt denial in policies and legislation but also through the manipulation of public opinion. Those in power do not of course only necessarily control the processes of legislation and enforcement of this, but also, often, the access to the media and channels of public communications.

In the early years of the regime the use of the non-Castilian languages was very heavily suppressed with their prohibition in any public use, including teaching, and with fines and even prison sentences being the penalty for disobeying. As the decades went by, however, this did slacken to some extent. From the 1950s publication in non-Castilian languages became more common. By the 1960s it was more possible to find classes teaching these mother tongues, although only in private centres. The 1960s are in fact characterised generally by a certain opening up and greater pragmatism as foreign investment and foreign tourism began to affect cultural and social norms. In particular, 1966 saw the passing of the so-called law of Freedom of Expression. The latter, which would hardly be described in this way by many human rights groups, did do away with the previous system of censorship and introduced instead self-censorship prior to publication, issuing, however, very clear guidelines on a wide range of topics and principles which could still not be challenged or discussed.

During this somewhat more liberal era, it was more common to hear the non-Castilian languages even in such places as the theatre and cinema. In the case of Catalan, the media started to include some use of this. By the 1970s Catalan was being taught – as a subject of academic curiosity like Greek or Romance philology – at Barcelona University.

However, it is in the area of public attitudes and opinion where the Francoist language policy is most evident and, arguably, most effective. The decision to allow a certain relaxation towards the use of the non-Castilian languages, and especially to allow their publication, is not the sign of a newly-discovered tolerance and respect, rather it displays the regime's confidence that these were indeed such marginal acitivities that they did not in fact in any way threaten the central state hegemony. Moreover, this was strengthened by the regime's careful portraying of the minority languages as inferior and inconsequential. The non-Castilian languages were always referred to as 'dialects' which, as we have commented earlier, is a term normally associated with an inferior status in the linguistic hierarchy. The recognised national language, on the other hand, was associated with all the trappings of the Spanish nation and with its values, to the extent that a common play on words was to conflate 'castellano' with 'cristiano' (people were exhorted to 'hablar cristiano') and thereby a sense of moral superiority. More subtle still was the way in which the growing use of the non-Castilian languages was carefully confined to their use for less 'serious' activities. For example, the state television in Catalonia would give national and international news of politics and current affairs in Castilian, and then finish with items where the vernacular language was used to talk about local folksy events of a more trivial nature.

Whilst it is true that mother tongue speakers of non-Castilian languages were still able to transmit these languages to their children, the development and full acquisition of these were stilted by unfavourable attitudes, the sense of inferiority and even guilt, and the lack of teaching to consolidate and reinforce their use and learning.

Despite these negative attitudes surrounding the languages, which might have followed a typical path of language shift and language death, the regime's clever propaganda drive made one costly mistake: the rejection and even ridicule of the minority languages became so closely associated with the ideology of the Franco regime that it also served as a point of reference around which to build the opposition to it. Language became a symbolic standard bearer for and against the regime. As we shall see later, this has had an important legacy in the post-Franco era.

Significant examples of this anti-regime role of language during the Franco dictatorship can be seen both with the role of Basque identified by the terrorist movement ETA which was formed during this time, and under the dictatorship attracted substantial sympathy. Also, the tolerating of performance in non-Castilian languages led to the wide success of a pop/folk music movement in Catalonia known as *Nova Cançó*. Active at the same time as American (and British) anti-war song movements, this group of Catalan artists singing in Catalan took their records and concerts to audiences well beyond Catalonia, and served as a tangible focus for anti-regime protests. Many of their concerts had to be broken up by riot police and they proved a real thorn in the flesh of the highly authoritarian regime.

The unexpected prestige which this political identification gave the non-Castilian languages also helped them in another potentially threatening area. In Catalonia and the Basque Country the future of the respective languages (in the case of Basque already very uncertain) was further affected by the large influx of Castilian-speaking migrants from poorer areas of Spain, particularly in the late forties and through the fifties. These waves of newcomers tended to concentrate around large urban areas where there were possiblities of work, particularly around Barcelona and Bilbao. In Catalonia the effect of this immigration was to bring the proportion of non-native Catalans living in Catalonia to around fifty per cent from the 1970s (Ninyoles, 1977). It is obvious that this could have an enormous impact on the survival of Catalan and Catalan identity. Given this immigration was taking place at precisely the time when the Spanish state was downgrading the status of minority languages and inhibiting their use, plus the fact that the migrants were usually very under-educated and often illiterate, it is no small cause for surprise that, particularly in Catalonia, attitudes towards integrating into the new community and even learning the local language were very favourable. Clearly this was fuelled by the association of this regional identity with opposition to a regime that was increasingly hated by many sectors of society, and in particular by those who had suffered politically, socially and economically under it.

Towards the end of the Franco years much of the regime's recent confidence began to dissipate with resulting renewed repression. This was normally at the level of political and judicial struggles, which nonetheless were often sited in the linguistic minority communities, such as the Basque Country and Catalonia. The increasing impact of these regions' opposition to the regime was closely associated with their badge of distinct languages and cultures.

Las lenguas españolas *and the 1978 Constitution*

With the end of the Franco dictatorship in November 1975 came the end of one of Spain's most highly centralised and authoritarian regimes and the very speedy moves towards the present Western-style democratic system of government. A key point in this transition to democracy is the 1978 Constitution and the ensuing legal framework this established. This constitution was passed by the *Cortes* in October 1978, widely endorsed in a national referendum in December that year, and immediately brought into effect.

This document embodies the new post-Franco conception of Spain, most significant of which is the paving the way for the introduction of the system of the *estado de las autonomías*. A cornerstone in this new definition and the concept of 'autonomies' is the overt linguistic policy and its interpretation of language rights.

Below we will discuss Articles 2 and 3 of this constitution as being the two which most essentially define our areas of interest: nation/state-building and the role of language in this.[2] After the constitution's Preamble and Article 1 enshrining sovereignty with the people, establishing the notion of a constitutional monarchy and describing Spain as a democratic state, Article 2 reads:

> La Constitución se fundamenta en la indisoluble unidad de la Nación española, patria común e indivisible de todos los españoles, y reconoce y garantiza el derecho a la autonomía de las nacionalidades y regiones que la integran y la solidaridad entre todas ellas.[3]

Unlike the history of the Castilianisation process that we have observed earlier, here is an attempt, albeit full of contortions, to reconcile the concept of a highly centralised Spain with the reality of its diverse parts (Brassloff, 1996). In an awesome example of political compromise and consensus, polar contrasts like 'Nación' and 'nacionalidades', 'unidad' and 'autonomía', 'patria común' and 'regiones' are placed together. Terms are offered – and understood – in very particular ways: what is a 'nacionalidad'? How is it different from a 'Nación'? It is to be understood from the constitution that 'nationalities' in Spain refer to the sense of nationhood experienced by the substate level regions or 'nations', whereas *the* nation is written with a capital 'N'. Clearly this is not the English meaning of 'nationality' as a legal term associated with citizenship, the right to a passport and other legal documents. In fact it is not clear that 'nacionalidad' in this Spanish sense has any legal weight or legitimacy, but it has enormous symbolic significance. Another term with a very particular Spanish meaning is that of 'autonomía' which is, arguably, less extreme than the English concept of 'autonomy'; a possible British equivalent might be 'devolution'. Even self-determination may only partially describe the actual position on close examination of the *'comunidades autónomas'* that now make up Spain, which in practice have much in common with the US states.

As Tamames (1992: 13) indicates, the pivotal word that allows the apparently incompatible terms to fit together in this article is that of *'la solidaridad'*. It is the 'solidarity' between the different 'nationalities' which effectively creates the 'indivisible' unity.

If defining what Spain is turns out to be so delicate, it will come as no surprise that the role of language in this balancing act is equally crucial and potentially ambiguous. Article 3 reads:

1 El castellano es la lengua española oficial del Estado. Todos los españoles tienen el deber de conocerla y el derecho a usarla.
2 Las demás lenguas españolas serán también oficiales en las respectivas Comunidades Autónomas de acuerdo con sus Estatutos.
3 La riqueza de las distintas modalidades lingüísticas de España es un patrimonio cultural que será objeto de especial respeto y protección.[4]

This is a much-quoted and much-discussed article,[5] commonly applauded as underpinning a new recognition of Spain's multilingualism and its linguistic rights. Close examination of this text, however, does not entirely bear this out.

Examining each clause individually, we can see from the very first sentence the significance of this article. The decision to call the official language 'Castilian' is a brave and controversial one. This had also been the case with the Constitution of the Second Republic, and it had met with the same reaction (see Tamames, 1992: 14). At that time figures as prominent as Unamuno and Ortega y Gasset had argued that the name should be 'Spanish'. A similar debate took place in the lead up to the latest constitution (see, especially, Salvador, 1987). To these opponents, all strong defenders of the concept of centralised Spanish national identity, Castilian *is* Spanish. They argue it is not possible to have a 'Spanish language' or 'Spanish languages' as the constitution goes on to refer to. The Francoist notion that 'cristiano' = 'castellano' = 'español' = 'España' has been firmly buried. It is also significant that the official language is attached to the 'State' and not to a 'nation', that elusive and controversial entity.

However, the radicalism takes one step forward and then one step back. By insisting that all Spaniards have a 'duty' to know Castilian, the law is prescribing a very clear and strong message. Few national constitutions legislate for the duty to know a particular language; 'right' is the more normal term.[6] 'Duty' may of course be an implicit consequence of other laws, such as the right to vote in some Latin American states depending on the ability to read and write – in Spanish. But, what is meant by 'know' a language? This might be an entirely passive and receptive ability, that of understanding but not producing or speaking/writing the language. Is this also a liberalising compromise?

The clause concludes by stating that all Spaniards have the right to use Castilian, which is a more familiar formulation of linguistic rights, but one that must, of course, depend on wider participation and interaction. To actively use it requires others knowing it.

The second clause takes a huge step forward towards the model of a multilingual society by implicitly recognising the existence of 'other' Spanish languages, and stating that they will be official in their 'respective communities'. However, it is worth noting that the constitution does not actually name these languages, leaving their identification open. It is generally accepted that this is now defined by those languages in which the constitution and organic laws are published, which are, besides Castilian, Catalan, Basque and Galician. However, as ever, the issue of how to define a 'language' proved controversial as the Valencians also insisted that they spoke a separate language, into which the constitution and other official documents should be translated and published. This demand was successful, reflecting, perhaps, the economic and political pressure a community like Valencia was able to exert, even though the resulting version of the constitution is almost exactly the same as the Catalan one.

The official status is of course co-official, as clause 1 has already decreed that Castilian is official throughout the Spanish state. But it should also be noted that this status – and the resulting support and legislation – is dependent ultimately not on the central state policy, but on the individual community's desire to identify and endorse their own language. The statutes of Catalonia, the Basque Country, Galicia, the Balearic Islands, Valencia, Navarra, Aragon, the Canary Islands, and Andalusia all make mention of their linguistic situation. On the other hand, such places as Leon, where Galician is spoken, or Zamora, where Portuguese is found, have no mention or protection in their local statutes of autonomy.

The most significant policy underpinning this clause is the granting of the territoriality principle to the inhabitants of these linguistic minority communities, as opposed to the personality principle that underlines the right to speak Castilian. The use of Catalan, Basque, Galician, etc., is restricted to the regions where these are spoken as mother tongues. Castilian, on the other hand, can be used anywhere within the Spanish state. The potential for conflict then between these two principles is obvious, and we will discuss the debate concerning language rights and the education system in Catalonia in Chapter 8.

If language rights for those whose mother tongues are not Castilian are only protected in certain parts of the Spanish state, it seems to me that there is a real inconsistency within the constitution between this article and Article 14 which claims:

> Los españoles son iguales ante la ley, sin que pueda prevalecer discriminación alguna por razón de nacimiento, raza, sexo, religión, opinión o cualquier otra condición o circunstancia personal o social.[7]

If one is denied the right to use one's mother tongue, for example in state education or in the courts, anywhere on Spanish territory, it is hard to see how this cannot constitute a form of discrimination on grounds of personal circumstance, and maybe even birth and race.

The first clause refers to the official language of the state and the second to co-official languages in certain defined areas, whilst the third clause of this article identifies a further category to be recognised as part of the state's language policy, that of *'modalidades lingüísticas'*, or 'linguistic varieties'. Once again exactly what these are is left unanswered. It has generally been assumed that the constitution is referring here to those varieties of language which are not usually identified as separate languages, rather dialects of Castilian, which, nonetheless, are held dear by their communities and are clearly markers of their particular identity. The reference to their importance and the promise to respect and protect them, has given rise, in some regions, to a greater confidence and pride in particular regional varieties.[8] The Andalusians have promoted important research into the variety of the Spanish they speak, and are encouraging its use. The Canary Islands have produced examples of their dialect of Spanish, such as the *Léxico del español usual en las Canarias* (Gobierno de Canarias, 1986). In both these latter cases there have been efforts to encourage the use of the local variety in such public communication as the local media and schools. Until now, the central Spanish variety of Castilian, originating in the Burgos area and commonly heard in Madrid, has been considered the standard norm to which all educated Spaniards should aspire. To some extent the third clause of Article 3 has encouraged those interested in language use to recognise that many forms of Spanish used on the Peninsula can serve the purpose of a community's prestige form of Spanish for public and educated use.

However, the formulation of words used in the third clause is extremely vague, as terms such as 'respect' and 'protection' are admirable in spirit but difficult to translate into binding action. Above all, it could be argued that unless central, or local, government resources are forthcoming, such high-sounding objectives will simply remain wishes. Conversely, of course, a proactive approach would be one that interprets this clause as meaning that the resources *must* be forthcoming to underline such respect and protection – that is to say, the necessary means for funding language research, producing new teaching materials, or mounting media campaigns. This is, of course, the responsibility of Language Planning, as we have seen. The radical and innovative policies of Article 3 can only be judged ultimately in the light of their implementation through, above all, Language Planning activities.

Vernet i Llobet (1994) in an excellent critical commentary of Article 3 suggests that underpinning this article are four constitutional principles: those of *'diversidad de tratamiento'* (differentiated treatment), *'territorialización impura'* (impure territorialisation), *'plurilingüístico'* (multilingual), and *'oficialidad'* (officiality) (Vernet i Llobet, 1994: 118). He endorses what we have already argued, that the treatment of languages in Spain is unequal, with the hierarchy of Castilian, the recognised 'other' languages, and the 'modalidades lingüísticas'. As we have also noted, he discusses how this leads to what he describes as 'territorialización impura', with the inevitable mismatch between Castilian and the other languages. As regards Spain's multilingual character, which has often been the interpretation given to this article, Vernet i Llobet argues that it is in fact the interpretation of Clause 3 which might lead to this conclusion. He claims that the 'respect' and 'protection' offered to Spain's linguistic variety could be applied to those languages which are otherwise protected as co-official in designated territories only. In other words, he is arguing that Clause 3 allows the state to over-ride the restricting territoriality concept as regards non-Castilian languages. This is an interesting interpretation, but one that has yet, to my knowledge, to be tested.

On the principle of official languages, Vernet i Llobet makes a particularly important observation. The recognition of the co-official status of the languages of certain autonomous communities alongside the state's language, Castilian, represents parallel languages having the right to be used in public domains, but, he suggests, this means that 'el régimen establecido es el de la doble oficialidad y no el de bilingüismo' (Vernet i Llobet, 1994: 124). As equal bilingualism is precisely the goal of much of the Language Planning in most of these regions, this is a very contentious claim.

These, and other, criticisms of Article 3 tend to revolve round disappointment or scepticism as to how truly radical it actually is in terms of a new definition and recognition of language rights translated into policy directives in post-Franco Spain. However, the critics of the article can be found also from those who believe the constitution has gone too far from the historic position of Spanish-Castilian as sole language of Spain. One such opponent is Gregorio Salvador, a linguist and member of the RAE, who has written endlessly of his dislike of Article 3 (e.g. Salvador, 1987, 1992). Besides his strong opposition to the use of 'Castilian' instead of 'Spanish' and the reference to 'Spanish languages', Salvador is overwhelmingly unsympathetic to the encouragement of multilingualism in general:

> Las repercusiones políticas del plurilingüismo son de todas las épocas y ahí siguen, si no gravísimas sí al menos bastante graves. . . . España es un país con zonas bilingües y el bilingüismo es siempre problemático.
> (Salvador, 1987: 103)[9]

In the euphoria of the early post-Franco period and the very positive reception given the constitution, it is important to be reminded that significant figures, and not only those who had been traditionally Francoists, did not accept moves towards multilingualism and improved language rights for the minority languages. Like Salvador, they saw this as potential conflict and problems. The solidarity and consensus that had been created by the opposition to the Franco regime had papered over differing attitudes and beliefs about language politics in Spain. It is quite amazing that only three years after his death the constitution could enshrine so many sentiments which would have been punished under the law during the dictatorship. It was easy to forget that not everyone even in the new Spain necessarily agreed with the promotion of the minority languages, and this expedient compromise has gradually begun to fall apart in the years since the end of the Franco regime. Nowhere is this more evident than in the debate over language education in Catalonia, as we will see in Chapter 8.

As a result of the 1978 Constitution, however, the way was opened for Spain to move from a highly centralised political regime to one of the most decentralised in the Western world. The so-called *estado de las autonomías* is the result. Spain has devolved much of the day-to-day political decision-making to the autonomous communities. The first to be granted their own statutes and to be given the most powers were what are commonly called the *'comunidades históricas'*, that is, Catalonia, the Basque Country (or Euskadi as it is often called nowadays) and Galicia. It is of course no coincidence that these are also the communities where a non-Castilian language is spoken. In line with Clause 2 of the third article of the constitution, too, these three not only included statements of policy regarding their local languages in their statutes (which, as we have seen, occurred with other communities), but also enacted 'laws of language normalisation'. These latter laws form the basis of the energetic Language Planning that has since taken place in their regions and will be the subject of discussion below.

Language Planning in Spain's comunidades históricas[10]

Whilst there may be debate and ambiguity about the exact nature of the language policies underpinning the 1978 Constitution, the three regions with the most active non-Castilian mother tongues were quick to take advantage of the new legal framework and to set about implementing what they considered the 'normalisation' of their community's language.

In both the Statutes of Autonomy and in the later Laws of Linguistic Normalisation a new term emerged to refer to the local language which was to be normalised: *'lengua propia'*. Whilst 'propia' means literally in English 'own', once again Spanish legislators have coined a term to fit a particular purpose. The use of this adjective avoids the ambiguities of 'national' and the inferiority of 'regional', etc., it also allows them to distinguish this status from 'official'. The statutes instructed their communities to promote and protect these *'lenguas propias'*. In the specific language laws this is spelt out in detail with sections on the use of the languages in the education system, in local government and administration, in the media, and in the community as a whole. Language Planning tends to operate under the auspices of the departments of culture in the respective communities, as well as, of course, the regional ministries of education. In Catalonia besides setting up a Directorate of Language Policy, the local government, the *Generalitat*, also established an Institute for Catalan Sociolinguistics.

The aims of the language laws in Catalonia, the Basque Country and Galicia, and therefore the goal of the Language Planners can be summed up by quoting from the 1983 Catalan *Llei de Normalització Lingüística*,

The restoration of Catalan to its rightful place as Catalonia's own language is the unquestionable right and duty of the Catalan people and must be respected and protected. In this regard, knowledge of the language must spread throughout the whole of Catalan society, to all citizens regardless of the language they normally speak, within a global framework in which everyone will accept the use of both languages and recognise and contribute to the recovery of Catalan as one of the fundamental aspects of the reconstruction of Catalonia.

(Generalitat, 1983; English version)

The implementation of these aims would obviously involve those different areas of LP that we observed in Chapter 4. That is to say status planning would work towards improving the prestige of the language in its local community (and outside) and to create respect and encouragement for its use. Acquisition planning was the work of the ministries of education who were to be active not only in the compulsory education systems but also in adult education courses (see Chapter 8). Corpus planning created new terminologies, standardised forms and norms, and published materials. Given the concept of the 'recovery' of the language which is shared in these regions and the ultimate goal of equality with Castilian within the respective territories, we can also apply the term used in the last chapter of 'normalisation' which is the preferred way the Language Planning programmes are referred to throughout Spain.

The legal texts regarding Language Planning in the three communities are very similar, and the aims and objectives and the areas where activities are to take place have much in common. However, as we would expect given the different economic and social nature of the regions, their histories and the distinct language situations, the implementation and the success and weakness of the Language Planning programmes in each of them is very different.

It is no surprise that the language normalisation programme of Catalan conducted in Catalonia is, by any criteria, the most successful of the LP projects. An early campaign to raise public awareness, plus an active education programme conducted in schools, adult education centres, and through the media has been highly successful. The large non-Catalan native population here has made the work particularly challenging, but the self-confidence of the region, its economy and the fact that the local middle classes all speak Catalan means that there is little problem persuading newcomers that learning Catalan is a passport to integration and upward social mobility in Catalonia.

Today it is difficult (some would say impossible) to live in Catalonia without speaking and certainly understanding the language. Catalan is normally heard now in shops, in offices, on public transport, in all government activities. Menus are in Catalan, as are street names, bank cheques, and all public notices. Much of the vibrant cultural activity of Barcelona takes place through Catalan, from theatre and cinema, through musical events to leading design work. Normally, but not always, notices, public announcements, etc., are produced bilingually. It is not unusual, however, for only Catalan to be used unless a request is actually made for Castilian.

The language censuses over the past fifteen years show how the language has gained ground in all four areas of understanding, speaking, reading and writing. In the census for 1996, 94.9 per cent of Catalonia's population is reported as understanding Catalan, with 75.3 per cent claiming to speak it (Strubell and Romani, 1998). In 1986 these statistics were 90.3 per cent and 64 per cent respectively (Ajuntaments de Catalunya, 1986). Even more impressive, perhaps, is the difference from the figure of only 79.8 per cent claiming to understand Catalan in the 1981 language census.

The undeniable success of the Catalan LP programme, however, serves to whet the appetite of many Catalanists. As self-confidence in their Catalan identity grows, many feel that the earlier LP goals were set too low, and because of this in fact likely to fail. The argument is that if only equality between the two languages is sought, the inevitable global superiority in terms of numbers and extension of use, puts Castilian always in a dominant position. To address this unequal balance, it is argued that the goal of superior status for Catalan, i.e. near monolingualism within the territory, should be aimed at.

This is of course highly controversial, both in terms of its constitutionality and for the mother tongue Castilian speakers living in Catalonia. The language politics of Catalonia have been further complicated by national politics. In the past years a minority government in Madrid (first Socialist PSOE and later centre-right Partido Popular) has depended on the Catalan regionalist party Convergència i Unió for support for their political programmes. As we shall see in the language education debate, this has led to important demands from the Catalans (and to some extent also from the Basques).

The most important outcome of the present language debate in Catalonia has been the lengthy discussions on and the eventual enactment of a new language law in January 1998, the *Llei de Política Lingüística*. The change in name seems to me to underline the emphasis away from Language Planning to the more delicate area of language policy and philosophy. Whereas the original 1983 law mainly fleshed out the policies of the 1978 Constitution, this new law is seeking to define new areas which were – perhaps deliberately – vague in the earlier legislation. In particular the concepts of 'llengua pròpia' and 'llengua oficial'[11] are clearly defined in the new law. Unlike the broad and overwhelming support for the 1983 language law, the new law met with far greater opposition. This indeed reflects the change in attitudes towards many aspects of the new Spain since the death of Franco. The consensus of the early years is now challenged, and in particular the centre-right Partido Popular wanted explicit statements about the guarantee of bilingualism and the importance of its role in Catalan society. The PP also wanted wording that confirmed that to speak Castilian in Catalonia was not 'alien' or 'foreign'. These demands were not agreed to, but the Preamble is careful to refer to the right to use both languages.

Whilst LP in the Basque Country works within the same legal framework as that of Catalonia, it has a much steeper hill to climb towards its so-called 'normalisation'. Barely a quarter of the population of Euskadi speak the Basque language, and only ten per cent in the other Basque-speaking region, Navarra (Garmendía, 1994; Tejerina, 1996). An important trend here, however, is that amongst the younger generations there is an increase in bilingualism in the two languages (Garmendía, 1994) which would appear to point to some success both in the status planning (improved attitudes and wider acceptance of the language) and, above all, in the teaching of Basque in the compulsory sector of the education system.

Basque is by no means so widely used and heard as the case of Catalan in Catalonia, and its total distinctiveness from Castilian makes this less likely. However, there have been strong efforts to ensure the increasing use and competence in Basque in the local administration (Badiola Astigarriaga, 1989; Cenoz and Perales, 1997), and, significantly, in the media (Cobreros Mendazona, 1989).

An important part of the LP activities in the Basque Country had to be at the level of corpus planning in order to reconcile the many different dialects of Basque still spoken in this region. The decision to treat the Batua dialect as the standard form and to codify this in its written form has both supported the implementation of teaching Basque and using it in the media, but has also left a certain amount of resentment amongst speakers of other dialects. This is a familiar problem for language planners and politicians when a single norm is selected. Inevitably that crucial link between language and identity is threatened by political decisions regarding status and prestige.

In Galicia, too, corpus planning has played an important role, whilst the promotion of the use and prestige of the language has been less vigorous than in the Basque Country and, certainly, Catalonia. Without the phenomenon of immigration to alter the sociolinguistic picture, the vast majority of Galicians are mother tongue speakers of Galician, with over 80 per cent reporting they can speak the language, and even more passive bilinguals able to understand it. Its closeness to Castilian of course helps the latter figure, but is also one of its principal threats as borrowings and switchings between the two languages to the detriment of Galician is significant, particularly in the urban areas. With, as we saw earlier, an overwhelming aspiration on the part of Galician parents for their children to be fluent in Castilian, seen as the language of social and economic mobility, the desire to use Galician in public life is not strong amongst much of the population. A very important factor in the campaign for positive attitudes is the role of the local government. In Catalonia and the Basque Country the local governments are fully committed and anxious to promote the local language, through laws and regulations, use in the administration and providing resources. In Galicia there has been throughout this period a right-wing local government of the Partido Popular, and their support for the language normalisation programme is correspondingly lukewarm. Given the link between the prestige of the local language and its role as marker of a separate identity, then it is no surprise that the Galician Government, the *Xunta,* whose ideology is strictly centralist, is keener to promote ties with the central – Castilian-speaking – state.

There has been some significant activity in the area of corpus planning insofar as work has been directed to produce norms for the writing of Galician. This in itself reflects an important debate within Galician LP. A small but vocal group, calling themselves 'reintegrationists', maintain that Galician should recognise its former identity as a part of Portuguese. They insist that Galician should be written exactly the same as Portuguese and have produced alternative norms to those developed by the Xunta's language planners (Henderson, 1996). In a community which is already relatively uninterested in promoting the wider use of Galician the existence of this minority debate and the two sets of written norms serve to further weaken attempts to expand the language's use, particularly through education.

Summary

Enormous advances have been made since the end of the Franco dictatorship in Spain in terms of recognising the symbolic and political importance of language and of establishing linguistic rights for the non-Castilian mother tongue communities. The 1978 Constitution and the *estado de las autonomías* have created a totally different picture, one where the regions that make up Spain have considerably more powers. However, the language policies still favour Castilian and whilst respecting other languages, have created a legal framework which ultimately restricts language planning activities even in the most aggressively distinct 'autonomous' communities. Whilst the existence of multilingualism in Spain is now recognised, the dominance of monolingualism is still implicitly encouraged.

Latin America: invisible nations

In this part we will trace the framework in which language rights are or are not recognised in Latin America. We will examine the consequent policies particularly in recent national constitutions. It will be clear that considerably less overt policy-making has encouraged Language Planning in Latin America, the most significant of this being in the area of education, which we will discuss in detail in Chapter 7. Here, we will see that very little has been carried out in the way of status planning, but comment on some recent corpus planning.

The linguistic rights of Latin America's indigenous minorities

In the previous chapter we argued that linguistic rights only become an issue when exploring the rights of minorities. For this reason, in this part we will concentrate almost entirely on the indigenous groups in Latin America, who, as we have seen in Part I, were by the twentieth century severely marginalised, and therefore, minoritised within the post-independence republics. This extreme marginalisation has meant (more perhaps than in the Spanish context) that rights in general of these communities are inextricably bound up. In other words language rights cannot really be discussed in isolation from other fundamental rights such as land rights, educational rights, access to political processes, freedom of expression of different cultural and social norms, etc. In many cases linguistic rights are more commonly expressed through education rights, as we will see in Chapter 7. As Hamel (1994b: 297) suggests, whilst claims specifically about language rights are rarely at the forefront of the demands being increasingly articulated by indigenous groups, language difference is in fact frequently one of – or even *the* – key marker of different ethnic boundaries. For this reason, if none other, language remains of crucial interest to us, even when the discussion of rights of the indigenous communities in Latin America does not always place it high on the overt agenda.

We have seen how the marginalisation of the indigenous communities and therefore the repression of their rights not only suffered from colonialisation, but continued into the independence period because of the policies of nation-building which sought to ignore difference in order to unite the peoples as one hegemonic entity. This project, which developed from the liberal-democratic thinking of the post-French Revolution philosophy, can be found underlying the various constitutions of the new republics. As Hamel writes when discussing Mexico in particular:

> The Mexican case shows with particular neatness some of the general characteristics which are typical of a certain type of Latin American indigenist policy and legislation: a liberal constitution that places formal equality of all citizens over and above all other principles, and above the reality of economic, social, ethnic and cultural inequality, the effort to build a homogenous, centralized, monolingual and monocultural nation-state, and the consequent orientation to assimilate ethnic minorities into the dominant society via education and other programmes. All this means that minority rights in general and linguistic rights in particular only benefit from comparatively weak protection.
> (Hamel, 1994b: 294)

This objective of total assimilation or integration has led many Latin American states to deny that their population is multiethnic nor made up of marginalised minorities (Banton, 1996). Moreover, when the UN was in the process of drawing up the Declaration of Human Rights in 1945 many Latin American representatives successfully fought against the inclusion of a clause which would have given protection to minority rights on the grounds that such needs were regional only and not universal. Since many indigenous communities also deny that they are 'minorities' which they see as a further way of isolating and marginalising them, but separate communities, even nations, we can see that the definition of such vulnerable groups and their rights is difficult. As Banton explains:

> The indigenous peoples do not see themselves as minorities and some believe that were they to be so described the colonisers would have achieved their ultimate goal. . . . They insist that their rights are grounded upon their prior occupation of the territory.
>
> (Banton, 1996: 94)

However, many Latin American states have also refused to recognise this difference in terms of distinct ethnicities or race. This attitude has been demonstrated by the participation over the years of some Latin American states in the UN's International Convention on the Elimination of All Forms of Racial Discrimination (passed in 1965). Banton (1996) offers an interesting survey of how individual Latin American countries reacted to this convention over the past twenty years. In their earlier reports, states such as Chile, Venezuela, and even Peru, Bolivia, Colombia and Mexico – the latter containing sizeable indigenous communities – all claimed that racial discrimination simply could not exist in their countries. Failure to recognise any such discrimination towards their minority groups demonstrates a likely failure to recognise other differences involving rights, such as linguistic rights. Representative of this kind of response is the Peruvian report of 1974 (written, significantly, during one of the most enlightened periods of Peru's history in terms of ethnic awareness):

> Since there does not exist, nor has there ever existed, any racial discrimination in Peru, no legal provisions exist on the subject and, obviously, no study or report is called for on racial discrimination in Peru.
>
> (cited in Banton, 1996: 96)

Banton explains that this reflects the Latin Americans' particular interpretation of 'racial discrimination' which is revealing in terms of these states' (in)capacity to identify the needs and rights of their populations. He writes:

> Latin American officials derive their conception of racial discrimination from the paradigm case of apartheid in South Africa. They thought it meant institutional or legally established differential rights and treatment and could not see how socio-economic differentiation and the

unequal development of culturally distinctive groups could occasion discrimination in the Convention's sense.

(1996: 96–7)

A further implication of course from this attitude was that inevitably the states were aiming to assimilate their indigenous groups rather than protect them or even award them any self-determination, the latter being a basic premise of the Declaration of Human Rights. Banton does, however, note changes in attitudes over the recent years, and cites such examples as Colombia's 'policy of self-administration' and Nicaragua's Indigenous People's Autonomies Act. Chile, Ecuador, Mexico and Peru have also made moves towards greater recognition and self-determination.

An important aspect of the discussion of rights in the Latin American context is once again that of collective versus individual. Language rights, in particular, are crucially centred in collective rights, as language cannot operate in individual isolation. Most indigenous communities understand that their strength and likely success for their claims must lie in a recognition of their group rights, and recently this is often articulated as a demand for real or near autonomy as separate 'nations' (Hamel, 1994b: 297). As we noted in the previous chapter the early declarations by international bodies regarding rights tended to protect and identify individual rights, and only more recently have directives and convenants attempted to address collective rights. Hamel (1994b: 297) argues:

> Indian movements . . . thus question the legitimacy of the state to organise their lives, and invade the arena of politics and the law, demand-ing autonomy and self-determination as peoples, even as nations. . . . The key obstacle to a recognition of such claims is the deeply rooted doctrine of the homogenous nation state that establishes formal equality among its citizens as individuals and denies a specific legal status to any collectivity, at least on an ethnic or linguistic basis.

(Hamel, 1994b: 297)

We argued in the previous chapter that collective rights tend to be attached to and identified with a sense of territory. Broadly speaking Latin American indigenous peoples can be categorised into the following three groups: those who are easily associated with a definable and well-bounded territory, particularly, for example, the tribes of the Amazon basin. Here, a territoriality principle would be easy to apply, if, arguably, illustrative of the 'enclave' type cautioned against in the previous chapter. The second group is still identifi-able with a territorial base, such as the Quechua or Aymara peoples in the Andean regions, but who, nonetheless, share this space with non-indigenous peoples. In this case, a territoriality policy, similar to the Spanish autonomous communities, may coexist with the individual and personality rights of, for example, Spanish speakers. The third group is probably the least protected and most invisible: those from indigenous communities who have migrated to the urban centres in search of employment and social advancement. Whilst significant numbers, they are still minorities – numerically and socially – and have to accept assimilation and integration into mainstream Western-style life to survive. Whilst some attempts exist to teach non-Castilian literacy to such groups (as we will see in Chapter 7), in places such as La Paz in Bolivia, the most common pattern is mother tongue loss and Castilianisation.

To the overwhelming majority of indigenous people in Latin America, however, a sense of place or territory is extremely important, and inextricably tied up with their sense of identity and claims for rights. Defining this territory, however, is a complex issue. Geography is no more a value-free academic discipline than any other in the social sciences. The political geography which has identified and described Latin America, like everything else, is eurocentric and Western in its origins. In the case of geography, in particular, it has also been frequently the work of the military, from the conquest onwards (Barton, 1997). Who draws up maps, who publishes these, and who gives places names and delineates boundaries are those in positions of power and dominance. With increased opportunities to make themselves heard in the latter part of the twentieth century, it is becoming clearer that many indigenous communities dispute the imposed boundaries and geographical interpretations of their lands.

Radcliffe and Westwood (1996) critically discuss at length the significance of space and territory in Latin American contexts:

> The range of words for 'place' in Latin America is relatively wide, with the nuances of individual terms illustrating the creation of identity through the juxtaposition of boundaries and places, and even the 'playing off' of one place against another. . . . [N]ames of places also significantly refer – to varying degrees – to people-in-place, populated spaces, with specific connotations about the *kinds* of communities located there. . . . A sense of community relies upon and refers to particular places, whereby a community makes references to itself and the national society and space through a series of practices (festivals, boundary-marking, graffiti, and so on).
>
> (Radcliffe and Westwood, 1996: 107–8)

They discuss how differing perceptions of parts of the shared national state are linked to the internal groups' different experiences, histories, power relations, etc. Often this is also a link of race and region. Radcliffe and Westwood cite the 'imagining' of white (interior) and black (coastal) Colombia, for example; or the role of the Amazon (hub of the lucrative rubber industry at one point) to Ecuadorean identity; or the Nicaraguan 'nation' as seen by those from the Pacific coast as opposed to those from the Atlantic coast. They also stress how this link with identity and territory can be fluid, giving the case of the Aymara community in Bolivia. In particular the enormous migration from the rural areas to the urban centres by indigenous communities has challenged their perception of their identity. In this situation language has often replaced territory as the first marker to outline their ethnic boundaries. The vast migration by Quechua and Aymara speakers in Peru to Lima is a particularly good example of this. But with this settlement in the capital city Quechua speakers are also often reluctant to teach their children their mother tongue, wanting them, instead, to have immediate access to Spanish, the language of social mobility in their new surroundings.

Language rights for Latin American indigenous peoples, then, are completely tied up with other such rights as land/territorial rights, political self-determination, recognition of separate ethnicity, and so on. The deliberate failure to recognise this difference in a desire to create a unified national identity on the part of the elites was mirrored in the early constitutional and legal frameworks throughout Latin America until at least the twentieth century. In the following discussion we will see that attitudes have begun to change in some parts of Latin America more recently.

Language policies and national legislation[12]

Hamel (1997b) identifies what he calls three different ideological formulations or orientations toward Indian peoples in Latin America since the time of the conquests. These correspond to different periods in Latin American history and are, according to Hamel, 'monoculturalism', which we have seen as being the clear policy of both the Spanish Crown and the newly independent republics in the nineteenth century. The second he calls 'multiculturalism' and the third 'pluriculturalism'. We will be mostly concerned here with the policies and legislation that emerged during the second two periods.

According to Hamel[13] 'multiculturalism' as the ideological position of many states emerged in the twentieth century as a result of the change in attitude towards the existence of indigenous groups. Whereas before they had been ignored, marginalised and exploited, they were now more likely to be recognised, but their existence was considered a challenge to modernisation and that the objective should be assimilation. Indigenist policies were created with a view to integration into the modern state. Hamel describes his term as referring to

> a recognition of the existence of indigenous populations as a factual state that needs remedy, usually oriented toward assimilation. . . . This perspective may include both language-as-a-problem and a language-as-a-right orientation.
>
> (Hamel, 1997b: 108)

This coincides with the time when national consitutions were beginning to acknowledge language explicitly in terms of status. As Alvar (1986: 298) notes the first time a Latin American constitution mentions the official (or national) language is in 1929 (Ecuador) and it is, of course, referring to Spanish. The perceived need to identify Spanish, however, reveals an awareness that there are, indeed, other languages. Alvar examines the important difference between 'official' and 'national' and offers a useful distinction:

> Hay que distinguir nacional de oficial, el primer concepto afecta a todos los idiomas de una nación, mientras que el segundo es un concepto mucho más restrictivo por cuanto sólo privilegia a una de todas las lenguas nacionales.
>
> (Alvar, 1986: 303)[14]

Alvar shows how the distinction is used during this period of what Hamel has called 'multiculturalism' to distinguish between Spanish and other major languages spoken in the Latin American states. He notes that, for example, Ecuador described Spanish as the 'national' language in 1929 but alters this to 'official' language in its 1945 constitution. In this later constitution Quechua and 'demás lenguas aborígenes' are termed 'national' languages.

> Lo que se consideró *idioma nacional* queda amparado en el nuevo concepto de *oficial*, por cuanto las lenguas indígenas son elementos de *cultura nacional*. Cuando en 1946 se vuelva a la oficialidad, se reconocerá la del castellano, porque, aun silenciando a las demás lenguas, ya no se podrán considerar ajenas a la idea de nacional.
>
> (Alvar, 1986: 302)[15]

Paraguay also uses the term 'national' language to refer to Guarani, and the Guatemalan constitution calls their non-Castilian languages an important part of its national patrimony. This latter definition is also given to the Amazonian languages in Peru, where, in one of the most enlightened constitutions in terms of language rights, the Andean languages Quechua and Aymara have co-official status with Spanish in certain territories where they are principally spoken.[16] This application of the territoriality principle to indigenous languages is also followed by the Nicaraguans in their Atlantic Coast autonomous regions.

Rather than refer specifically to linguistic rights or language status Latin American constitutions tend to make reference to indigenous communities in terms of their existence and, therefore, to a lesser or greater degree, their protection. This is the case in the constitutions of Guatemala (Richards, 1989), Peru (Alvar, 1986; Cerrón-Palomino, 1989), Ecuador (Alvar, 1986), Mexico,[17] (Hamel, 1994b; Nahmad, 1998), Chile and Panama (Hamel, 1994b). Nicaragua and Paraguay have specific statutes concerning the status and rights of their indigenous groups (Hamel, 1994b).

However, as Hamel (1994b) and Alvar (1986) both emphasise even in more recent periods when such cultural diversity is recognised and applauded, these are not usually seen as contributing in their own right to the cultural richness of the nation as a whole, nor are these sentiments backed up with the necessary means and resources. In particular, it is doubtful that cultural and linguistic rights can be protected without the necessary corresponding political and economic rights.

The recognition and granting of the latter would constitute what Hamel refers to as the third stage in ideological policies towards indigenous communities, that is to say, what he terms 'pluriculturalism', which he says 'not only recognises cultural diversity but assesses it positively as a resource of enrichment for the whole nation and the state' (Hamel, 1997b: 108). Hamel claims that the late twentieth century is beginning to see more articulated demands by indigenous movements for a recognition of their differences and their right to exist alongside, rather than to be integrated or assimilated into, majority national groups:

> The more advanced movements have developed strategies that integrate specific claims (territory, resources, justice, education, language) into the overreaching striving for local and regional autonomy. Autonomy in turn is conceptualized as the specific modality to exercise the right of self-determination as indigenous peoples and nations. Accordingly, language-related policies and legal regulations have the best prospects of success if they are incorporated into that general framework and attempt to create the necessary conditions (including resources) for language maintenance and growth.
>
> (Hamel, 1997b: 108–9)

This is, of course, an argument for Language Planning to improve the languages' status and expand their use. The reality is, however, that except in the area of acquisition planning in education, little Language Planning and the resources for it has yet been forthcoming in most Latin American states. It is interesting to see that the Latin American indigenous peoples are increasingly conceiving their needs and rights within the framework of 'autonomy' which is precisely the term used and model developed for the minority linguistic communities in Spain.

Language Planning in contemporary Latin America[18]

On the whole, Latin American states have not enacted the kind of legislation that we observed in Spain which established a basis for a Language Planning framework. Many of the statements in national constitutions are as vague as those we discussed in the third clause of Article 3 of the recent Spanish constitution. It is easy for such sentiments to be forgotten and ignored, in particular insofar as any real implementation of them will necessitate financial and material resources. In Chapter 7 we will examine how far resources have been made available to support bilingual and intercultural education programmes. Here we will briefly comment on some status planning that is taking place in a few Latin American countries. We will also examine some interesting cases of corpus planning. Whilst our main interest and emphasis is on the indigenous languages, we should not ignore the fact that some Language Planning activity continues to take place as regards the majority language, Spanish.

Besides the education system the other main focus for some status planning of the non-Castilian languages in Latin America has been through certain channels of the media. The use of, for example, Mayan in Guatemala, Aymara in Bolivia, and Nahuatl in parts of Mexico on local radio, has had a significant impact in terms of increasing these languages' prestige. Widening the use and reception of the language that such transmissions give, plus linking them with modern technology, are viewed by the communities as confirmation of the improved status of their languages. The perception that only Spanish is associated with social mobility and integration into modern (urban) life is somewhat diluted by this contact with indigenous mother tongues through the media.

The prestige of the languages also receives a boost with the setting up of bodies to research and promote them. In the past these have tended to be activities carried out by (often foreign) anthropologists who tended to reify the languages and treat them as things of the past. More recently such bodies have been more practical and, importantly, staffed by indigenous people themselves.

A particularly good example of this is in Mexico with the work done by the Instituto Nacional Indigenista (INI), and its associated department, Dirección General de Educación Indígena. These organisations, run largely by members of the indigenous communities, have raised the profile of the debates on the role and status of Mexico's non-European ethnic groups (recognised officially as fifty-six), and the most appropriate forms of education and language maintenance. This has resulted in the proposal for the Mexican constitution to include the following amendment:

> The Mexican nation has a pluri-cultural composition which is based originally on its Indian peoples. The law will protect and promote the development of their languages, cultures, usages, customs, resources, and specific forms of social organisations. It will grant their members effective access to the jurisdiction of the state. In the agrarian judgements and processes in which they are a party, their practices and legal customs will be taken into account in terms that will be established by law.
>
> (cited in Hamel, 1994b: 293)

In this case, work on indigenous cultures and languages has led to the necessary political pressure to produce proposals for legislation, both at national level (as seen above) and also by the work of the state of Oaxaca whose state laws have been adapted to support language rights and greater respect for the indigenous communities (Nahmad, 1998). It will be interesting to see whether such national legislation leads to the resources and support needed to translate the policy into planning initiatives.

Recalling Glyn Williams' (1992) contention that status and corpus planning should not be viewed as two entirely discrete activities, I shall discuss three examples of corpus planning in Latin America which all have an important role to play in the social and political attitudes to the languages involved: Mayan in Guatemala, Quechua in Peru and Bolivia, and Spanish in Mexico.

Richards (1989) describes the corpus planning that has taken place in Guatemala in order to develop materials for use in the bilingual education programmes. In order to achieve this the first goal had to be the elaboration of a 'general Mayan' language which would become accessible to speakers of the various different Mayan dialects. The goals of this corpus planning are quite obviously simultaneously relevant to the improvement of the language's status because they are to:

> fortify the identity of the indigenous population of Mayan origin, with its own cultural values, so that it may respond to its authentic needs and legitimate interests . . . [and to] fortify, consolidate and preserve the purity of the indigenous languages of Mayan origin of Guatemala.
>
> (cited in Richards, 1989: 104)

As part of the corpus planning process there has been a need to establish the alphabetical norms for writing Mayan. Richards recounts the debates this has entailed, showing how the early writing of Mayan languages, usually by missionaries, followed the Spanish alphabet, for reasons of convenience and to facilitate the transfer to using Spanish, i.e. as part of the Castilianisation process. However, as Richards (1989: 104) writes 'many Mayan sounds are different from Spanish sounds, and by using Spanish orthographic symbols to represent these sounds, an inaccurate portrayal of the native language occurs.' She highlights too the role of the Summer Institute of Linguistics (SIL)[19] in maintaining this usage during much of the twentieth century, and the attempt by native Mayan speakers and the unofficial Mayan language academy to counter it with an alternative set of norms. Here again can be seen a clear example of the political nature of corpus planning; the decision as to which set of norms to use reflected the underlying objectives of promoting Mayan as an independent language, or the teaching of indigenous mother tongues prior to transition to literacy in Castilian.

The controversial nature of this aspect of corpus planning and its consequent close relationship with status planning and attitudes in general to the language in question occurs with other Latin American indigenous languages. The debates over the correct orthography and alphabet for

Quechua has also been problematic. The use of the name 'Quichua' rather than 'Quechua' in Ecuador, as the preferred form by the indigenous speakers there, is symbolic of the underlying tensions in this debate.

Plaza and Albó (1989: 81–4) describe similar experiences to the Mayan one in the elaboration of alphabets in Bolivia for both Quechua and Aymara. Once again the different norms competing for acceptance range from those closest to Spanish to those most authentically indigenous. Plaza and Albó describe the areas where most disagreement takes place in the elaboration of these alphabets, which include: the number of vowels (whether three, or, as in Spanish, five); the use of *x* instead of *j*; and the use of inverted commas instead of *h* to denote aspiration (Plaza and Albó, 1989: 82).

The debate over the number of vowels in Quechua has also been fiercely fought in Language Planning discussions in Peru (Hornberger, 1995; Niño-Murcia, 1997). Hornberger (1995: 187) comments that 'what might at first appear to be a trivial matter of language corpus planning turns out to have far-ranging social, cultural and political implications.' Niño-Murcia writes:

> Societies shifting from a predominantly oral system to a written one undergo a controversial, even painful process of standardization. This process, a crucial arena for negotiation of power relations in any language, has become hostile in Peru, where standardization is perceived as an attack on regional identities. On the other hand, since language standardisation is one of the processes during which concerns about purity are heightened, in the Andean speech communities standardization has also contributed to the exaltation of puristic attitudes.
>
> (Niño-Murcia, 1997: 151)

Hornberger explains how the decision in 1985 to adopt an official alphabet with only three vowels caused ongoing controversy, and one in which, again, the Summer Institute of Linguistics was involved. Hornberger (1985) describes the different actors in this debate and the areas round which the controversy ranges. She points out the different viewpoints taken depending for example on the regional (and in the case of the SIL, national) background – Lima versus Cuzco, urban versus rural – whether the individuals are members of the Quechuan language academy or the Peruvian department of education, to which generation the proponents belong (i.e. to what extent have they been active participants and supporters of the 1975 revolutionary government), and, of course, whether they are native Quechua speakers or not. Disagreement revolves round such issues as the true structure of the language and the difference between the spoken and written norm; who has the ultimate authority to make decisions; the legitimacy of history to decide, given that the five vowels system had been used for nearly five hundred years based on Spanish orthography. As Niño-Murcia argues, 'Positions adopted range from support for creation of a single alphabetic system to insistence on maintaining differences among language varieties by adopting several alphabets' (1997: 152).

And Niño-Murcia adds that 'The extremes of these positions reflect opposing ideological tendencies' (1997: 152). She discusses how this debate is not just about tensions between Quechua-speakers and Spanish-speakers. She examines the internal conflict in the Quechua-speaking community over attitudes to standardisation and language purity, and explains how the competition between Cuzco and Lima has helped fuel a desire to defend the Quechua of Cuzco as the 'best' Quechua, legitimised, its defenders argue, by its historic legacy from the Inca empire. It is, they claim, the imperial and rightful language. This has led to an elitist position over which form of the language, and which alphabet, therefore, should be the official one. The debate pits the Cuzco elite in the form of the Academy of the Quechua Language, supported by the SIL, against language planners and bilingual educationalists wanting to integrate a far wider Quechua-speaking community with more inclusive norms. As we can see, all these debates involve far more than simply corpus planning decisions; as always, they in fact reflect positions of power – power to make and impose decisions.

Finally, whilst this chapter has focused primarily on minority languages, we should not forget that there is Language Planning activity to support Spanish. That much of the legislation supports Spanish is obvious, but some corpus planning, and even a form of status planning also takes place. In Latin America this can be seen with the work of the local language academies, loosely associated to the RAE in Madrid. In the effort to enhance Spanish as the unifying national language, states such as Mexico also emphasised the particular characteristics of their own form of Spanish. The status, then, of local varieties over the distant Iberian variety had to be promoted (Hornberger, 1994: 222).

A further example of corpus planning closely linked to raising the status of a non-Peninsular variety of Spanish is with the production of the *Diccionario del español de México*. Lara (1992) gives an interesting account of this, stressing that the dictionary is a product of the social usage of Spanish in Mexico and reflects the standard norms of this particular context. Lara compares the dictionary's aim to be like the famous US English dictionary, a 'Webster mexicano'. He claims that the Spanish vocabulary in it is based on 'su uso integral en México' (1992: 21). As providers of perceived norms and standards, the pinnacle of corpus planning, dictionaries play a highly influential role in the sociolinguistic life of every state, and are far from being the apparently neutral scientific creations sometimes claimed.

Summary

In this overview of language policies and language planning in Latin America we can see that apart from the statements found in national constitutions which have led to relatively little in the way of further language legislation, the role of the state in the development of linguistic rights in the region has been limited. In fact until recently it has often led the campaign to ignore and suppress the diversity of indigenous groups. However, an important aspect of the recent moves towards claims for greater autonomy reflects an important characteristic of Latin American minority groups in the latter part of the twentieth century: initiatives which generate from entirely grassroots, non-formal organisations. The Chiapas rising in Mexico is of course an extreme example of this non-state (anti-state), grassroots movements, but there are countless other examples of small community-based groups, often one-issue groups, frequently in recent years, women's groups (Archer and Costello, 1990; Freeland, 1998; Radcliffe and Westwood, 1993). We will examine more examples of this when we discuss some of the literacy projects in Chapter 7.

Conclusion

At the end of the twentieth century linguistic minorities both in Spain and in Latin America are increasingly finding their voices and are claiming rights, including recognition of their separate mother tongues. Many too are demanding some form of autonomy or self-determination which would allow them to pursue alternative cultural, social and political organisation from the dominant hegemony of the state. The extent to which these demands have been successful reflects inevitably the nature of the political system in which the communities reside. The degree of autonomy granted the Spanish linguistic minorities was clearly enhanced by the general overall constitutional and democratic transition after Franco's death; the Indigenous Peoples' Autonomies Act was granted in Nicaragua by the Sandinista government after the downfall of the Somoza dictatorship.

In much of Latin America in particular, however, an awakening to the rights and needs of non-Castilian speaking communities is only beginning, and still in many quarters unwelcome. The construction of national identity of the nineteenth century post-independence period is still fragile and per-ceived as threatened by too much fragmentation if internal groups are allowed autonomy. Increasingly, both in Latin America and Spain, some degree of the recognition of individual rights is apparent, but the granting of collective rights and the related recognition of communities and, in particular, their territorial base, is still frequently problematic. Moreover, individual rights are limited largely to encouraging the minority community member to make the transition to membership of a majority community. The Galician in Madrid or the Quechua-speaker in Lima are encouraged to leave behind in their territorial homelands their markers of linguistic (and other) differences.

An analysis of the recognition of language rights and language policies in the contemporary Spanish-speaking world confirms the contention that language behaviour is ultimately controlled by those in power. As Glyn Williams repeatedly asserts, majority groups do not give up their dominance voluntarily. Where minority groups have made inroads into the nation state hegemony it would seem to be because of a series of reasons beyond the state's control including economic strength (e.g. the Catalans), demographic size, once this becomes more obvious as the result of modern technology, such as TV and improved transport (the Mexican indigenous communities), international pressure from groups concerned with ecological issues (such as the support for some of the Amazonian tribes in the threatened rain forest), or with political rights (Mayan-speakers in Guatemala to some extent benefited from the coverage of the award of the Nobel Peace Prize to their compatriot Rigoberta Menchú).

In all the areas we have examined, however, Spanish remains the favoured and dominant language, which is reinforced by its world language status. Whilst it is not unduly challenged by the teaching of more mother tongues in the education system, it is in this area where the linguistic minorities might most hope to protect their languages and cultures and ultimately maintain their survival, although the enormous number of indigenous languages which have already become extinct in Latin America, as in many other parts of the world, does not bode well for them.

Part III

Language and education

6 Bilingual education, literacy and the role of language in education systems

So far in this book we have traced the close relationship between language and identity, and particularly national identity. We have seen how the realisation of the significance of this relationship has led governments and politicians to formulate overt policies which either seek to deny linguistic rights or to recognise and promote them. We have also noted how in the Spanish-speaking world, nation-building has been at state level a conscious, planned project in which language has played a prominent role. As for Language Planning in particular, so for nation-building in general, the education system is one of the (if not *the*) most central agencies available to the state. Through the curriculum, values of citizenship are underlined, patriotism is legitimised through particular views of the nation's history, and binding all this is the particular language or languages in which the curriculum is offered. A basic premise underlying education in the Western world is that teaching, learning, communication and preparation to participate in society as a whole rely on a competence in and access to literacy, which, in turn, will be principally (if not exclusively) in the majority language of the state. Education, then, both directs the population in an interpretation of national values, national symbols, and national space, and also effectively controls who can participate and have access to this national imagined community. Once again we are reminded of Anderson's assertion that it is print-language that allows the nation to imagine its geographical limits and its shared markers (see Chapter 1). Access to this print-language, and also to *which* print-language, is decided by the state through the education system. Clearly not all education is state-administered, but even when it is in the hands of other bodies, these are usually themselves other representatives of the national establishment, such as the Church or army, and, therefore, have similar hegemonic agendas. As we will see in later case studies, it is very difficult for non-governmental groups to have much success in promoting alternative, and sometimes anti-government, educational programmes and curricula.

In this section we will examine education policies and practice in case studies from the Spanish-speaking world. In particular we will focus on examples of how this does indeed reflect the nation-building aims of the state. As the constant challenge to homogeneous nation-states is the existence of minority communities within their borders, we will be especially interested in examining the fate of minorities (and above all, linguistic minorities) in terms of their recognition by the national education systems. Much of the legislation and constitutional framework which we observed in the previous chapter depends for its success on its enactment and interpretation through the education systems. We will want to raise questions such as whether the teaching of Catalan in Catalonia's schools is achieving the aims of the Language Normalisation Law, or whether in fact, as some argue, it is denying Castilian-speakers their linguistic rights; whether bilingual education to Latin America's indigenous children is only designed to facilitate the quick conversion and assimilation to Western, Castilian-speaking lifestyles or whether it is allowing these children to value their language and cultures on a par with Spanish; and whether the organising of adult literacy classes in indigenous languages will simply have the effect of further isolating and disenfranchising these communities from the dominant Spanish-speaking society around them.

First, in this chapter, we will look at the broader issues behind language and education. In particular, we will discuss the power of language in education systems, the models of bilingual education and their objectives and successes, and the role of literacy in empowering marginalised groups.

Bilingual education: assimilation or maintenance; exclusion or empowerment?[1]

The issues surrounding language and education of course cover both which languages are *used* as well as which languages are *taught*. But they also involve *how* languages are taught and *to what extent* the teachers and the curriculum offer an overall awareness of and sensitivity to the importance of language during a child's development.[2] Remembering once again the dual function of language – for communication and as a symbol of identity – then clearly the school curriculum would be expected to provide both the means to perfect communication, and, at the same time, the opportunities to understand the individual's and community's relationship with a particular language or languages.

In the case of a state's majority language and its speakers this is simply not an issue. Obviously children who are majority language speakers expect to learn to read, write and articulate their needs, opinions and transactions through the language of the state as they progress through the education system. In turn this system's curriculum will reflect all the values of the state's sense of national identity through the majority language. Where the role of the language in reinforcing this identity has been significant, this too will be imparted through such subjects as history, literature and mother tongue teaching.

Where, however, the education system is challenged is with the way in which it does, or more often does not, reflect the pluralist nature of the state's society, and includes the languages and cultures of communities other than that of the majority group or groups. Is competence to communicate in the minority languages of a state taught, to either the mother tongue speakers of these languages or to them and the majority language speakers? Is respect for and awareness of the importance of these minority mother tongues understood and reinforced by the education curriculum? In other words, are the linguistic rights that we outlined in Chapter 4 recognised, respected or ignored and/or repressed through the education system?

As we have already seen at a general level, the answers to these questions are very frequently no. Sometimes the state education system has deliberately ignored its minorities as part of an explicit policy of nation-building and a drive for monocultural unity. On other occasions the exclusion is more the result of ignorance and naive oversight. In either case the result is the same: children from minority communities enter the education system to find themselves treated as outsiders, where the most immediate and obvious factor is the inability to use their mother tongue and the need to communicate through a language they do not know. Inevitably this is likely to create a sense of alienation, of inferiority, of incompetence, and of marginalisation.

It should be stressed that this experience is not exclusively that of mother tongue speakers of languages other than the state/official language. In most parts of the world a similar, if less extreme, experience is often encountered by children whose variety of the dominant majority language differs to a greater or lesser extent from the standard norm generally offered in the school curriculum.

In the latter situation (as well of course as in the former) the need to train teachers and syllabus designers to a high degree of linguistic sensitivity and awareness becomes important. The content, then, of teacher training programmes is as crucial as the content of the curriculum itself (Nunan and Lam, 1998: 127–38). This further confirms the argument that the power of language should never be underestimated, and no less in the education system than in society as a whole. In other words, it is not only a matter of which languages or varieties of languages are used and taught, but also how much teachers and educators consciously or unconsciously create access to opportunity and to social or power hierarchies through the way they manage language.

Bilingual education models

So-called bilingual[3] education programmes have developed in response to this awareness of the difficulties for minority children, and only in very restricted situations have they ever been aimed at the majority group.[4] We will, therefore, concentrate on examining how far these programmes go towards making minority community children's entry into the national education system easier, and what ultimate objectives they entail.

116   *Language and education*

By 'bilingual' education we are referring to schools and education systems which include a second (or more) language as a means of instruction and even means of general communication. We are not including in this the normal provision for the teaching of foreign languages as part of the curriculum. In the type of bilingual education that we are examining, this second language will be the mother tongue of a community which forms part of the national territory. This may be an indigenous community, such as Basques in Spain or Quechua-speakers in Bolivia, or immigrant groups, such as North African Arabic-speakers in Spain or some German-speaking communities in Latin America.

It is usual to divide the models of bilingual education into four types: assimilationist (or transitional), maintenance (sometimes also called 'pluralist'), submersion, or immersion. A further type sometimes encountered is that of 'segregationist', although this may only be a version of the maintenance model but one that does not operate in a pluralist sense. These categories are defined by their methods, exposure to the language(s), and, above all, their objectives.

It might be supposed that the objective of bilingual education was obvious: that is, the achievement of bilingualism. 'Bilingualism' is a much-debated and variously-defined term, but for the discussion here I will follow Skutnabb-Kangas:

> A speaker is bilingual who is able to function in two (or more) languages, either in monolingual or bilingual communities, in accordance with the sociocultural demands made on an individual's communicative and cognitive competence by these communities and by the individual herself, at the same level as native speakers, and who is able positively to identify with both (or all) language groups (and cultures) or parts of them.
>
> (Skutnabb-Kangas, 1984: 90)

As we will see below, if this is the ultimate goal for students in bilingual education programmes, then very few in fact are likely to be regarded as successful. In fact, only two of the models at the most come close to claiming this as their goal, and certainly the notion of being 'able to *positively* identify with both . . . languages' (my emphasis) is absent in many bilingual education programmes.

The assimilationist model

Certainly the central goal of the *assimilationist model* as its name suggests is very far from encouraging such an equal competence and attitude to both the languages and cultures. These programmes – and they are probably the majority amongst bilingual education programmes – are designed to make the child's entry into formal education less alienating by offering the first years of schooling in the mother tongue. However, their aim is then to shift the emphasis gradually but surely away from this language by introducing more and more use of the target language, that is, the language of the state.

Such programmes have become more common in the second half of the twentieth century. Before this, bilingual education programmes were few and far between. But in 1951 UNESCO agreed to recommend to the international community that ideally all children should have the opportunity of being taught, at least in the primary school years, in their mother tongue. Much of the thinking behind this was based on the acknowledgement of the harshness of the experience for young children of attending school where their mother tongue could not be used, as well as the apparent effectiveness from a psycho-pedagogical point of view of teaching first in the mother tongue, and rather less on a commitment to the respect for everyone's mother tongue *per se*.

There are real practical problems to the implementation of the UNESCO directive, not least being the reluctance on the part of many national governments to recognise any rights, including educational and linguistic ones, of their minority communities. It is also difficult to make decisions as to which languages might be favoured in this way; such problems arise as to how large a group of children is needed to justify the resources, and also how to distinguish a 'language' from a (mere) 'dialect' of another (majority) language. Other obstacles include the lack of resources available particularly in developing countries (who in many cases are emerging from their colonial conditions and trying to forge somewhat fragile national unity). Resources are needed to train teachers in languages which until now have not been used in the curriculum, and this training also requires making teachers in all curricular subjects, not just languages, become aware of linguistic issues in the widest sense. Often, as in the case of many Latin American indigenous languages, the languages in question have never been standardised or developed in a written form. Elaboration work is costly and time-consuming, not to mention potentially controversial, as we saw in the previous chapter. Basic materials, textbooks, etc., do not exist, and publishing in minority languages is once again an expensive exercise. Above all, it is often necessary to introduce such education programmes in parallel with the kind of status planning that would improve attitudes towards the prestige and therefore use of the languages. If not, often the very community whose mother tongue is to be promoted, is the most opposed to its use in the education system. They view their language as 'inferior' and want their children to make progress in society by learning the majority language as quickly as possible.

Whilst the UNESCO directive did not specifically advocate transitional or assimiliationist programmes of bilingual education, in many cases this was the interpretation adopted. A few years of primary school mother-tongue education met the concerns of UNESCO and helped pave the way for a more integrated move into 'mainstream' education in the majority state language. Clearly with this view of bilingual education comes also a particular ideological view of the nature of the nation-state. If multiculturalism is viewed as undesirable, for reasons of ineffiency of communication, cost, and fragmentation of national unity, then a successful and quick move towards monolingualism in the state's official language, but without first having alienated linguistic minorities by completely denying them some exposure to their mother tongues, is considered the ideal policy. To differing degrees this has been the position all over the world, not least in many parts of Latin America and, particularly, in the US.

The maintenance model

On the other hand, in a few cases bilingual education has been structured on a *maintenance model*, that is to say, one that provides instruction in and of two languages (the majority and minority mother tongues) to an equal extent throughout the child's education. The minority mother tongue in this model is not phased out, and in some cases its use is even increased. In one version of this model the aim is seen as being that of achieving bilingualism in both languages as defined in the Skutnabb-Kangas quotation above, with a genuine desire to prepare the student with an equal competence and equal positive respect in both languages. In some instances of this model it is not just the minority child who is educated bilingually, but the majority child too, although this is very rare.

In a more negative version of this model, the emphasis on the instruction in the non-state language for children of this community may increase to the extent that leads to what Skutnabb-Kangas (1988: 23) has termed 'segregationist' aims: to condemn the child to marginalisation outside of mainstream society where the official language is used, but for which the child has limited proficiency. This situation can occur in communities where the non-state language is not in fact a minority language in numerical terms.

The immersion model

Another model of bilingual education which could be said to have as its goal the achievement of bilingualism in Skutnabb-Kangas' terms is the *immersion model*. This form of bilingual education is widely used in Catalonia and therefore of particular interest to our discussion. This kind of programme is run for speakers of the dominant or official language of the state for their children to learn a target minority language. Usually, in practice, this minority language is widely spoken within a particular region, frequently as a consequence with a relatively high status and prestige, such as French in Quebec or Catalan in Catalonia. The main features of this programme are that the programme must be voluntary[5] on the part of the participating parents (and where appropriate, students). Children, from the start of their schooling, experience all instruction and general communication in the target minority language. Many will not speak this at all. The teachers, however, are bilingual and there is an understanding and willingness to allow the children to use their mother tongue on occasion as they learn to move towards fuller competence in the target language. The point at which the mother tongue is introduced into the curriculum will vary from programme to programme and country to country. It is usually, however, around about seven to ten years of age. After this, the programme generally resembles the kind of *maintenance* bilingual programme described above.

One of the important issues implied by the immersion programmes is that their success must question the basic UNESCO premise that it is better for children to start their schooling in their mother tongue. It has been frequently argued that this is not only less intimidating, and therefore more respectful of the child's identity, but also psychologically better for the child's learning development. In fact, research in this area is extensive but inconclusive (Appel and Muysken, 1987: Chapter 6; Fasold, 1984: 13–20; Tucker, 1998) with results having been obtained to support arguments both in favour and against the use of the mother tongue in purely pedagogical and psychological terms. In the conclusion to their chapter on bilingual education, Appel and Muysken offer a useful and relevant assessment:

> We want to emphasize that research results indicate that bilingual education for children from low-status linguistic minorities *can* be profitable, but no *predictions* can be derived from these results, because of the many varying social situations. A point of considerable interest is the social and political attitude of the majority towards minority groups. If this attitude is too negative and too many segregative trends exist in society, it may not be advisable to organize separate bilingual education for children from linguistic minorities. Probably it is always a good idea to integrate bilingual programmes into regular schools in order to further the relations between minority and majority students. Bilingual programmes should not be organized to bring about a kind of 'splendid isolation' for minority groups, which will often turn out to be dangerous isolation as well, but should guarantee that students from minority groups gain better educational and social opportunities, while at the same time maintenance of the minority language is fostered.
>
> (Appel and Muysken, 1987: 71)

In our later examination of bilingual education programmes in the Spanish-speaking world it will be important to observe how much this sense of isolation has been allowed to exist, consciously or unconsciously. In particular, we will see that parents can be divided in their views on whether separate systems are good or bad, usually along the lines of whether they are majority-language speakers or minority-language speakers.

The submersion model

The fourth category of bilingual education is the *submersion model*, which is normally not even a particularly conscious model. This is the situation that occurs when the national education system makes no allowance whatsoever for mother tongue provision for children of minority groups. This may be simply because these children are ignored by education planners, or it may be a deliberate education and language policy which seeks to assimilate non-majority language speakers as quickly as possible (and as cheaply as possible) into the mainstream education system. This is of course the situation in many parts of the world, and is always the case with individual children who for some reason attend schools in countries where their mother tongue is not spoken but without necessarily forming part of a wider group. Sometimes in these cases some extra classes in the majority language is given them, such as English as a Second Language (ESL) classes offered in many British schools. On some occasions too children experiencing this kind of system of education may have mother tongue classes organised for them outside the school curriculum, occasionally by the education authorities, but more often by local community groups (often religious groups). In Europe this latter situation has often been the outcome of the response to the 1977 European Community directive recommending the teaching of the mother tongues of children of immigrants living in the EC. As with the earlier UNESCO directive, this could only have the strength of a suggestion to national governments in their education planning. Many chose to ignore the directive or implement it in a very minimal sense, such as with a token offer of extra-curricular classes.

Summary

In summarising the aims and implications of bilingual education programmes in terms of their impact on minority communities, we can say that these run on a continuum from segregationist-isolationist (maintenance of the mother tongue without integration into the majority community as well), to basically transitional and assimilationist (largely discarding the mother tongue), through to maintenance of the mother tongue and culture to the somewhat limited extent of ackowledging separate ethnicity but, in the words of Skutnabb-Kangas and Cummins, 'to the exclusion of societal questions of economic and political power' (1988: 394), to the complete pluralist approach which recognises minorities' cultural and linguistic rights and educates their children to take an equal role in a pluralist society. In this latter, more holistic, method of bilingual education language is not simply a competence to be taught and learnt but an instrument through which the world is understood and interpreted, which gives the students access and, ultimately, empowerment.

Education systems and the politics of literacy

In this part we will develop the idea of empowerment and the role that language and education have to play in this. By 'empowerment' I am referring to access and participation in decision-making processes and the institutions and sectors of society that implement decisions. In other words we are talking about the role in society available to individuals and communities if they are accorded the rights that we discussed in Chapter 4. As commented earlier, Western society operates its political institutions, its legal system, its economic infrastructure and its social welfare through the mechanisms of literacy. Anderson (1983, 1992) has described this as print-capitalism and as being the outstanding characteristic of modern (Western) society. Without this access to the printed word, we cannot read legal documents, understand rules, regulations, and instructions; an important part of our information channels is through printed media (although the role of television and radio will be commented on later), and today an increasing necessity to operate in society is to be computer-literate, which also entails deciphering writing. Literacy is therefore an immensely important part of being able to operate in any social community. But literacy is not value-free. We will therefore examine below what is meant by literacy, who decides this and controls it, how this is closely related to language issues, and, in particular, how literacy is taught and learnt. For the discussion below we will focus principally on adult education, whilst recognising that for many, it is as children that literacy practices are first learnt. However, as one of the greatest gaps between the developed and developing world is in the degree of formal education that has been available, the role of literacy in this situation is also significant. As much of our interest is in the relationship between dominant majority communities and subordinate minority communities (often in under-developed countries), we will note that access to education, access to literacy, and, ultimately, access to power and participation in the wider society have been the privilege of the majority communities. In a desire to improve this situation, adult education can play a very important part in the consciousness-raising process which enables people to participate more and to have more confidence in their social role.

Below we will look in turn at the questions we have posed concerning literacy and its relationship to power. This discussion of literacy practices is well framed by a quotation from the beginning of a book on this subject by Mike Baynham (1995: 1), where he states certain basic premises for the examination of literacy practices.

- literacy has developed and is shaped to serve social purposes in creating and exchanging meaning;
- literacy is best understood in its contexts of use;

- literacy is ideological: like all uses of language, it is not neutral, but shapes and is shaped by deeply held ideological positions, which can be either implicit or explicit;
- literacy needs to be understood in terms of social power.

What is literacy?

In recent years an enormous range of literature and studies have been published discussing this question. The uncritical belief held for so long in the Western world that literacy was only the mechanical ability to read and write has been widely challenged:[6]

> A large body of work, in a number of different disciplines has begun, over the last decade or so, to replace the traditional notion of literacy with a socioculturally situated alternative formulation. This new formulation stresses the sorts of social practices in which reading, writing and talking are embedded and out of which they develop, rather than the private cognitive 'skills' of individuals. . . . The new literacy studies has its origins in the collapse of the old 'oral culture-literate culture' contrast. Out of the deconstruction of this contrast comes more contemporary approaches, not to literacy as a singular thing, but to *literacies* as a plural set of social practices.
>
> (Gee, 1990: 49)

To understand the new literacy studies it is necessary to re-define what is meant by 'reading', and 'writing'. In the past these have usually been associated with the static practice of the use of alphabets to communicate language which is then read. This has of course normally been on paper, but could also be on screen or on other physical objects (such as packets, containers, cloth, or walls, for example). But if we interpret these processes in a fuller, more metaphorical sense, we can see that 'reading' can refer to 'making sense of', or 'understanding' and 'interpreting' the environment around us. And 'writing' can be the signs that this environment around us uses to represent what needs to be understood and interpreted. If we follow this broader definition, then the different forms of representation can include the traditional forms of writing, as well as other ways of graphic communication (through painting, textiles, architecture, sculpture, film, etc.). Even the so-called 'traditional' writing is potentially far wider than the restricted Western definition often includes. It is significant that the word used to translate 'literacy' in Spanish is *'alfabetismo'*. Such a limiting association with a letter-based script is in danger of excluding other scripts which are not based on individual letters, such as, for example, the Chinese script. It excludes pictorial alphabets and fails to recognise the legitimacy of alternative systems of communication. This very Westernised and Eurocentric view of literacy is relevant for us to examine when looking at the teaching of non-Spanish languages in Latin America.

In order to move beyond this limited concept of literacy, writers are now talking about, for example, radioliteracy, or computer-literacy, or recognising such practices as Chilean tapestry-making and Peruvian bean art, Mexican murals and Cuban graffiti, all as legitimate forms of literacy practices. At the same time, as Gee and Baynham in the quotations above point out, these practices are shaped by their contexts, and are, therefore, intrinsically part of their social settings.

The move away from the more traditional conception of literacy and literacy learning to these new approaches can be represented (perhaps a little simplistically as all such categorising is inclined to do) by the two approaches to literacy, reflected in their teaching as we will see below, of *functional literacy* and *critical literacy* (Barton, 1994a; Baynham, 1995). The former has been in the past the interpretation that has underpinned much of the literacy provision offered by UNESCO which is a very important international provider of literacy teaching in particularly the developing world. The latter approach characterises much of the recent discussion and projects of the 'new literacy' movement, and, as we will see, is found with many radical, independent literacy programmes being experimented with in recent years, including Latin America.

With *functional literacy* the emphasis is on learning to read and write (in relatively traditional terms) in a mechanical way, in order to acquire a skill in order to perform certain functions (the need for which is largely determined by those other than the learners). Literacy is offered as a static, finite product to be got 'right' or 'wrong'. The emphasis is on being reactive rather than proactive, on 'doing' rather than 'thinking'. The activity is routine rather than creative.

On the other hand, *critical literacy* emphasises the relationships between the learner and the world that they are learning, in the broadest sense, to read and write. The emphasis here is essentially on questioning, exploring and thinking. Literacy is seen as a form of access to a world that can be interpreted, enjoyed and challenged. In the discussion below on how literacy learning is provided in formal and non-formal education systems, we will concentrate on the methods being developed to offer critical literacy learning to adults. In doing this, to some extent we will also be critiquing much conventional schooling for children because for many adult learners for whom these programmes have been designed, it is their initial experience of the school system that has been inadequate and unsatisfactory. In the majority of these formal school systems literacy is viewed in its functional sense and taught accordingly, often thereby disenfranchising more vulnerable children, such as those from minority communities for whom the whole school experience is intimidating and even irrelevant.

Adult literacy projects: learning to read the world

As we have already argued, in societies where the culture, values and lifestyles are Western-based, access to literacy practices (in the widest sense) is absolutely crucial to empowerment. This is normally offered through formal schooling, but for many, particularly in developing nations, this system creates a sense of failure and worthlessness. This may be, as we saw above, because the curriculum is carried out in an unfamiliar language, limiting confidence and competence by the linguistic minority child. It may also be because the whole process and experience is predicated along power structures which confirm the relationships in wider society of dominant and dominated groups, where the linguistic (or other) minority child is repeatedly made aware of their subordinate role. Schools and school systems are institutions organised around administrative rules and regulations. The buildings, the management hierarchy and the documentation can be thoroughly alienating to children and their parents from marginalised groups. Moreover, the language or variety of language used is often unfamiliar to them.

For this reason many adults believe that they have failed in their school days. It is, of course, arguable, that it is in fact the school system which has failed them. Many may have therefore dropped out early; in some cases, children may not have attended at all. Their lifestyles may have been too different, and the need for them to help in the home or in working to keep the family alive may have interfered with their availability. Schooling seems to them an irrelevance. It is only as adults that increasingly they are made aware of their lack of access to the society around them because of their limited education and literacy.

It is for this type of adult that community literacy projects have been developed to help them regain their self-esteem and to have access to and to participate in society around them. Whilst this situation is particularly acute in developing countries, such as in Latin America, it is not by any means confined to such countries. In the more developed parts of the world such failure in and by the state education system is a common experience for children from poorer families, and from minority communities. Language is often one of the key reasons for this, either because a totally different language is spoken and used in all the curriculum, or because the variety and forms used are unfamiliar to the experience of these children. The latter experience becomes even more relevant for adults trying to operate in modern, literate societies:

> Literacy education for community users can . . . engage with the whole range of ways in which power is exercised through language in the institutions of everyday life: banks, social security offices, college offices, law courts, the public spaces that are associated with public discourses.
>
> (Baynham, 1995: 88)

To address this situation of inequality and disempowerment, literacy classes are to be found in further education courses and sometimes in the workplace. But these are in themselves often reinforcing the alienation felt by those who are intimidated by public institutions and threatened by hierarchies. Community-based projects, particularly in rural areas, have proved more successful, and are often, too, the point of access to the more formal and institutional education for those who wish to continue their retraining and entry into life-long learning. As well as the work of UNESCO, in many parts of the world, including Latin America, these have often been organised by non-governmental organisations (NGOs), and also by religious organisations. In analysing the programmes' aims and methods, then, it is important to identify the ideological positions on which they are based. We have already seen that the UNESCO programme is best described as essentially functional and skill-oriented, conceived for context-non-specific environments. The UNESCO campaigns have also linked literacy very closely with employment and, therefore, economic development. The result, according to Barton, is that:

> Literacy has been treated as a variable, which is measurable and then related to other variables of development, such as economic development and modernity. The idea has been that resources are put into literacy and this then aids development. It has been seen as something external which is brought into a society. In Unesco campaigns and in industrialised countries, unfortunately, functional literacy is associated with imposing literacy on others, rather than starting from people's own perceptions of their needs.
>
> (Barton, 1994a: 194)

Religious organisations obviously also have very specific objectives for their literacy programmes: that is to provide the tools through which the reception and understanding of their particular religious message can be transmitted. Protestant missionary groups today, as Catholic ones at the time of the Spanish conquest in Latin America, are leaders in writing down previously unwritten indigenous languages, in order to translate and publish the Bible in these languages. We have already noted the activities of the US-based Summer Institute of Linguists, which is the missionary wing of the Wycliffe Bible Translators (Barton 1994a: 190). The SIL is very active in its work, which whilst producing a large body of publications in and elaboration of unwritten indigenous languages, has a very obvious agenda of spreading Christian (and Western, particularly American) values. As Barton stresses:

> The organisation has been the centre of controversy in several parts of the world. It has often been criticised for failing to respect other cultures. . . . Throughout history maps of the spread of different literacies have

reflected patterns of political and religious domination. This is no less
true today.

(Barton, 1994a: 190)

It is certainly true that many of the recent community-based literacy projects,
including Latin America, have a clear political and ideological basis. They
are constructed out of a particular way of analysing the situation of the
adult learner and of conceiving of the learner's rights and potential. As Gee
(1990: 42) says 'Literacy always comes with a perspective and interpretation
that is ultimately political.' One of the most important educators in this field,
himself a Latin American, is the Brazilian Paulo Freire.

Freire (1921–1996) was brought up in the Northeast of Brazil and begun
his professional career as a teacher of Portuguese in his hometown of Recife.
He started to work voluntarily with Catholic charity movements to help those
living in extreme conditions of poverty in Recife. From this experience, however, he began to learn the problems of middle-class charity, with its capacity
to analyse from its own perception and to 'walk away' when it suited. He
became increasingly engaged with the needs of the people he was working
with and convinced that literacy was one of the principal roots of their disempowerment (for example, to vote in Brazil then, it was necessary to be
able to read and write). From this experience he developed his particular
critique of literacy education and his aclaimed methods which have since
been implemented to varying degrees in many parts of the world,[7] not
least in Latin America as we shall see in Chapter 7.

Freire writes:

> All educational practice implies a theoretical stance on the educator's
> part. This stance in turn implies – sometimes more, sometimes less
> explicitly – an interpretation of man and the world.
>
> Teaching adults to read and write must be seen, analysed and under-
> stood in this way. The critical analyst will discover in the methods and
> texts used by educators and students practical value options which betray
> a philosophy of man, well or poorly outlined, coherent or incoherent.

(In Maybin, 1994: 252)

Freire, and his followers, criticise traditional literacy teaching methods and
textbooks for the relationship these set up between teacher and learner,
that is, a hierarchical one which treats the learner as inferior and 'empty'.
The state of lacking literacy is portrayed as like an illness or an affliction
needing to be 'nourished' and 'saved'. In this framework the learner[8] has an
empty mind waiting to be filled by the teacher. Freire creates his well-
known 'banking' metaphor to explain this teacher-student relationship.

> Education thus becomes an act of depositing . . . Instead of communi-
> cating, the teacher issues communiqués and 'makes deposits', which

the students patiently receive, memorize and repeat. This is the 'banking' concept of education . . .

In the banking concept of education, knowledge is a gift bestowed by those who consider themselves knowledgeable upon those whom they consider to know nothing.

(Freire, 1972: 46)

Freire discusses how this relationship has led to so many people feeling marginalised and on the edges of mainstream, dominant society, which is presented to them as the core social and political reality. He argues that there is a need to see how this perception is imposed by those in power and that it must be deconstructed in order to allow the learner freedom:

From this . . . point of view, the illiterate is no longer a person living on the fringe of society, a marginal man, but rather a representative of the dominated strata of society, in conscious or unconscious opposition to those who, in the same structure, treat him as a thing. Thus, also teaching men to read and write is no longer an inconsequential matter of *ba, be, bi, bo, bu*, of memorizing an alienated word, but a difficult apprenticeship in naming the world.

(in Maybin, 1994: 255)

Freire advocates a new relationship between learner and teacher (or facilitator, as he prefers to see this role). This is a relationship of respect, equality, dialogue and the desire to learn together about the world around them. In this, language – and therefore literacy – is crucial, as language determines the way we think and therefore the way we see the world around us. 'The cognitive dimensions of the literacy process must include the relationships of men with their world' (in Maybin, 1994: 256). Reading, then, becomes a form of codification between the 'concrete and the theoretical concepts of reality'. Learning to read is learning to 'decode'. Freire amplifies this position when he writes, 'reading the world always precedes reading the word, and reading the word implies continually reading the world' (Freire and Macedo, cited in Gee, 1990: 41). We can see here the link with the earlier discussion of what literacy encompasses: the codification is not just actual physical writing but metaphorical forms of representation. To 'read' them requires understanding, interpreting and naming what they represent.[9]

Obviously this process as proposed by Freire and his followers has a strong political and ideological underpinning. It is a particular view of society and analysis of power relations. Freire does not deny this. Gee sums up this belief in his chapter on literacy education from Plato to Freire in the following strong terms:

A text, whether written on paper, or on the soul (Plato), or on the world (Freire), is a loaded weapon. The person, the educator, who hands over the gun, hands over the bullets (the perspective), and must own up to the consequences. There is no way of having an opinion, an ideology, and a strong one, as did Plato, as does Freire. Literacy education is not for the timid.

(Gee, 1990: 42)

This linking of the ideological and political intentions behind policies and objectives of language and literacy education is a constant theme in this book. Freirean practitioners see literacy as a form of emancipation and empowerment, but the very same methods can be used to manipulate learners to particular interpretations of the world around them, be these left-wing or right-wing in political colour. As we shall see in the next chapter, this is an accusation that has been levelled against the Nicaraguan and the Cuban literacy campaigns. Moreover, whilst in the early days of Spanish domination of the American colonies, illiteracy and poor education were viewed as a way of marginalising the indigenous population, in this century, some literacy has been acknowledged as being a necessary skill to operate within an industrialised and modernised society, even in a subordinate and inferior role.

'Literacy and language education need to be understood as potential tools for social control rather than automatically as a means to social emancipation' writes Pennycook (1998: 82), and he goes on to quote Street (1993: 24) as warning that 'literacy itself does not promote cognitive advance, social mobility or progress: literacy practices are specific to the political and ideological context and their consequences vary situationally' (cited in Pennycook, 1998: 82).

The impact of literacy on language politics

Literacy and language politics are closely related. Literacy practices can for all the reasons mentioned above, and others, affect linguistic behaviour. Literacy also requires decisions concerning in which language education and publications should take place. Below we will briefly discuss these two aspects of the relationship between literacy and language, before examining them in greater detail in the Spanish-speaking context in the next chapters.

Mühlhäusler is one commentator who has developed the discussion regarding the impact of literacy on linguistic behaviour, in particular in the Pacific region. But his discussions are generalisable, especially for the Latin American context where, as in the Pacific, the pre-colonial languages are unwritten and have since been 'made literate'.

Mühlhäusler writes about the use of literacy as an instrument of social change and argues that it is 'a mode of behaviour which can radically affect the linguistic structures and practices of language use in a community' (1996: 212). As languages are codified and written down, he identifies certain characteristics that occur: the promoting of low-information to high-information societies; offering the possibility of storing information over long periods of time; and the supplementing face-to-face interaction with written communication over long distances (Mühlhäusler, 1996: 213). All of these changes can have profound effects on their societies, and we are reminded of the discussion by Anderson (1983, 1992) of how society was changed by the introduction of print-language in the sixteenth and seventeenth centuries. Anderson also notes changes in popular conceptions of time and space, as well as personal relationships. An underlying theme in this book is the importance of print-language to the capacity to 'imagine' a community, and thereby help form a certain kind of nationalism or political unity.

Both Anderson and Mühlhäusler stress how the introduction of literacy into a society changes that society from a time-focused sense of its identity which is cyclical and based on history, myths, customs and traditions, to a space-focused society once time has become linear and chronological. Because of the capacity to communicate quickly and easily over large areas without actual physical contact relationships, hierarchies and therefore a community's sense of identity dramatically alter.

The capacity for storage permitted through literacy (including modern technological media) has also, according to Mühlhäusler, led to great changes. Information can now be kept more secret and out of the public domain. Public memory becomes less important than written – often legal – documentation. Moreover, this new situation leads to the issue of access to information, which previously was equally available to the public as a whole. This has led to what Mühlhäusler calls 'the creation of communicative inequalities and decreasing heterogeneity' (1996: 213).

The decreasing heterogeneity refers to the other aspect of the impact of literacy on language, that is, the issue of in which languages there should be literacy and literacy practices. Once languages are elaborated, standardised and materials are published or broadcast in them, questions of economy of scale arise, and an acceptable minimum to make these activities viable emerges. The result is the decline in dialectal differences but eventually, too, in small languages in their entirety. Inevitably it is the languages of world powers, of colonisers and ex-colonisers, and of power elites which hold the position of language of communications, publications and information-storage. Literacy is often, then, the cause of language death. This is an issue we will examine for the specific case of minority languages in the Spanish-speaking world.

The introduction of literacy (writing systems, technological media, etc.) into languages which have hitherto not been written down is an ambiguous issue, as we have seen. As Barton (1994a: 207) points out,

> Literacy in a vernacular is . . . two-edged in that, although it seems to give status and value to a language and widen the range of practices, all too often it is a stepping-stone to literacy in a language of wider communication. Literacy can then become a way of escaping the vernacular and

having access to a broader range of cultures. Initial literacy is not in itself enough to protect a language.

As Barton argues, the consequences of small languages being squeezed represent an ecological loss on a global scale. He bemoans this potential disappearance of language diversity because 'different languages embody different values, experiences and sources of ideas' (1994a: 207). How far governments want, or can even afford, to protect linguistic diversity, is of course an issue we have discussed in various contexts already, and have noted that education is often a tool for enforcing national unity and homogeneity rather than diversity and heterogeneity.

Conclusion

The power of language in education has been traced in this chapter, specifically through examining its position in bilingual education programmes and in literacy programmes. But language is an underlying force throughout the curriculum, as we have also noted, and the presence or lack of access to the accepted form of language can bring power – or powerlessness – to students. Perceptions too about educational institutions and practices can reflect back on the status of language. The availability of materials in a given language, or the decision as to which curricular subjects will be taught in which language can enhance or reduce a language's prestige. In many countries such decisions are controlled by governmental policy makers and by those who have access to the necessary resources to produce and disseminate materials and train teachers.

In the following two chapters we will analyse these issues in the specific context of the Spanish-speaking world in order to see what models of educational practice exist and what ideologies underpin educational linguistic policies.

7 Latin American educational policies in the struggle for linguistic rights

In this chapter we will explore some of the issues raised in the previous one in terms of how they are relevant to the Latin American context. As we suggested in earlier chapters, it is above all in the realm of education that Latin America's indigenous populations have attempted to establish certain cultural and linguistic rights. As we saw in Part I policies and attitudes to the education of the marginalised indigenous peoples were a significant aspect of the Castilianisation process from the beginnings of the Spanish conquest through the early independence era. The decision whether to teach Spanish or whether to use indigenous languages in the Church's early evangelising work, and, later, the role of the national education system in enforcing post-independence national identity and national unity were deliberate and conscious political considerations.

The discussion here will be of the contemporary situation in Latin America, and in particular through an examination of the nature of the two strands outlined in the previous chapter: that is, the nature of bilingual education in compulsory-age schooling, and initiatives to educate adult learners through literacy programmes. This is linked with the situations we outlined in Chapter 5 in terms of the degree of political autonomy or state centralisation that the different indigenous groups experience. How far these groups influence policy-making and control their own resources and the management of them will largely determine the aims and objectives of the separate programmes. The gap we have seen that can exist between legislation and implementation is also crucial. We have already noted that all the constitutions in Latin America make some reference to respecting the rights and equality of their citizens – and therefore, implicitly, the rights of the minority communities – and that many also explicitly mention the right to some kind of protection for the indigenous groups. However, as we commented, this is very vague, and only rarely specifically expressed in terms of educational rights. According to Hamel (1994a: 276) only the constitutions of Bolivia, Peru and Mexico 'stipulate that literacy should be achieved through L1 [the mother tongue indigenous language] to facilitate transition to L2 [Spanish] as soon as possible', whilst Colombia, Ecuador, Panama and Guatemala 'decree bilingual intercultural education without any specific definition of purpose'.

In Paraguay education in the indigenous languages is mainly 'limited to the audio-oral skills'.

Even today language education in much of Latin America still builds on the nineteenth century policies of aiming for national unity by means of efficient integration or assimilation of all groups into the national Western-based hegemony. One important difference from the earlier educational policies outlined in Chapters 2 and 3, however, is the increased awareness of the need to provide more basic education, and especially literacy to the large indigenous populations. From perceiving these groups as marginal to society's needs, and for whom education was unnecessary and even an impediment, the new thinking since the 1960s has evaluated their role in the labour force and as potential consumers differently. According to Campos Carr (1990: 52) writes:

> The new goal was to gear content and method of formal and non-formal education to the demands of the economy. . . . Not surprisingly, the millions of illiterates in Latin America in 1960 were proclaimed to be a barrier to economic development. Illiteracy became 'dysfunctional'.
>
> (Campos Carr, 1990: 52)

This increase in the provision of education has meant that whilst there are now far more examples of some form of bilingual education and functional literacy for the minority communities, this is nonetheless essentially assimilationist and transitional. Children and adults from the minority communities were to be educated as quickly as possible for their integration into mainstream society where their role of subordination within the workforce was still clearly defined. In quite a few cases too this bilingual education is merely a submersion form. However, since the 1970s in particular there have been signs of education programmes (both for school children and for adults) based on principles of maintenance and respect for separate cultures. These programmes, normally described as bicultural or intercultural rather than simply bilingual, have varying degrees of success. Hamel describes these initiatives:

> Clearly opposed to previous models, the new programmes are based on a pluricultural conception of the state and full respect for the Indian peoples and their ethnic rights. They claim as their target the maintenance or revitalization of Indian cultures and languages . . . According to the new philosophy, indigenous culture in the curriculum should not be restricted to content (Indian folktales and songs), but cover the range of material, social, cognitive and linguistic aspects of culture. The consequent pursuit of such a perspective has even raised doubts about the appropriateness of formal education – an occidental dominant institution par excellence – for Indian peoples as such.
>
> (Hamel, 1994a: 275)

We can see here some of the same critical deconstructing of traditional educational frameworks that we analysed as relevant to literacy programmes. The challenge, however, that this might pose to the existing state institutions and conceptions of education is enormous.[1]

The discussion which follows will be restricted to looking at some of those countries in Latin America where issues of bicultural-bilingual education and radical literacy programmes have taken centre stage. We will analyse how far their aims are truly pluralist and empowering, and how successful they appear to be. In doing this, we will inevitably limit the discussion to a few selected case studies. For more exhaustive summaries of bilingual education frameworks throughout Latin America readers should consult the studies by Amadio and López (1991), Chiodi (1990) and Von Gleich (1989).[2]

The countries to be chosen include Mexico, Peru and Bolivia (where in the latter two, programmes for Quechua or Aymara speakers can often be discussed in a cross-border sense), Nicaragua, Cuba and Guatemala. For the discussion on bilingual-bicultural education we are focusing on the position and rights of the minoritised indigenous communities. However, when examining the new literacy programmes we will also look at an example of a monocultural, Spanish-speaking country, Cuba, where poor Spanish-speaking people have also been marginalised.

Whilst indigenous education programmes are our prime concern here, many of their characteristics and their challenges are shared by immigrant communities also marginalised from the national core. There is also an under-provision and lack of recognition for the rights and needs of these communities in Latin America, as in so many other parts of the world. Puiggrós (1994) describes the position of the immigrant in Argentina, a country with only a small pre-Conquest indigenous population but which in the nineteenth century accepted the need to populate its land with immigrants (many from Italy) in order to support its agricultural economy. As with indigenous communities in other parts of Latin America, the immigrant was to be assimilated as quickly as possible with, above all, the aid of the education system:

> Immigrants shared with the Argentine oligarchy the belief in a myth: that national unity was possible only through socio-cultural homogeneity. Argentine society as a whole was unable to conceive of national unity as a product of the articulation of differences, preferring to be accomplices to educational strategies that tended towards concealment, censure or elimination of these differences.
>
> (Puiggrós, 1994: 161)

Even in countries, then, where large indigenous populations were not present to challenge the dominant state identity, the role of the national education system was seen as essential in the nation-building task based on ironing out difference and creating homogeneity.

Below we will first examine bilingual education programmes in Mexico and the Andean republics of Peru and Bolivia, and then look at literacy projects in Guatemala, Nicaragua and Cuba. We will, above all, be interested in seeing what the overall aims of these programmes are and how these are manifested in the resourcing, the curricular content, and the pedagogic methodology. These aims are of course linked to and products of Language Planning – overt or covert – and ultimately of (language) policies which enshrine the state's view of its national identity.

From bilingual to bicultural and intercultural

Mexico[3]

As we have already seen in earlier chapters, the history of the Castilianisation process in Mexico follows the same pattern as in much of Latin America. An area containing very many distinct mother tongues is progressively conquered by the dominant use of the Spanish language. This is made easier because of the prestige of Spanish, its position as the language of power and of the elites, and because it contains a well-developed written form. The indigenous mother tongues are pushed to the edges, and many disappeared altogether by the end of the nineteenth century. During the early years of independence, the drive for national unity is particularly responsible for the deliberate rejection of the use of the indigenous languages in public life.

In the twentieth century particularly from the 1930s, however, bilingual education was introduced more widely into Mexican schooling. The underlying belief was that to allow some use of the mother tongues would help indigenous children move more quickly to learning Spanish and having some success in the education system. The methods, then, were purely those of transitional bilingual education. Usually literacy in the mother tongue was not offered, the bilingualism being limited to the oral use of the L1 until children became more competent in Spanish. According to Hidalgo:

> One of the objectives of BE [Bilingual Education] . . . was not to maintain and preserve the IMTs [Indian Mother Tongues]. Instead, the objective was to accelerate the process of Castilianisation, a process better accomplished by the mother tongue in the first two years of elementary education. . . .
> Estimates between 1880 and 1980 confirm that while the absolute number of speakers of IMTs increases with the normal population growth, they decrease in connection with the national population. . . . Whereas the percentages of bilinguals grow dramatically, that of monolinguals decline. . . .
> In fact, critical evaluations of BE have shown that all methods are equally successful in helping speakers of IMTs *shift* to Spanish.
>
> (Hidalgo, 1994: 193)

The goal of Castilianisation was not necessarily one only imposed from the state on the indigenous peoples. As we have noted in the previous chapter, one form of bilingual education can lead to segregation, and particularly in the 1950s and 1960s there was a fear amongst indigenous activists that this form of education could deliberately isolate their communities from mainstream culture and politics (Brice Heath, 1972). They were keen that their children should have the earliest opportunity to learn Spanish.

However, from the 1970s an important shift has taken place in the discussions of Mexican bilingual education and the role of the indigenous communities in the nation (Coronado, 1992; Hamel, 1994a; Hidalgo, 1994). From 1978 the running of indigenous education programmes became the direct responsibility of the Dirección General de Educación Indígena (DGEI) under the auspices of the Mexican public education department (SEP), supported too by the Instituto Nacional Indigenista (INI). Coronado quotes the objectives for bilingual-bicultural education as described by the SEP,

> La educación bilingüe significa conocimiento y manejo de la lectura y escritura así como la estructura de las dos lenguas, la propia y el castellano . . . El aspecto bicultural implica tomar en cuenta la cultura materna (filosofía, valores y objetivos indígenas) de los educandos en la planeación educativa tanto en el contenido como en los métodos psicopedagógicos.
>
> (SEP, cited in Coronado, 1992: 54)[4]

This change in focus has partly arisen from a critique of the objectives of the earlier bilingual programmes, which many radical groups no longer share, preferring maintenance bilingual education to transitional. Partly, too, it is a reaction against the methodology and quality of the bilingual education being offered (Bravo Ahuja, 1992). The teachers were often poorly trained and uncommitted to the status of the mother tongues. The methods employed were traditional and inappropriate, with rote learning and a heavy dependence on writing and irrelevant, academic content (Hidalgo, 1994). Children were alienated from this curriculum and the teacher–pupil relationship, leading to drop-outs and educational under-achievement.

From the mid-1970s educationalists began to explore ways of improving both the learning of the mother tongues and literacy skills in them, as well as the place of the indigenous cultures in the school curriculum. This discussion introduces the concept of biculturalism as well as bilingualism as part of the education for indigenous children. The main characteristics include besides a maintenance goal for the use of the mother tongues and greater teaching of and use of literacy in these, the redefining of the curricula away from colonial and post-colonial discourses which rejected the existence of indigenous cultures except in the most reified of forms. An important aspect to the bicultural approach is that the planning and delivery of the education should involve the indigenous communities themselves. Teachers should themselves be bilinguals of the communities, and methods should correspond more closely to the cultural norms of the indigenous peoples. As Hamel constantly points out, to achieve such participation and direction from the indigenous communities also implies greater autonomy in the control and management of their lives and societies in general, at a political as well as social level.

Hidalgo (1994) mentions some signs of positive aspects in Mexico's language policy as a result of the shift to bilingual-bicultural objectives in indigenous education. The state now recognises the existence of its fifty-six minority languages, and the newest constitution guarantees individuals' rights to use their mother tongues. The education programmes are being directed largely by qualified indigenous personnel. Other positive measures mentioned by both Hidalgo and Coronado include 'los albergues escolares, la radio bilingüe, las brigadas de mejoramiento comunitario' (Coronado, 1992: 68), which have an influential effect on community attitudes amongst all age groups, not only those of school age.

Hidalgo quotes the long-term goals of 'balanced bilingualism' sought by these education planners,

1 It is proposed that by the end of six years children will be fluent in all four skills in two languages. . . . By doing so, the indigenous languages of Mexico will be rescued, preserved and developed.
2 It is also proposed that a writing system for the Indian languages should be promoted in order to link the languages with modernization.
3 Indian languages should be used as both a subject and a medium of instruction, because the old practices of alphabetization proved to be decontextualized. (*Fundamentos para la modernización de la educación indígena*, cited in Hidalgo, 1994: 200)

Hamel (1994a) also notes an upturn in the number of trained bilingual indigenous teachers and the publication of more textbooks in mother tongues. Coronado (1992), however, is less sanguine about either of these aspects saying that often the indigenous teachers are relatively insecure in their grasp of both languages, and further suggesting that

el dominio que los maestros tengan de las dos lenguas no garantiza, sin embargo, que tengan el conocimiento técnico que les permita enfrentar los problemas de la enseñanza de las lenguas tanto al nivel oral que escrito. (Coronado, 1992: 63)[5]

And, she argues, even those who are better qualified have not normally specialised in the understanding and methods of bilingual education. Whilst Coronado accepts there have been efforts to produce more books in indigenous languages, she points out that these are often nonetheless simply translations (literally and culturally) of existing texts in Spanish. The lack of much standardisation work of the indigenous languages has also led to the inevitable imposing of Castilian norms and an insensitivity to vast dialectal variation, according to Coronado.

Hamel (1994a) points out the increase and acceptance of a greater use of literacy in the mother tongues from the 1980s. However, he also suggests that the signing of the NAFTA agreement and the consequent closer ties with the US and Canada in the 1990s have led to renewed pressure to learn Spanish and English as languages of wider communication internationally, to the detriment of the mother tongues.

Hamel (1997b) is sceptical too of the true bicultural nature of these education programmes in that he points out that the curricular content must remain homogenous for Spanish or mother tongue learners in terms of overall objectives, and particularly as far as the underlying philosophy in the Spanish language materials and curriculum. This is further reinforced by the fact that the majority population is still being taught a curricular programme based on the dominant view of the Mexican nation and designed to be homogenising.

Hidalgo's assessment of the progress to date of the bicultural programmes is somewhat pessimistic:

> It seems that the ideal goal of BBE (Bilingual Bicultural Education), balanced bilingualism, will be difficult to achieve given the number of IMTs, the functional inbalance vis-à-vis Spanish, and the reduced number of speakers of some groups. Moreover it appears that the objectives of BE are purely restorative, inasmuch as Mexicans are trying to restore the languages spoken in the country, the limited functions they have had since colonial times, the confidence and identities of their speakers, the values of oral traditions, etc. The goal of BBE seems to be de-marginalization.
>
> (Hidalgo, 1994: 201)

This negative evaluation of bicultural education in Mexico is shared too by Lastra (1992) who cites various assessments of the experience. She concludes that a major part of the problem lies in the fact that the goals of the bicultural programmes are conceived by 'indigenistas' who are essentially eurocentric and Western in their thinking (even when they are actually members of the indigenous community) which, amongst other things, encourages them to construct educational programmes along formal Western lines, and above all, through the development and use of mother tongue literacy. Lastra, like Mühlhäusler, as we saw in the previous chapter, sees the danger to survival of over-Westernising indigenous languages. She emphasises the decontextualising experience that schooling can be for minority children and how the invention (as she sees it) of mother tongue literacy is a false device as it cannot represent the true cultural life and norms of the indigenous community society outside school. Like Hidalgo, Lastra has an explicit scepticism for the appropriateness of traditional formal education as the right place to nourish and promote the indigenous people's sense of identity.

The highly centralised nation-building project began in the nineteenth century, combined with the internationalising dimension from Mexico's northern neighbours and trading partners, certainly seems to outweigh the attempts at creating a pluralist and multicultural society in Mexico, despite the recent efforts through the education system. The recent events in the predominantly indigenous region of Chiapas[6] serve to confirm that the sense of marginalisation and disempowerment continues. The interwoven link between language, education, politics and national identity is total in the Mexican experience. It is reasonable to share Coronado's gloomy evaluation of bilingual-bicultural education in Mexico.

> Afirmar que en México existen programas de educación bilingüe para la población indígena es hablar de buenos deseos y pocas realidades. Efectivamente la educación para los grupos étnicos ha ido transformándose hacia el reconocimiento de las lenguas y las culturas como legítimas e importantes como constitutivas del patrimonio cultural de la nación, y se reconoce hoy la necesidad de partir de la realidad lingüística y cultural de cada grupo como base fundamental de los procesos educativos dirigidos a estos sectores, en el marco de su inserción económica y política en el sistema capitalista mexicano. Las prácticas concretas, sin embargo, muestran que la historia de dominación representada en la castellanización ha dejado una profunda huella en la sociedad y el efecto ideológico de la imposición lingüística ha marcado de diversas maneras a las poblaciones que demandan el acceso a la educación . . .
>
> (Coronado, 1992: 68)[7]

Peru[8]

Peru is one of the cases most thoroughly documented in terms of description, analysis and evaluation of its education programmes, and particularly that of bilingual projects for the Quechua and Aymara speakers (see, for example, Hornberger, 1988; Hornberger and López, 1998: López, 1988; Paulston, 1972). This is not surprising insofar as the recent history of language policy and planning in Peru has been amongst the most interesting and potentially radical to be found in Latin America.

At the start of the twentieth century Peru began to become more concerned and conscious of the need to involve its large indigenous population in the education system, from where it had mostly been excluded. The 'education impulse' as this move is called (Portocarrero, 1992: 69) was however entirely aimed at Westernising the indigenous peoples in order to integrate (or assimilate) them into Peruvian national society. As Portocarrero says, 'The role of the school was to form the citizen and train the worker – in other words, the school was a laboratory where national unity was crystalized'

(1992: 71). This educational project not only taught the indigenous children to be ashamed of their culture and to want to aspire to Westernised, Spanish-speaking ways, it also indirectly encouraged migration to the cities by holding out the prospects of social mobility and integration.

> The school . . . became an agent of deculturation. Indigenous children learned to devalue their culture, their education served them only if they migrated to the city. If they remained in the rural areas, . . . the use of education was almost null. The school in fact fostered emigration and depopulation of rural areas, interfering with the reproduction of the Andean traditions.
>
> (Portocarrero, 1992: 76)

One of the most important consequences of this kind of education being given to the indigenous communities was the rapid decline in the use of non-Spanish mother tongues. On entering school Spanish was the medium of instruction; mother tongues were only used at home, and if the children then left for the cities, they tended to abandon the use of the vernacular.

Although a significant indigenist movement had emerged in the early part of the twentieth century in Peru, which argued for greater dignity for the indigenous people and was (in its rhetoric at least) concerned with their basic social and economic rights, this was not translated, in the main, into education policy.[9] However, in 1968 a coup d'etat, led by Velasco Alvarado, brought in a radical left-wing military junta with a very different philosophy and conception of Peruvian identity to those it succeeded. A renewed interest in 'indigenism' appeared. The legislation of this period reflected a belief that Peru was indeed a nation formed from its indigenous peoples, as well as Europeans. As Cerrón-Palomino comments its 'popular reformist program was a complete breakdown of the traditional structure of Peruvian society' (1989: 25). These reforms included agrarian reform (1969), social property reform (1974), education reform (1972) and the officialisation of the Quechua language (1975) (Hornberger, 1988; Portocarrero, 1992).

The 1972 education law tried to introduce sweeping changes to the ideology of Peruvian education:

> The main principles of this law was the sensitization and opening of the school to the social dimension of its environment; the establishment of nonauthoritarian norms of pedagogic practice . . .
>
> (Portocarrero, 1992: 81)

As Hornberger writes:

> The intention of the Education Reform was to create an educational system that would build up the Peruvian nation along humanistic, demo-cratic and nationalistic lines. While emphasizing the unification of the

nation, Reform documents also recognized the existing diversity in the nation . . .

(Hornberger, 1988: 23)

Velasco was himself overthrown in 1975, and the second phase of the military government was far less radical, with the result that many of the reformist objectives of the earlier period were never completely realised.

Incorporated into the new education law was a national bilingual education policy, or *Política Nacional de Educación Bilingüe* (normally referred to as the PNEB). However, this still saw language as a 'problem' rather than a resource, and advocated bilingual education as a way of respecting indigenous culture, but also facilitating indigenous particpation in Peruvian society, by learning Spanish (Hornberger, 1988). Hornberger sums up the three principal objectives of the PNEB as '1) consciousness-raising; 2) the creation of a national culture; and 3) the use of Spanish as the common language in Peru' (1988: 26).

As a result of the PNEB various projects in bilingual education were set up throughout the country, some entirely government (local or national) backed, and others largely independent (such as ones by the SIL, and the important involvement of the German Technical Co-operation Society – GTZ). Following the objectives of the Education Reform, these projects were in their majority forms of transitional bilingual education. However, a few – such as that run in Puno and analysed by Hornberger (1988) – were in fact full maintenance models. As Hornberger argues, whilst these may not have followed the principles of the education law, they were consistent with the newly declared officialisation of the Quechua language.

As we have noted in earlier chapters, Quechua was declared co-official with Spanish in 1975, but later, in 1979, this was watered down to having, along with Aymara, official status in certain regions. Hornberger (1988) describes in detail the significance of the 1975 constitutional statements. In particular she claims that the earlier decree 'represented "language-as-resource" orientation in status planning'. In this phase of legislation, the government was expected to defend, promote and develop Quechua. In the later constitution Hornberger describes the emphasis now as 'language-as-right' (1988: 30). The latest constitution, of 1993, also 'supports the application of bilingual education (Article 17) and accords official status to all Amerindian languages spoken in the country (Article 48)' (Hornberger and López, 1998: 207). The implementation of this latter provision has not yet been obvious.

Hornberger (1988; and López, 1998) amongst others discusses and evaluates at length the Puno bilingual education initiative which was a direct result of the educational reforms. It is an interesting case study because Puno is a highly indigenous-populated region, has two strong indigenous mother tongues spoken there, Quechua and Aymara, and has much in common with the indigenous communities across the adjacent political border with Bolivia. The project sought to maintain a high degree of use of the mother tongues, using them as the only or one of the languages of instruction right through the six grades of primary school. Spanish was introduced gradually, starting in second grade as a reading language. An important part of the project was the complete re-designing of the curriculum, across all subjects. The materials developed were deliberately responsive to the local communities, in terms of reflecting cultural practices and the agricultural economy surrounding them. The curriculum and materials for the two languages of Quechua and Aymara were developed in parallel – the project was not conceived as a multilingual experiment, which it might well have been – but with cooperation and discussion between the planners and designers of both. Teacher training programmes for bilingual teachers were introduced in the Teacher Training institute (the 'Normal School') in Puno, as well as a postgraduate course in Andean linguistics in its university (Hornberger and López, 1998).

The Puno project has had profound influences on thinking regarding bilingual education in Peru and in other parts of Latin America. The projects have been widely evaluated, by Peruvians and by others, and the successes and failures of the project have been taken on board in other project planning of this kind. Success in terms of the actual use and acquisition of language(s) is summed up by Hornberger and López as indicating 'increased use of indigenous languages in the classroom . . . , improved student participation in oral, reading and writing activities, and by improved teacher techniques' (1998: 217).

The social and cultural outcomes of the project are also important. During the early period of the project positive results were noted in involving the community in participating and accepting the objectives of the programme. Attitudes to maintenance bilingual programmes improved, but exactly at a time when nationally, support for bilingual education was retreating. The political environment in Peru during the later years of this project – with the terrorist activities of the Maoist Shining Path made the success of the work more difficult.

As far as long-term bilingual education policy is concerned Hornberger and López sum this up as only partial success. In 1996 the Peruvian government re-established a Bilingual Education Unit to oversee bilingual education in primary education. The message that such education would stop after this level is clear.

> Gone are the days when Peruvian academics thought intercultural bilingual education could become an important cross-sectional component of the Peruvian educational system and permeate all levels and modalities of Peruvian education. [The Puno Project's] admirable record of success in overcoming numerous technical challenges to present a panorama of new possibilities in indigenous education was not enough to overcome the weight of political failure.
>
> (Hornberger and López, 1998: 219)

Bolivia

The proportion of the overall Bolivian population who are indigenous people is around 63 per cent, the highest for any country in South America (Hornberger and López, 1998). This figure includes over two and a half million Quechua speakers and over one and a half million Aymara speakers, as well as a sizeable Guarani speaking community. Given that the European-originated population in Bolivia is a minority, but, nonetheless, controls the economic, political and social direction of the country, it makes a particularly interesting case study in terms of ethnic integration, multilingualism and lingusitic rights. The exclusion of the majority indigenous population from the education system until this century was particularly severe and deliberate in Bolivia (Howard-Malverde and Canessa, 1995; Rivera, 1992). This situation improved somewhat in the early part of the twentieth century. The date heralding significant change is 1952 with a popular-supported Nationalist Revolution. As well as agrarian reform, nationalisation of the mines, this new political movement brought important educational changes, enshrined in the Bolivian Educational Code.

> The code established basic principles for national education: education was free, compulsory, democratic and unified. Politically, education was expected to be a national and collective enterprise, anti-imperialist and anti-feudal.
>
> (Rivera, 1992: 25)

In a similar way to the 'education impulse' in Peru, the objectives of this new education were to integrate the indigenous people into national life by making them 'Bolivians', rather than 'Indians'. And, as Howard-Malverde and Canessa comment 'An ideology of equality also meant repressing difference' (1995: 233). In this discourse of national identity construction the use of *'indio'* was to be replaced by *'campesino'*. Education was the core of this creation of the new Bolivian, and the expansion of educational provision, building of schools, etc., as a result of the 1952 legislation was impressive. Essential to this project was the teaching of Spanish to the indigenous children because this was accepted as being the passport to citizenship. Since the fifties, then, any bilingual education programmes had been designed to be transitional with the ultimate aim of full competence in Spanish.

Plaza and Albó (1989) describe the various bilingual education efforts of the 1970s and 1980s. They point out that quite a substantial amount of bilingual education and educating of the indigenous communities in general after the 1952 revolution was carried out, nonetheless, by religious groups, including the local Catholic Church on the one hand, and the SIL on the other. An interesting feature of the work of the former was the use of local radio in community education, both to school children and to adult learners. These transmissions frequently took place through the use, at least in part, of the appropriate mother tongue (Plaza and Albó, 1989: 71). The majority of the projects described by Plaza and Albó whilst far more sympathetic to the needs and values of the indigenous communities, and introducing the use of and literacy in their mother tongues, were all essentially transitional. One project of the 'maintenance' type is discussed, however. All the projects suffered to some extent from a lack of resources, including well-qualified teachers and sufficient appropriate materials. In the case in particular of the maintenance project, unfavourable attitudes from within the communities to the teaching and promotion of the mother tongues were a further obstacle. With Spanish perceived as the language of empowerment, the need to learn literacy in the mother tongue was not supported by many parents.

The 1980s saw the introduction of important initiatives towards more bicultural education in Bolivia, following on the pronouncements to this effect by the Bolivian government in 1983 with its *Plan Nacional de Alfabetización y Educación Popular* which set up the SENALEP (*Servicio Nacional de Alfabetización y Educación Popular*) (Plaza and Albó, 1989). This carried out important work and changes in the area of literacy work and adult education for the indigenous communities. A shift in language and education policies generally could be seen, with a greater understanding of the different needs for rural as opposed to urban school curricula, and with an increasing emphasis on diversity and multilingualism. In fact the election to the vice-presidency in 1993 of an Aymara, the educationalist Victor Hugo Cárdenas was achieved on the basis of a campaign platform of 'unity in diversity' (Hornberger and López, 1998; Howard-Malverde and Canessa, 1995). Much of this change in attitude remained at the level of rhetoric and expressions of hope given the need for expensive resources to bring about change, and the entrenched position of Spanish as 'superior' language in many people's eyes.

Since 1982 Bolivia has returned to a democratic form of government after various military and civilian dictatorships (which followed the 1952 revolutionary movement). This has led to much reflection and examination of the country's national identity and increasing awareness of its multicultural nature. It is a logical part of this process, then, that in 1994 a new conception of Bolivian national identity was reflected in the Bolivian National Education Reform. As with other areas of political life in Bolivia in the 1990s the Reform starts from the premise of reflecting the country's diversity through far greater decentralisation and more popular participation in the organisation and running of local communities including the schools.

The Reform advocated 'the introduction of *all* Bolivia's indigenous languages (alongside Spanish) as subjects and media of instruction in *all* Bolivian schools' (Hornberger and López, 1998: 221 – the authors' emphasis). This is a huge and radical enterprise which must entail amongst other considerations designing curricula, training teachers, standardising non-European languages (especially those from the Amazonian areas). For this work some of the lessons and developments from Peru's Puno project were invaluable. According to

Hornberger and López many of the teachers had been trained in the Puno institutions. Hornberger and López also point to the extensive use of indigenous mother tongues as languages of instruction as well as learning, and they describe the curricula and materials being designed.

> The Reform places the learner at the centre of the educational process and emphasises modifications to social relationships in classrooms and schools through changes in pedagogical practice, the reorganisation of classrooms, the reconsideration of learning time and space, and the use of learning modules, learning centres and cooperative learning strategies. . . .
>
> The Reform explicitly foresees and invites the inclusion of indigenous knowledge and culture in the national curriculum. Similarly the inclusion of Quechua, Aymara, Guarani, and other Bolivian indigenous languages as languages of instruction is intended for both indigenous language speakers and Spanish speakers nation-wide. For the first time, Bolivians encounter a real possibility for two-way intercultural education.
>
> (Hornberger and López, 1998: 225)

It is probably not an exaggeration to say that this is a first in Latin America, not simply in Bolivia. Particularly radical – and potentially controversial – is the expectation that the majority language speakers should learn minority languages, and about indigenous cultures. At present the indigenous languages are taught to Spanish-speakers within a monolingual Spanish environment as foreign/second languages. The materials available for this are even fewer than those for mother tongue teaching of the indigenous languages, and so need developing. Children need to be convinced, too, that learning the indigenous languages is relevant and enjoyable. Attitudes until recently amongst the dominant language speakers have regarded such languages as inferior, particularly in urban areas.

It is still too early to see how successful the radical education programme in Bolivia is. However, unlike in the Mexican and Peruvian cases we examined, in Bolivia the objectives and methods of the present education system are supported, resourced and promoted by the government. Whereas in Peru local success was viewed as undermined by a lack of commitment at national level, and in Mexico, rhetoric and legislation seemed to exceed implementation, in Bolivia there is a slow but sure application of the aims of the Reform.

Summary

Latin American states have shown little interest in the education and rights of their indigenous populations until well into the twentieth century. Even then, reactions have varied and measures taken are of patchy effectiveness. In most states the overwhelming view has continued to back the idea that national unity should be sought through homogenising integration. Gradually states have begun to see the need to educate indigenous children and to teach them in their native tongues – but only in order to facilitate their transition eventually to competence in Spanish, and thereby assimilation into mainstream society. Much of this bilingual education was not even provided by national governments, but by international (NGO) bodies or religious organisations. The 1970s saw a change throughout much of Latin America in terms of appreciation of indigenous rights and the possibilities of plural societies. This thinking, however, did not produce significant change in all parts of the region. But many of those states with sizeable indigenous populations were pressurised to consider new models of education, bicultural/intercultural education which aimed to maintain indigenous languages and cultures in parallel with Spanish and Westernised culture. We have examined three of these examples to see how far bicultural/intercultural education is really taking place.[10]

Of the case studies that we have examined, only the present Bolivian one can be described as truly intercultural in its objectives, methods and view of the national society around it. A crucial factor in this success appears to be related to the degree of popular participation in the management and design of the Bolivian programme. Alongside the Education Reform, Bolivia introduced a Popular Participation Act to encourage far greater local involvement and responsibility in running the political and social affairs of the community. Such participation is only possible with a degree of decentralisation, or autonomy, as advocated by many commentators, such as Hamel (1997a and b), and indigenous activists. But Latin American republics since independence have tended to be highly centralised as part of the homogenising and nation-building process.

Participation, too, is a feature of the kind of Freirean methodology outlined in the previous chapter that characterises the kind of adult education which provides access to empowerment. In the following section we will examine specific examples of this kind of adult education programme in Latin America and discuss whether there are examples of practice here that, like the Bolivian Education Reform, give rise to expectations of a more multicultural, multilingual and participatory society for indigenous as well as European-origin peoples.

Enabling and empowering: radical adult literacy progammes in Latin America[11]

In the vast majority of the case studies and discussion in this book issues of linguistic rights and language policies have revolved around the rights of minority linguistic communities, such as the indigenous peoples of Latin America. However, other marginalised groups are also disenfranchised from the core of their state's political and economic life through lack of education and inappropriate linguistic skills. Even where the existence of indigenous communities is not an issue, poor working class people, both in urban shanty town environments, and, above all, in isolated rural areas, are denied participation in much of their country's day-to-day life. Illiteracy (in the relatively traditional sense of the term) is often the main cause of this marginalisation. According to Campos Carr:

> In 1980 there were 45 million adult illiterates . . . in Latin America and the Caribbean . . . out of a population of 159 million adults. In the majority of these countries nearly 50 per cent of those who enter primary school do not complete their early education. And in the rural zones of many countries or the high Andean region, the adult illiteracy rate may reach anywhere from 50 to 85 per cent.
>
> (Campos Carr, 1990: 50)

The Westernised cultures and societies that control the decision-making, the power, and the economy of many Latin American states require literacy skills for their inhabitants to be able to take part and to have the rights and advantages of citizenship. Of course in the case of the indigenous groups this is also compounded by the issue of competence in Spanish. However, we will begin the discussion here of the role of literacy in offering groups greater participation and empowerment in society by looking at a Spanish monolingual country, Cuba, where until the 1959 revolution, however, illiteracy was extremely high and much of the population was thereby outside the benefits of mainstream society. This is one of the earliest examples of radical literacy programmes in Latin America. We will follow it with a look at some more recent literacy projects, principally in Nicaragua and Guatemala, where multilingualism and ethnic diversity are once again important factors, and the idea of biliteracy must be included.

Cuba

In the years leading up to the 1959 Revolution in Cuba education provision was poor, particularly in the rural areas, and illiteracy rates were high. As Torres observes, 'At the time of the revolution only 24.2 per cent of the total population aged 15 years and over had ever gone to school.' Illiteracy accounted for 23.6 per cent of the population but was much higher in rural areas' (Torres, 1990: 72). In these rural areas there were few schools and few and badly-trained teachers. It is therefore not surprising that the first foothold of the revolution was in the Sierra Maestra mountains and not in the towns or cities. Even then, an important part of the recruitment and training of the insurgents was a basic education programme, including the teaching of literacy.

Cuba's post-revolutionary literacy campaign is famous worldwide, partly because of the priority and high profile given it by Fidel Castro, partly because of its innovative content and conception, and partly because of its undeniable success (Bhola, 1984; Torres, 1990). Castro announced this campaign in a speech to the UN General Assembly in September 1960, when he spoke of 'the great battle of illiteracy' and his intention to see Cuba 'the first country in America which, after a few months, will be able to say it does not have one person who remains illiterate' (cited in Bhola, 1984, and Torres, 1990). From the start this literacy campaign was inextricably part of the new socialist agenda.

> If socialism was to be more than a mere idealistic aspiration, if the revolution was to build a socialist reality meeting the needs of the people, the educational level of the people had to be raised so as to improve technology, production and culture. Illiteracy had to be eliminated because it deepened and reinforced class differences produced by economic conditions and gave the exploiting classes a justification for their privileges.
>
> (Bhola, 1984: 93)

For this reason, and unlike previous literacy campaigns in Latin America, the content of the primer written for the campaign, *Venceremos*, was designed round different sociopolitical themes relating to the revolution. Bhola gives some examples of these topics covered by the primer's fifteen chapters: the Revolution, the Cooperatives, Racial Discrimination, Housing Rights, etc. This was not simply to be literacy education, but political education too. In this way the leaders of the revolution hoped to reach the population at large and involve them in the enormous and radical changes the country was undergoing.

The campaign was planned to last over one year and to mobilise all Cubans, either as teachers or learners. We can see how the metaphors and discourse of fighting and victory is evident. Besides being a 'campaign', the teachers were 'brigadistas' and the organisation was to military-like precision. Young city-bred students were given a little training and then sent off to the countryside to teach in people's homes. The reading level being aimed for was approximately that of first grade level, but, as we have seen, the experience was about far more than just learning to read and write. Bhola describes the pedagogy underlying the teaching:

> Methodologically, the primer combined the analytical and the synthetic approaches and taught recognition and writing of both printed and cursive letters. Each lesson began with a photo and a sentence describing the event or subject of the photo. The sentence was divided into words; words were divided into syllables; and these were, in turn, combined to make new words and sentences.
>
> (Bhola, 1984: 100)

According to, for example, a UNESCO report in 1965 and Bhola (1984), whose study of the project is published by UNESCO, illiteracy in Cuba went down from 21 per cent to 3.9 per cent during the year-long campaign. This is indeed spectacular, and made Cuba the country with the highest literacy rate in Latin America. However, some words of caution must be voiced. Firstly, in terms of how transferrable to other contexts this project might be, it is important to note the lessons of success when the government is totally committed and ready to give resources. But it is also important to remember that Cuba has a relatively small population compared with other Latin American states with high illiteracy rates, and, above all, to remember that Cuba is a monolingual country where the only language spoken is a high prestige European language. The materials are readily available to back up the literacy work, and a culture of literacy in Spanish is long-established. The same is not the case for Latin American indigenous languages. The problem (or challenge) of bilingualism is not an issue.

Moreover, we need to remember that the highly ideological nature of the project was not received well by all commentators (especially in the US administration). It could be argued that far from emancipating sectors of society who had previously been marginalised through their illiteracy, the campaign would simply indoctrinate them into another government-led conception of national (in this case, socialist) identity.

Another criticism of the campaign was of the low level of reading that was considered realistic to aspire to in the first phase. Without follow-up pro-grammes and more advanced materials, it is rightly argued that the little that has been mastered can easily be forgotten. This is when the counter-argument of the relevance of the sociopolitical nature of the programme is used to claim that this makes the programme relevant and memorable because its usefulness is understood. Torres quotes Fagan (1969) 'The cam-paign . . . was intended to mobilize and change Cuban political culture' (1990: 78).

> Other effects of the campaign were the provision of medical services for the poor (including the free supply of spectacles to illiterates needing them) and the contact between two social groups that had been separated by dependent capitalist development: the illiterate peasants and the educated urban residents.
>
> (Torres, 1990: 78)

When the 1961 campaign was over, some of its work was carried on through adult education provision which the government set up, particularly in the workplace. This, coupled with a reformed education system in general which placed far greater emphasis on providing children with the skills they would need to find and keep employment, contributes to the excellent quality of Cuban education today – amongst the best in Latin America. It has also, paradoxically, contributed to some of the current political unrest in Cuba as, forty years or so on, Castro's leadership is in its last years. There are those who might argue that the Cuban population is over-educated, with expectations amongst the graduating students being unrealistically high and impossible to satisfy.

Nonetheless, the level of political and social awareness in Cuba, linked with and coming out of the literacy rate, is admirably high, allowing the population to feel part of its society, and sharing in the project of nation-construction. This awareness, participation and creativity is certainly characteristic of the 'new literacy' we discussed in the previous chapter, and will observe in more recent examples of literacy programmes in Latin America.

Nicaragua

Almost exactly twenty years after the Cuban revolution, Nicaragua experienced a similar revolution with the overthrow of the despotic Somoza family and the installing of the Sandinista government with its radical social and political programme. Like the Cubans, the Nicaraguans considered education an important part of their programme for change, and, also like the Cubans, from long before the actual overthrow of the Somoza dynasty, Sandinistas had been giving popular education and literacy classes in 'liberated' areas. The Nicaraguan literacy campaign and subsequent adult education provision was part of what Lankshear (1997: 109) calls 'the complementary motifs of national development and social justice . . . evident across a rich array of entirely new (for Nicaraguans) policy initiatives, laws and social programmes'. Although the aims and objectives and the political environment of the Nicaraguan literacy campaign has much in common with the Cuban one, it also has some very important differences which we will comment on later.

As in Cuba, the level of educational provision and uptake in Nicaragua at the time of the revolution was very low, even in Latin American terms. Less than 40 per cent of the school age population attended schools, and around 50 per cent were illiterate, rising to 76 per cent in the rural areas (Torres, 1990). For this reason, the Sandinista government saw education and literacy as a priority on taking over power, and their minister of education (Catholic priest and poet) Fernando Cardenal was asked to lead a literacy campaign within two weeks of the overthrow of Somoza (Archer and Costello, 1990). The Sandinistas saw the need for such education in the wider context of their revolution.

This kind of social change and national development cannot simply be *donated* to a people, but must be created with and through the committed activity of marginalized groups, and be answerable to their needs and in tune with shifts in their social awareness and their capacity for informed and constructive social action. Consequently, a powerful literacy, capable of enlisting people in politically informed ways to projects of historical change was seen as absolutely central.

(Lankshear, 1997: 110)

The Nicaraguan Literacy Crusade was carried out in five months during 1981, and was described by the Sandinistas as a 'second revolution' (Archer and Costello, 1990; Torres, 1990). It was modelled on the Cuban campaign, and also the later Tanzanian one, and greatly influenced by the work of Paulo Freire who had by then been operating his methods in various parts of Latin America. Freire himself was invited by the Nicaraguan government to come to the country and advise on the literacy programme.

As with the Cuban campaign, young students were mobilised from the towns to go out to the countryside and teach in rural areas. A primer was devised, *El Amanecer del Pueblo* (The Dawn of the People), which, like its Cuban counterpart, was organised around social and political topics of the revolution. The method it followed was to take a picture or photograph and then a 'generative' word (as Freire called it), such as '*trabajo*' or '*revolución*'. The session would start by discussing the pictorial stimulus and the word's relationship to it. For this reason the words and pictures chosen were always selected to be central to the learners' experiences and to the objectives of the Sandinista social reforms. The words would then be broken down into syllables and learners would begin to recognise the different parts and rearrange them to make up different words (Archer and Costello, 1990). Freire describes his method of the generative word in a way which highlights the power and significance of language to people's daily lives.

> In our educational method, the word is not something static or disconnected from [people's] existential experience, but a dimension of their thought-language about the world. That is why when they participate critically in analysing the first generative words linked with their existential experience, when they focus on the syllabic families that result from that analysis, when they perceive the mechanisms of the syllabic combinations of their language, the learners finally discover, in the various possibilities of combination, their own words.
>
> (Freire, cited in Archer and Costello, 1990: 26)

As many commentators have noted, the literacy crusade (as it was known) produced excellent results. The illiteracy rate of around 50 per cent was reduced to at least half that number.[12] Perhaps almost as important was the way that the urban and rural communities came into contact and learnt to understand and respect one another to a far greater degree than previously. This is poignantly summed up by the comment from one *brigadista* from the city who said that after she had been living and teaching in a rural community for a while, she realised the meaning of the social change and the literacy campaign's role in it. She says 'My students learnt how to write *machete* and I learnt how to use one' (quoted in Archer and Costello, 1990: 31). The rural communities began to lose their mistrust for outsiders and to participate in the programmes. The urban dwellers began to learn about the cultural practices and beliefs of the rural communities, and to discuss these with them and learn to respect

them. In this way, the structured concept of formal classes starting at particular times with expected behaviour, gave way to the understanding that
campesinos do not necessarily use clocks, and that the day's work and the
year's harvest are more important points of reference. The common view
that women did not 'need' to become literate was discussed and challenged.[13]
Superstitions were often explained by such discoveries as poor sight requiring
glasses (Archer and Costello, 1990).

This new ownership of national identity was an important consequence of
this campaign, as we saw with the earlier Cuban one:

> The campaign produced . . . some significant results. To some extent it
> reduced the high degree of inequality between countryside and city,
> male and female, and the Atlantic and Pacific Coasts. It mobilized
> previously marginal populations into new roles related to national
> reconstruction.
>
> (Torres, 1990: 88)

It is particularly in relation to this inequality between Atlantic and Pacific
coasts that we need to draw attention to some of the significant differences
between the Nicaraguan and Cuban experiences. We may also be less certain
of how far the removal of inequalities did in fact take place as a result of the
literacy campaign.

Nicaragua is a diverse and, in places, highly inaccessible country in terms of
its geography. This has meant that over the centuries communications
between the Pacific coast and the Atlantic coast have been difficult, slow
and infrequent. As a result the two have developed from very different histories and with very different legacies (Archer and Costello, 1990; Freeland,
1993, 1995). The fact that after independence they came to form one
Nicaraguan republic is an entirely political and constructed outcome, with
few shared national characteristics apart from geographic proximity. The
Pacific coast was colonised by the Spaniards and shows all the usual
characteristics of Latin American *mestizo* (i.e. mixed-race) society with the
dominance of European-origin elites, alongside indigenous peoples, and the
inter-marrying between the two. On the Atlantic coast the colonising was
the result of the coast providing bases for British pirates originally. Britain
later established settlements along the coast to exploit some of the rich
resources found in this region, and imported African slaves to work there.
The result is a mix between the existing indigenous communities, the largest
and most dominant of which is the Miskitu one, and African-origin Creoles.
It is only really during the time of the Somoza regime that Spanish-speaking
mestizos migrated there from the Pacific coast. Until this century the
Managua-based government had little interest in the Atlantic coast and
little influence over it. Spanish, therefore, was hardly heard there. Besides
the obvious differences beween the Atlantic coast's indigenous peoples and
the Creole as opposed to the Pacific coast's Spanish-descent and *mestizo*

population – differences expressed culturally, politically and linguistically – there was also an important difference in terms of religion. The Catholic Church of the Pacific coast had not penetrated the Atlantic coast, where, invited by the British, the Moravian Church had set up a mission and led a Protestant ethos in the region since 1849. They set up schools and established a written form for Miskitu into which they translated the Bible. Up until the twentieth century also, and coinciding with a shift from British influence (and exploitation) to that of the US, the Miskitus were the dominant ethnic group in the area. Besides speaking their mother tongue, Miskitu, which was effectively a *lingua franca* in the region, many Miskitus also spoke English, which was the language of the elites. Gradually, however, the Afro-Creole community, speaking a creolised version of English, came to dominate the public life of this region. Neither, however, were Spanish-speaking and all the Atlantic coast communities resented the imposition during the Somoza era of Spanish in the local administration and the schools.

The Sandinista revolution did not immediately have the same impact on the Atlantic coast as elsewhere in Nicaragua. To this region the change of regime was just another change of government in dominant Managua. However, national integration and the spread of the revolutionary message was of course an important plank of the Sandinistas' programme which needed to include improved relations with the Atlantic coast. Initially, at least, however, the Sandinistas misjudged what this national integration might mean, displaying familiar analyses of the Indian-as-second-class-citizen who should be brought 'on stream' through Castilianisation, etc.

The Atlantic coast leaders set up a movement known as MISURASATA which brought together to fight this process activists from the three largest indigenous communities on the Atlantic coast: the Miskitus, the Sumu and the Rama. This movement fought against the imposition of Spanish as the language of the literacy crusade for the Atlantic coast, and successfully persuaded the Sandinista government seven months after the announcement of the campaign that instead mother tongue teaching (for children as well as adults) should be developed. Materials and primers were devised and classes organised, following radical Freirean methods. This indeed is the paradox, as it was precisely this experience that served to educate and sensitise the local population into understanding their position of inequality in Nicaraguan society and the lack of rights that they were accorded. As Freeland comments:

> It was a genuinely empowering experience, which so successfully applied the Freirean principles of the National Literacy Crusade that it became a turning point for Miskitu ethnic nationalism.
>
> (Freeland, 1995: 253)

The success of the political message of the literacy campaign amongst the Miskitus led to further demands for land rights which the Sandinista government interpreted as being the beginnings of a movement towards total autonomy. For this reason the Sandinistas arrested the leaders of the MISURA-SATA and brought to an end the experiment in biliteracy and bilingual education for two and a half years during which time ethnic war between the Sandinistas and the Miskitus as well as national war from the counter-revolutionaries often supported by Atlantic coast groups, took place (Archer and Costello, 1990; Freeland, 1995).

By 1987 the Sandinistas had been persuaded of the need to work with the Atlantic coast to protect Nicaraguan national identity, albeit as a far more plural and multiethnic project than they had originally conceived. In that year the Autonomy Law of the Atlantic coast was passed (Freeland, 1995). This law recognised as 'official within the region all the languages of the coast, regardless of their vitality or demographic strength, whilst maintaining Spanish as the official national language' (Freeland, 1995: 253).

The result of this Autonomy Law is to decentralise such governmental institutions as ministries of education. As a consequence education was now directed on the Atlantic coast and could respond to the Law's decree concerning languages. This has opened the way to both school-age bilingual/bicultural programmes, as well as non-formal adult education which can build on the earlier literacy campaign.

Resources to make realities of both the bilingual education and mother tongue literacy programmes on the Atlantic coast as well as the follow-up adult education programmes planned to build on the original Literacy Crusade in the rest of Nicaragua, have been severely restricted, first because of the drain on the economy of the *Contra* war, and, then, with the electoral defeat of the Sandinistas in 1990. With their fall from power and a rapid move by the new government to a free market economy, public services suffered enormous reductions in funding and support. Education, and particularly adult education, was no exception, with the adult education department shut down altogether. Schools have been starved of funds, and literacy programmes are almost non-existent. In particular the new government banned the discussion of politics in the curriculum believing the previous methods to have been too indoctrinatory. It is a sad comment on the success of the earlier Literacy Crusade that by 1993 illiteracy once again stood at 50 per cent of the population, obviously raising the question of how effective the earlier campaign really was.

The Nicaraguan experience, like the Cuban one, is clearly part of a particular political context and agenda. One question that needs answering is whether the kind of language and literacy programmes discussed here can only be successful if part of such an ideological framework. At the very least they indicate the way in which such teaching and learning is entirely dependent on the aims and objectives of the national government's agenda. In the following discussion of Guatemala, we will be able to contrast literacy work there with Nicaragua and Cuba in terms of a different national political environment.

Guatemala

Guatemala is another Latin American republic where over half the population is estimated to be of pure indigenous race. The country has rugged mountainous and tropical terrain, making communications difficult and rural isolation common. The lack of integration of this majority population into mainstream society has been reinforced by this inaccessibility. It also helps explain that, whilst the vast majority of the indigenous peoples speak languages of the Mayan family, there are marked dialectal differences, often to the point of incomprehensibility, as a result of such isolation.[14]

The marginalised Mayan population has been driven from the centres of Guatemalan society first by the Spanish colonisers, and then by the wealthy landlords of the republican period. In recent years, through particularly the 1970s and 1980s, a new repression by successive military governments forced landless peasants to join terrorist guerrilla movements in the inaccessible mountains. The violence that this led to and the murder of husbands and sons has had significant social and political consequences for the indigenous communities, many of which now find themselves led by women.

It is against this backdrop of civil conflict that various educational initiatives have taken place in Guatemala, as governments realised – as we have seen occur in other parts of Latin America – that there was a need for some integration of the vast indigenous population into mainstream Guatemalan life. Educational provision had been pitifully low in Guatemala. Richards (1989) cites Gonzales as reporting that in 1950 'almost 90% of the school-aged rural indigenous population did not attend school'. After 1965 a '*Castellanización Bilingüe*' programme was introduced in Guatemala to teach the indigenous children Spanish, but by starting out through their mother tongues (Morren, 1988; Richards, 1989). This entirely assimilationist programme was largely unsuccessful and unpopular, as it lacked appropriate materials and, especially, teachers who were bilingual in the children's mother tongues. Moreover, the indigenous communities were mistrustful of such initiatives conceived by the central government from whom they had suffered such bad treatment.

This lack of trust is an important obstacle in the various government-sponsored literacy programmes that have been tried out in the last few decades. The indigenous people had been too accustomed to ill-treatment from those known as the *Ladinos* (those of European/Spanish-speaking origin), which has been reported as taking such forms as the cheating out of land rights by using written legal documents in Spanish that the indigenous person cannot understand. Even recently this kind of treatment has been reported with women being underpaid for their goods because they cannot read the scales to know how much these weigh (Schirmer, 1993). Literacy programmes when they did exist were aimed at teaching functional literacy in Spanish and were entirely insensitive to the Mayans' cultural differences.

The National Literacy Programme at this time [1970s–80s] was, not surprisingly, committed to *castellanización*, 'adapting' the learner to different work environments and promoting an affirmation of national identity. Methods were mechanical and the programme was ignored by potential learners. . . . Reasons for failure cited by ministry sources included 'the existence of monolingual Mayan groups' and 'the lack of motivation amongst the people'. By blaming the learners and identifying self-improvement with *castellanización*, the programme failed to reach the people it was aimed at.

(Archer and Costello, 1990: 138)

A civilian government took over in 1986 (if army-backed and US-financed) which whilst not making great improvements in terms of real democratic processes did initiate a new education and literacy programme to improve the condition of the indigenous peoples. In particular, 1 per cent of the national budget was allocated towards this.

Alongside the government-backed initiatives other local self-help initiatives have also emerged. Two particularly of note for their conception and their position in the 'new literacies' mode are those organised by women's groups in reaction to their condition as widows of men murdered during the harsh counter-insurgent campaigns (Schirmer, 1993) and one using radio broadcasts (Archer and Costello, 1990; Graham-Brown, 1991). The women have set out to make certain that their movement obtain the necessary literacy skills to operate in the language of power, Spanish, and thereby defend their rights and dignity. However, as Graham-Brown (1991) notes, indigenous women are often less affected by central (Spanish) culture as they move around less and have less contact beyond the home. For them, literacy in their own mother tongues is a more sensible starting point in the discovery of the emancipating power of education. Originally this can be focused on issues of immediate relevance: the family, their health, managing their land. This has been recognised by NGOs (e.g. IDESAC) supporting women's needs in Guatemala. Later on, of course this will necessitate moving beyond their immediate locality and real empowerment will only come with access then to the literacy practices of Spanish.

The recognition of the role of learning through dialogue and discussion of real and relevant topics underlines the other interesting literacy project run by the local community themselves. This can be described as 'radioliteracy' (Archer and Costello, 1990) because it involves the setting up of a Mam (one of the Mayan groups) association ACUMAM who started to run and transmit from a local radio station. Initially they expected to broadcast in Spanish, but quickly changed to Mam, which has given this language enormously improved prestige, as well as an expanded audience. The subjects chosen for the broadcasts were all of immediate relevance to the community, such as advice on agricultural topics and on the weather. Overt discussion of literacy skills in Mam came after the relevance and interest in the broadcasts had been established. The link between indigenous language and modern technology has proved highly successful in raising the status of the language, and, therefore, people's desire to learn and use it. We might argue that this innovative experience in spreading the use of Mam (and we have noted similar experiments with Aymara and Nahuatl) could be described as a twentieth century version of Anderson's 'print-language' revolution in bringing together people in their imagined national communities. In this case, we can see a strengthening of the sense of identity amongst the Mam nation.

Conclusion

What has emerged clearly in this discussion of adult literacy programmes is that they are unlikely to succeed unless the learners feel they have some ownership of the programmes. This can often be achieved by the use of methods, such as those advocated by Paulo Freire, which emphasise participation and the taking of responsibility for the direction and objectives of the process. In order to do this, the same conditions that we suggested necessary for bicultural/intercultural education in general, need to prevail. That is, there must be some self-determination delegated to the communities involved. In the case of marginalised indigenous communities disenfranchised from mainstream (Westernised) society, this may need to take the form of decentralisation or some local government autonomy. In the case of such experiences as post-revolutionary Cuba or Nicaragua, it is the whole restructuring of social and political integration which led to a greater sense of involvement. Literacy, too, like education in general must be relevant and sensitive to the context and environments of the learners. Not only the structures and methods need to take into account local practices and cultural expectations, but the content too must seem appropriate to the life-styles and aspirations of the learners. Which language should be the medium and/or target of this learning experience will then be dictated by an analysis and understanding of what is sensitive, what is appropriate and what is aspired to.

8 Politics, language and the Spanish education system

In the previous chapter we saw how the indigenous communities of Latin America are only slowly being recognised as having rights that might be advanced through the state education systems. Whilst a few countries are beginning to pursue educational goals of bilingualism and biculturalism, most are still mainly concerned with providing efficient routes to integration and assimilation into the national core culture. In Spain, however, the radical changes brought about with the arrival of a democratic government following the Franco regime, and the introduction of the *estado de las autonomías* have meant that there is now general acceptance of the right to have educational provision in the minority languages – as long as the local government is prepared to facilitate and promote these. It also means, as we have mentioned earlier, that local governments can use the education system to promote new awareness of and respect for their community's identity in general, including linguistic features which while not actually amounting to separate languages, mark particular varieties of Spanish. The level and the quality of this educational provision does vary fairly widely.

In all the *comunidades autónomas* where a minority language is actively used some teaching of and in this language is provided for.[1] In places such as Galicia, Valencia, the Balearic Islands and parts of Navarra this usually means the teaching of Galician, Catalan and Basque respectively throughout children's schooling, with some subjects taught through the non-Castilian tongue. There are not, however, many examples in these regions of schools where the language is predominantly the non-Castilian one.[2] The curriculum does allow space and opportunity for awareness of the particular characteristics of the environment and context of that region to be enhanced. On the whole, in fact, there is a strong sense of regional identity emerging from the education systems of many of the autonomous communities, which, whilst not always focusing on language, can certainly be described as fostering a greater awareness of cultural diversity.

In Catalonia and the Basque Country the education system has been a core part of the local governments' language planning and identity-building project. The experiences and results are different in the two, as would be expected given the important differences between the two communities culturally, linguistically and historically. The role of language in the education system, and the role of the latter in local politics, however, is high profile in both. Insofar as these local education policies are potentially in conflict with the Spanish majority linguistic group, the politics of language education in the two communities take on a national focus. In both, but especially in Catalonia, the teaching of the minority language has become symbolic of many of the tensions and frictions between the autonomous governments and the central government in Madrid. The successes and failures of these policies are read by many commentators as reflections on the success and failure in general of the new Spanish political system, a system which is also watched closely by many countries under pressure to accept their multi-cultural and multilingual reality. For these reasons, the following discussion of language and education in Catalonia and the Basque Country has a significance for more than just the Spanish case.

'Igual que Franco pero al revés'? Catalan language education policies

As we have noted in earlier chapters, during most of the Franco dictatorship the teaching of Catalan was prohibited. During the sixties it became legal to include some teaching of Catalan in private schools. After the 1973 Education Act Catalan was allowed to be taught in the state sector, but only as a foreign language (like English or French, which inevitably were more popular in this role). There were, however, very few materials in Catalan, and even fewer trained teachers. This apparent softening by the regime, then, was little more than a gesture. From 1968 Catalan philology was offered at Barcelona University.

However, with the death of Franco and the *Transición* to democracy there was an immediate rush to bring Catalan fully into the education system as soon and as comprehensively as possible. In what follows we will trace the steps taken to achieve this, which has been one of the most successful examples of language reversal in recent times. As we saw in Chapter 5 Language Planning has been remarkably effective in Catalonia, the heart of this activity centring on the education programme. So successful in fact has the impact of Catalan in the local education system been that a backlash from Castilian-speakers has grown. The demands of Catalans after years of Francoist repression, on the one hand, and the opposition from some Castilian-speakers to what they interpret as an infringement of Article 3 of the 1978 Constitution, on the other, have created a debate that crystalised in the struggle to pass the new 1998 language law in Catalonia.

We will first describe the post-1975 framework that the new democratic system set up, and then examine the development of Catalan teaching in the schools and reaction to it. An important part of this provision has been a wide programme of immersion projects which we will discuss, showing how these hardened in their conception with changes in national education policy. Ultimately the discussion leads to an examination of the debates surrounding the new 1998 language law and how it has grown out of and contrasts with the 1983 law.

The legal framework for Catalan education[3]

In July 1978 a decree was issued that Catalan should form part of the official state curriculum in Catalonia. It was now a compulsory subject in all Catalonia's state schools, to be taught at least three hours per week. Courses to train teachers of Catalan were also set up at this time. It was further recognised that some schools would want to move towards a curricular programme largely taught through Catalan, in which case at least five hours of Castilian were to be offered.

In October 1979 the Catalan Statute of Autonomy was approved. Article 3 of this Statute confirms the status of Catalan as the *'llengua pròpia'*[4] of Catalonia and states in its third clause,

> The Generalitat will guarantee the normal and official use of both languages, it will adopt the necessary measures for it to be learnt and it will create conditions which allow Catalan to be completely equal in terms of the rights and duties of the citizens of Catalonia.
>
> (Catalan Statute of Autonomy; my translation)

Clearly the 'necessary measures' and 'conditions' to promote Catalan centre particularly around its provision in the education system. And as a result the Generalitat issued another decree in 1982 making three hours teaching a week of both Catalan and Castilian compulsory, plus one hour a week of a curricular subject taught through Catalan. No equivalent was stipulated for Castilian. With the drawing up of the 1983 *Llei de Normalització Lingüística* this anomaly apparently favouring Catalan disappeared.

The Normalisation Law was the most important part of Catalan language planning and formed the basis for the local government's language policies over the next fifteen years. Although it has recently been replaced by a new law, the 1983 one is the framework for much of the impetus for the development and promotion of Catalan in the years following the end of the Franco regime.

The Normalisation Law has a section dedicated to the role of the Catalan language in the education system (Articles 14–20). The underpinning principles of this role are expressed above all in Article 14, reproduced below in the English translation,

ARTICLE 14
1 Catalan, as Catalonia's own language [*llengua pròpia*], is also the language of education at all levels.

2 Children have the right to receive their primary education in their usual language,[5] whether this is Catalan or Castilian. The Administration must guarantee this right and put in place the necessary means to make this effective. Parents or guardians can exercise this right in the name of their child insisting that it should be applied.

3 The Catalan and Castilian languages must be taught as compulsory subjects at all levels and grades of non-university education.

4 All Catalonia's children, whatever their usual language on beginning their education, must be able to use Catalan and Castilian in a normal and correct fashion when they finish their basic studies.

5 The Administration must take appropriate measures so that a) pupils should not be separated into different teaching centres for reasons of language; b) the Catalan language should be progressively used as pupils start to master it.

A further interesting article states that,

ARTICLE 20
Educational centres are obliged to make Catalan the normal vehicle of expression, both in internal activities, including those of an administrative nature, and in external ones.

Embedded in these clauses are some interesting and potentially controversial principles. For example, the first clause underlines the recognition of the potential equal status of Catalan to its community by stating that it is Catalonia's 'own' language, whereas the third clause reminds us that Catalan is on no more than an equal footing with Castilian in terms of the duty to offer it in the state education system. Clause 2 enshrines the notion of the 'right to choose' in which language a child should be taught, but Clause 4 makes it clear that whichever language that might be, children must also eventually reach an equal mastery in both languages when they complete their basic (compulsory) education. Clause 5 is especially interesting as it stresses the idea that educational segregation should not be allowed to take place, and that children should be able to learn together regardless of their mother tongue and their language preferences. But it also implies that the expected expansion in the command of Catalan should be reflected by it being more widely introduced throughout the education system. Article 20 in fact makes it clear that Catalan should normally be the vehicular language in schools.

When the 1983 language law was passed, support for its objectives was enormous. Only one delegate in the local Catalan parliament voted to abstain from the new law. This was, after all, only eight years after the end of the Franco dictatorship and very many still identified political democratisation in general with the upgrading and promotion of the minority languages in particular.

Catalan teaching had initially to face various problems of the sort familiar to minority language communities when trying to promote their language: a shortage of trained teachers, a low level of literacy skills in the mother tongue amongst teachers, few materials, and the continuing dominance of the majority language throughout the Spanish state (and world-wide). A further problem was the uneven balance between private and public education in Catalonia. The former tended to be more Catalanised, and, therefore, to cream off the teachers and pupils who could provide the native Catalan-speakers' input into the state schools, which were attempting to integrate non-Catalan speakers into a bilingual/bicultural society. The distribution of Catalan and predominantly Castilian-speaking communities was not only uneven at the socio-economic level, but also geographically. Large concentrations of Castilian-speaking migrants from poorer parts of Spain meant that the pupils in schools in some areas (particularly in the industrial belt around Barcelona) were almost entirely Castilian-speaking.

In areas where there were high numbers of native Catalan-speakers, such as the province of Girona, the schools quickly moved towards predominantly Catalan environments and programmes in the schools, starting by introducing one or two more subjects taught through the medium of Catalan and moving towards the majority of the curriculum in Catalan. This often took the form of following a cohort through the school that built up the provision of Catalan as they progressed. It must of course be remembered that a minimum of three hours of teaching of Castilian and another hour of teaching a subject in Castilian had to continue, as was also the case for Catalan in the predominantly Castilian-speaking schools.

The incentives and means to create such Catalan-dominant environments in schools in areas where the migrant population was high were largely absent. The implementation of the new language education policy was, therefore, somewhat patchy initially. Nonetheless, the attitudes of parents to their children being taught Catalan were largely positive, recognising as they did that Catalan was indeed the dominant language within Catalonia itself in terms of prestige, local culture, and economic success. In 1986 a survey of parents found that 81 per cent believed that it was 'very beneficial' for their children to learn Catalan at school (Strubell and Romani, 1986). It is significant that a survey commissioned by the Catalan daily *Avui* in 1994 showed that 98 per cent of those interviewed wanted their children to be taught Catalan, and in the same year another by the Madrid-based *Centro de Investigaciones Sociológicas* showed that 96 per cent believed that everyone living in Catalonia should understand Catalan (Mar-Molinero, 1995).

In order then to meet this need to learn Catalan but in environments which were not always particularly conducive to this, the Catalan department of education decided to introduce immersion method schooling in Catalan. As we saw in Chapter 6 this method of teaching children through the target language, which is not their mother tongue, from the start of their schooling, with bilingual teachers, should be a voluntary commitment between school and parents. This programme was originally introduced in the school year 1983–84 in schools in Santa Coloma de Gramanet on the outskirts of Barcelona with a very high Castilian-speaking working-class population. This model has been developed and expanded enormously over the years since then (Arenas, 1986; Artigal, 1993).

In the same sense that the Spanish state had accepted the principle of decentralisation and '*autonomía*' after the death of Franco, so too was this explored in education policies. Apart from substantial delegation of education organisation to local government level, educational thinking at national level underwent important reform in the early nineties. The resulting new law was the *Ley Orgánica de Ordenación General del Sistema Educativo*, or LOGSE. One of the reforms implied in this law was the recognition that school curricula should be able to reflect more explicitly the features of their immediate environments and respond to their local community needs. The exact nature of the curricular goals and content was to be left to individual schools following basic principles outlined in the LOGSE. The Generalitat immediately interpreted this as encouragement for the promotion of Catalan culture, language and identity. The Generalitat issued a decree in March 1992 that underlined the link between Catalan as '*llengua pròpia*' of the region and the need to reflect this in the school curriculum. To this end it declared the immersion programmes as an essential part of the community's education policy. As a result these programmes have become the core of the local government's policy in setting out to extend the learning of Catalan more aggressively amongst predominantly Castilian-speaking communities in Catalonia. From the school year 1993–94, the Generalitat brought into force also its decree that Catalan 'would normally be used as the vehicular language and the language of instruction in compulsory infant, primary and secondary education' (cited in Milian i Massana, 1992: 352). This constitutes an important change in the apparent level of compulsion to learn Catalan. Of course much depends on the meaning of 'normally' which, in theory, taken in conjunction with the constitutional right, both under the national constitution and under the 1983 language law, for children (or their parents) to choose in which language they should be educated should mean that children can still demand to have the major part of their education in Castilian, so long as they learn Catalan and reach the necessary standard in it. However, in practice, the Generalitat's main way of implementing the decree for this extended use of Catalan was through a more rigid use of the immersion system. It seems to some that the voluntary aspect of this method has been discarded, despite that being one of the main cornerstones of the method (see Artigal, 1993 and the discussion in Chapter 6).

It was inevitable that this change in attitude by the local government towards the teaching of Catalan would lead to some tension amongst non-Catalan speakers in Catalonia. It also coincided with changes in the political configuration of the central government in Madrid which moved the tensions to a more centre-stage position in terms of Spanish politics. In the following part we will examine the debate that emerged both as it was conducted (some might say, directed) in the media, and how it was challenged in the courts.

The language backlash[6]

As a result of this marked change of attitude in the policies regarding promoting Catalan through the schools, various individuals and organisations began to campaign against what they regarded as an unacceptable level of obligatory Catalan teaching. Some of this opposition came from Catalans within Catalonia, most came from non-Catalans, both within and outside of Catalonia. Much can be seen as a direct consequence of national politics, whilst some is at a more personal or a more ideological and philosophical level.

At the political level it is important to note that in June 1993 the socialist PSOE government of Felipe González which had been in power since 1982 lost its overall majority and in order to retain control of the government had to rely on the votes of smaller parties. In particular the PSOE and the ruling Catalan Centrist party in Catalonia, Convergència i Unió, led by the skilful Catalanist politician Jordi Pujol, arrived at a pact. It was widely claimed in certain quarters that part of the deal was a more aggressive and proactive language policy in Catalonia to promote Catalan, in return for CiU support. This was certainly the opinion of the Madrid right-wing daily *ABC* which published on 12 September 1993 a now-famous condemnation of Pujol and his administration with the headline '*Igual que Franco pero al revés: persecución del castellano en Cataluña*' ('The same as Franco but the other way round: the persecution of Castilian in Catalonia'). In the following article and the newspaper's editorial of that date *ABC* argued that the level of Catalan teaching now being 'imposed' in Catalan schools made the situation in Catalonia comparable with that of the suppression of Catalan in schools during the Franco regime.

The debate that opened up at this time regarding the language rights of Castilian-speakers in Catalonia is important, and, at a more general level, unusual. It is unusual because it is very rare to find instances of majority language speakers (in terms of the national state configuration) feeling persecuted and oppressed by the minority language community. There is of course the potential for similarities in any part of the world where minority language planning is active and successful, as majority language speakers feel threatened. The case is already evident with English-speakers in Quebec, and to some extent English-speakers in Wales. Often it is a perception rather than a sustainable reality in terms of threat. The accusations that Spanish is beginning to dominate in parts of the US is a case in point. Many Catalans will refute the accusations in Catalonia too as being simply perception and not reality.

Most commentators have not seen the issue in such controversial and strident terms as *ABC* and there was a great deal of quiet support for the

Catalan language policies. Some in the Catalan media felt the need to counter the *ABC* campaign which continued over many months with articles by prominent critics of the language policies and with endless 'letters to the editor' on the subject. Those disagreeing with the *ABC* stance considered it politically-motivated and an implicit attack on the overall *autonomías* policy of which language was a symbolic element. *La Vanguardia* wrote the day following the initial *ABC* attack,

> Lamentablemente a estas alturas de la democracia española, las tintas siguen bajando turbias en una determinada prensa . . . La imaginación de estos anticatalanistas no se limita a cargar las tintas con una supuesta conspiración mercantilista del catalanismo. Cualquier campo es bueno. Y un ejemplo paradigmático es el duro ataque lanzado en su edición de ayer por el diario *ABC* contra la normalización lingüística en Cataluña.[7]

This is a Barcelona-based Castilian language daily which is centre-right in its political philosophy. It concluded the article by saying,

> Lo más grave del asunto es que manifestaciones tan irresponsables como éstas sólo contribuyen a echar más leña al fuego. . . . Ignoran la buena convivencia social existente . . . y alimentan la incomprensión hacia Cataluña y el Estado de las Autonomías.[8]

On 14 September 1993, two days on from the *ABC* article, the Barcelona-based *El Observador* declared, 'Detrás de estas difamaciones se esconde la intención de desestablizar la convivencia en Catalunya' ('Behind these defamations hides the intention to destabilise the coexistence in Catalonia'). And on the same date the Catalan daily *Avui* under the headline '*L'abc de la falsedat*', reported that all the Catalan political parties had denied that there was discrimination towards Castilian in Catalonia, including, even, the Catalan wing of the right-wing *Partido Popular* (Mar-Molinero, 1995). Even the Madrid-based national dailies *El Mundo* and *El País* maintained low-key positions regarding the debate, but generally supported the teaching of Catalan.

However, opposition, albeit from a (vociferous) minority, did now exist towards the language normalisation policy and the education programme in particular, and it was beginning to make itself heard. Amongst these were various organisations usually made up of active parents, or, in one case, teachers. The best known and most active have been CADECA (*Coordinadora de Afectados en Defensa de la Lengua Castellana*), *Acción Cultural Miguel de Cervantes*, and the *Asociación por la Lengua Española en la Administración de la Justicia* (Branchadell, 1997; Mar-Molinero, 1995). A leading spokesman for the campaigns launched by these groups is the lawyer Estéban Gómez Rovira. Gómez Rovira was instrumental in challenging parts of the 1983 language law through the Catalan High Court, the Spanish Supreme Court and ultimately the Spanish Constitutional Tribunal. The challenge was principally over the constitutionality of requiring children to learn Catalan (and thereby reducing the amount of Castilian they might learn) based on the first clause of Article 3 of the 1978 Constitution which describes Castilian as *'la lengua oficial del estado'*. Interestingly, whilst the Catalan High Court in February 1994 defended the normalisation law in general, it did criticise the Generalitat for not always enforcing the rights of Castilian-speaking children to be taught in their mother tongue. They did however endorse the principle of not having separate and segregated streams of schools for the two languages. Spain's Supreme Court was less convinced of the constitutionality of the normalisation law and referred it to the Constitutional Tribunal. This latter eventually upheld the disputed clauses regarding the language of education in December 1994. The argument revolved around the interpretation of the constitutionality of requiring children to learn 'official' languages other than that of the Spanish state, and the right of children (and/or their parents) to choose in which between the official languages they would be taught at different stages of their compulsory education.[9]

The contention regarding the consitutionality of the language laws and the disquiet on the part of some in Catalonia as the education system became more Catalanised, is based on various principles and beliefs. For example, the right to be taught in a child's mother tongue, which we have previously noted was supported since the 1950s by UNESCO amongst other international organisations, was considered by opponents to be denied by the immersion method. The issue of individual rights versus collective rights was also, once again, important to the debate. The opponents of the language teaching policies believed that the individual right of the Castilian-speaking child should take precedence over the collective right of Catalonia to pursue policies that defended its territorial entity. Attached to this territorial entity is the concept of the *'llengua pròpia'*: the connection between *'pròpio'* ('own') and *'propietat'* ('ownership'/'property') is made with the collective group 'owning' its language.

The 1998 Llei de Política Lingüística

On 7 January 1998 the Catalan Parliament passed by a majority of 80 per cent of its deputies a new law on language policy, replacing the 1983 Normalisation Law. This approval came after lengthy consultation and debate about the new law, including opposition from those groups who we have noted believed that the language policy in Catalonia was detrimental to their children's language education.

One of the most important changes in emphasis in the new law was a clarification of the meaning and significance of *'llengua pròpia'*. The second article of the new law states that *'El català es la llengua pròpia de Catalunya i la singularitza com a poble'* ('Catalan is Catalonia's own language and this [the language] distinguishes it [Catalonia] as a people') (my translation). In the Preamble to the law this is further expanded:

> La llengua catalana és un element fonamental de la formació i la personalitat nacional de Catalunya, un instrument bàsic de comunicació, d'integració i de cohesió social dels ciutadans i ciutadanes . . . A més ha estat el testimoni de fidelitat del poble català envers la seva terra i la seva cultura específica.
>
> (*Llei 1/1998 de 7 de gener, de la política lingüística,* reproduced in *Llengua i Dret,* 1998: 267)[10]

Such a defining role for language in the character of the nation is reminiscent of the relationship between language and national identity that we discussed in Part I, and follows the tradition of such Catalan politicians as Prat de la Riba. It is important in the discussion of education as it has been understood to mean that the 'normal' situation in the school environment should be the use of Catalan. Of course, there are those who claim that although they live and work in Catalonia, their mother tongue, and therefore their *'llengua pròpia'* is Castilian, and that Catalonia should acknowledge the existence of two such languages in recognition of its residents' personality rights, rather than identifying with collective territorial rights.

It is one of the most significant points in the new law that only Catalan is the *'llengua pròpia'* and that the status of Castilian is protected, instead, through a clear definition in this law of 'double officiality'. Article 3 of the new law states that 'Catalan is the official language of Catalonia, as is also Castilian'. The second clause of this article goes on to say,

> El català i el castellà, com a llengües oficials, poden esser emprades indistintamente pels ciutadans i ciutadanes en totes les activitats públiques i privades sense discriminació.[11]

In this way the law seeks to protect individual rights, whilst the concept of *'llengua pròpia'* protects collective rights of the territory of Catalonia. In the Preamble to the law it states,

> Pel que fa a l'ensenyament, aquesta Llei garanteix a tota la població el ple coneixement de les dues llengües i, alhora, garanteix que l'alumnat no sigui discriminat ni separat en grups diferents per raó de la llengua . . .[12]

Articles 20–24 of the new law refer to matters of education and language. Article 21 is in fact very similar to the earlier Article 14 of the 1983 law. However, one substantial difference is the fact that not only, as in the earlier law, are children expected to reach a level of mastery in the two languages, but students will now not be given their secondary school graduation certificate unless they can prove sufficient competence in oral and written Catalan and Castilian (Article 21, Clause 6).

> L'apartat 6 de l'article 21, quan estableix el requisit d'acreditació del coneixement de les dues llengües oficials per obtenir el títol de graduat en educació secundària, és probablement la clau de volta del model lingüístic de la doble oficialitat. D'una banda, garanteix a tots els ciutadans el coneixement de les dues llengües i, d'altra banda, garanteix a tots els ciutadans el seu dret d'elecció entre les dues sense subordinació.
> (Jou i Mirabent, 1998: 21)[13]

Article 20, clause 1, again states that as Catalan is the '*llengua pròpia*' of Catalonia, it is the language of education at all levels and in all types. Whilst this echoes what was said in the 1983 law, the more explicit and coherent meaning given to '*llengua pròpia*' in the new law, has greatly strengthened the interpretation here that Catalan will be expected to be the language of all communications as well as instruction in Catalonia's schools. For this not to be the 'normal' situation now would need to be challenged and justified. Whereas previously schools had tended to reflect their local community's linguistic profile in terms of which language dominated, although frequently with a willingness to introduce more Catalan, now the default position is clearly that of Catalan. And it is for this reason that the opponents of such strong support for Catalan are unhappy and claim that children in Catalonia are losing their opportunities to learn Castilian effectively. Recently this opposition has been joined at national level by the Minister of Education, Esperanza Aguirre, reflecting the more right-wing position of the new government which took over after the 1996 general election. This government is formed by the right-wing Partido Popular, but without an overall majority, once again depends on Jordi Pujol's CiU to stay in power.

The political role that the Catalans play in helping the central Spanish government of the day has, ironically, allowed them to exert significant pressure in maintaining and promoting the vigorous language normalisation policies, not least in the area of education. We are reminded, once again, of how politics always lies at the heart of language issues.

Since the death of Franco in 1975 there has been a marked change in the attitudes to and the provision of Catalan in the education system. From its tentative re-introduction in the seventies it has been transformed into the principal language of the Catalan education system. Some argue that this has a detrimental effect on the learning and use of Castilian, and thereby infringes both the child's constitutional rights and also their opportunities in the wider national (and international) arena. Those supporting the language education policies will argue that a 'normalisation' of Catalan is the native right of Catalans and that it can only be achieved by relatively aggressive action if it is to compete on equal terms with the far more widely spoken state language. They argue that no child in Catalonia can possibly be deprived of learning Castilian since it is still the dominant state language, widely heard and read in the media and the mother tongue of nearly half Catalonia's population.

The debate over language education policies in Catalonia challenges many of the issues of linguistic rights that we have already outlined: the conflicting rights of a community over an individual's rights; the need for political autonomy in order to influence linguistic rights; the role of the education system in determining the sociolinguistic profile of the community. A further complicating factor in the tension between Catalan and Castilian is that of the increasing presence of North African immigrants. Until the seventies Spain had virtually no experience of the non-European immigration which in other parts of Europe is so common. The relative economic buoyancy of Catalonia in the seventies attracted particularly Moroccans, often illegally, to live in above all Barcelona and surrounding areas. The children of these immigrants often spoke neither Castilian nor Catalan and have presented major problems to the local education policy makers in terms of curricular philosophy (Boogerman Castejón, 1997). Whether Catalonia wants to, or can, offer a truly multicultural education to its citizens is acutely challenged by these newest arrivals, although, for the moment, numbers are small. It is a challenge which could potentially be very uncomfortable for the more aggressive Catalan-teaching policies. Those counter-arguments used to dismiss demands for more mother-tongue rights for Castilian-speaking children on the grounds that Castilian is the state's majority language and widely-spoken and heard simply cannot be asserted in the context of demands for mother-tongue teaching for Moroccan immigrants. Many international bodies are firmly committed to the teaching of such community languages to the children of immigrants, and these are precisely the same international bodies to whom the Catalans look for support and approval in their campaign to promote their own (minority) language.

Bilingual education in the Basque autonomous community

The other area besides Catalonia where language planning has been most active since the death of Franco is the Basque Country. Although much of the process and trajectory is similar to that outlined in the case of Catalan, the foundation on which the teaching of Basque was based, the progress and the resulting successes and failures are inevitably different. Judged within its own context the education programme here is no less radical than the Catalans', but compared with the latter, the changes and statistics are far less spectacular. For this reason, too, the impact on the politics of the region, and of the state in general, has been less felt than the consequences of the Catalan education programmes.

Below we will outline the steps that have been taken in recent decades to teach Basque and assess its effect in the overall language normalisation effort in particular, and to the Basque autonomous community in general. Although Basques consider Navarra a part of the Basque Country, and parts of this region do contain Basque-speakers, we will not include Navarra in the discussions here. Some Basque education is certainly offered in the Basque-speaking areas of Navarra, but, given the very minority nature of the language there, this has not developed to anything like the level of provision found in the Basque autonomous community (BAC), and considerably less than in Catalonia.

The demand for Basque teaching: from Ikastolas *to the normalisation programme*

Unlike Catalan, Basque did not have a strong tradition as a written, literary language of the educated elites, and therefore the suppression of the language in the majority of the Franco years was an even greater threat to its survival. Nonetheless the very harshness of the repression of Basque culture and its language served to make people aware of the need to protect the symbols of their culture. As we noted earlier, the Basque language had not originally formed a major part in the sense of Basque national identity, but its potential elimination and the general hostility from the Franco regime to all things Basque persuaded many of the need to teach their children Basque before it was too late (Tejerina, 1996).

In response to this perceived need and indeed as an act of political defiance towards the Franco dictatorship a series of semi-clandestine Basque medium schools were created (or in some cases, reactivated from the Republican period), known as *Ikastolas* in the 1960s. The popularity of these schools, which had eventually to be tolerated by the Franco government, can be seen in the increase in numbers attending them and the growth in such centres.[14] Tejerina (1996: 228) observes an increase from 596 students attending these schools in 1964 to 26,936 in 1974, and an expansion from three centres in 1960 to 160 in 1975. Nonetheless even these higher numbers represented less than 10 per cent of the BAC student population (Gobierno Vasco, 1990). It must be remembered that although there was now an increased political solidarity with the idea of teaching and learning the Basque language than there had been previously, there were still many, particularly amongst the urban middle classes, who were not convinced of the need to protect and use Basque. Less than a quarter of the population of the BAC spoke Basque, and, as we will see, this figure has only increased slightly since the death of Franco.

The constitutional and legal framework to emerge after the death of Franco upon which language policies and education policies could be developed is almost identical in the BAC as in Catalonia. In 1979 the Basque autonomous community was given its statute where, in Article 6, it states that

Basque [*Euskera*] as the Basque Country's own language [*lengua propia*] will have, as with Castilian, the character of official language within Euskadi, and all its inhabitants will have the right to know and use both languages.

It goes on to say that besides guaranteeing the use of both languages and regulating for their official status, that the autonomous community will also regulate and provide the 'necessary means and measures to ensure knowledge of them' (Article 6). This the local government must clearly provide through the education system.

In October 1982 the Basque Government published its own language law, the *Ley de la Normalización del Uso de Euskera*. With a slightly different title from the equivalent Catalan law, this, nonetheless, has a great deal in common with the Catalan one – as indeed it does also with the Galician one. As regards education, it decrees that Euskera and Castilian shall be compulsory subjects from kindergarten to pre-university studies. It also establishes three separate models of bilingual education from which parents and children may choose. These reflect the varying objectives of bilingual education that we have previously discussed, from a minimal provision of some second language teaching as part of the overall curriculum, to total immersion in the target language.

Because the letter 'C' does not exist in Basque the models were labelled A, B, and D.[15] Model A is a programme basically for Castilian-speakers but with Basque taught as a subject within the curriculum. Its objectives as regards the learning of Basque are summarised as follows:

- entender bien el euskera,
- capacitar al alumno para que pueda expresarse en los temas cotidianos más sencillos,
- afianzar la actitud favorable hacia el euskera,
- capacitar al alumno para que pueda insertarse en un medio eskaldún.
(Gobierno Vasco, 1990: 14)[16]

Model B offers a programme of roughly half and half in both target languages, although it is primarily aimed at making Castilian-speakers proficient in Basque. The languages are both media of instruction as well as curricular subjects. In this model the Gobierno Vasco (1990: 15) describes the linguistic objectives as:

- facilitar al alumno, además de un buen nivel de comprensión del euskera, una capacitación adecuada para desenvolverse en dicho idioma,
- capacitarlo para continuar sus estudios en euskera.[17]

And finally the Model D is an educational programme totally in Basque with Castilian only offered as a curricular subject. It was expected that this would primarily serve Basque mother tongue speakers, but, in fact, it has attracted quite a few Castilian-speakers wanting an immersion method of learning Basque. Its objectives are described as the following:

- afianzar la competencia en euskera, enriqueciendo su conocimiento de la misma y haciendo que sea su idioma coloquial además de lengua escolar vehicular,
- reforzar el colectivo de alumnos euskaldunes, a fin de contrarrestar la presión idiomática predominante en el entorno social y afianzar su carácter crucial en la consecución del bilingüismo generalizado,
- garantizar un conocimiento adecuado del castellano.

(Gobierno Vasco, 1990: 15)[18]

The challenges for the teaching of Basque are in many senses greater than for the teaching of Catalan, not only because the pool of native speakers is so much smaller and the prestige amongst the elites historically less, but also because with little literary tradition, the necessary materials for the education system did not exist. Even fewer appropriately trained teachers were available, requiring a major re-training programme. Also, Basque is a much more difficult language for Castilian speakers to learn than Catalan, with competence taking much longer to achieve.

Nonetheless, since the introduction of these types of bilingual education in the Basque Country from 1982, the most significant feature has been the decrease in students enrolling on the Model A programmes and the corresponding increase of those on Model B and D schemes (Artigal, 1993; Cenoz, 1998; and Gobierno Vasco, 1990). The models are in theory fully available throughout the region and in both the private and public sectors. In reality there are certain areas where the sociolinguistic context has meant less choice. Cenoz points out:

Model A currently includes less than half as many students as in 1982 (75% v. 34%) while Models B and D which use Basque as the language of instruction have seen a significant increase, from 25% in 1982 to 73% in 1996–97.

(Cenoz, 1998: 177)

In its own way this represents almost as dramatic an increase in the use of Basque as the language of education as the similar increase that we noted with Catalan in schools in Catalonia. In particular it must be remembered how relatively few Basque mother tongue speakers exist in the BAC, where there is also a significant proportion of the population who have emigrated from some other part of the Spanish state and are Castilian monolingual speakers (Fishman, 1991: 180).

The current vitality of Basque language education

The prestige of Basque is nothing like as high as Catalan amongst its community, but the vigorous Language Planning activities in the region have helped raise it. In particular the need to pass exams in Basque for certain desirable public sector jobs has been an important incentive. In general, too, a pride in the culture of the local region in an era where globally there is significant revival in awareness and respect for local identities has also encouraged parents to want their children to learn the local language, which many did not ever have the opportunity to learn themselves.

This interest in learning the language and about the culture is reflected too in the provision of and enrolment on expanding adult Basque classes and renewed celebrations of Basque festivals and games (MacClancy, 1996; Tejerina, 1996). In 1977 a group known as AEK (*Alfabetatze Euskalduntze Koordinakundea*) was established which coordinated night school courses for Basque literacy and education on a community and cooperative basis. As MacClancy notes:

> Teachers insert their groups into the social milieux of the area where the course is held, students being taken, for example, on visits to local organisations and businesses in order to practise their Euskera. . . . For a tenet of AEK is that a language dies, not because people do not know it, but because those who do know it do not use it, or do not use it in a quotidian manner.
>
> (MacClancy, 1996: 212)

This was a very successful and active movement, keen to promote Basque and Basque culture and to operate at the level of 'the people'. It was also a very radical movement and has sometimes been accused of only being interested in certain kinds of marginalised groups in Basque society. As demand for learning Basque grew, there was some criticism of the lack of professional underpinning of much of the AEK structure, and the Basque government set up a rival organisation, known as HABE, which was more expensive but offered the language qualifications required for public sector jobs. There has been a conflictive relationship between these two organisations which is symbolic of the tensions that can arise when local communities set out to expand and promote their cultures and languages. It is the tension between leading from the top with government resources or relying on grass-roots enthusiasm and energies. As MacClancy writes:

> At the root of this continuing controversy are contrasting conceptions of the roles the two Euskera-teaching institutions play in the contemporary Basque Country. We might say that while HABE has the restricted, somewhat 'technical' aim of promoting the speaking of Euskera, AEK has broader aims: teaching people *Batua* (the standardised Basque

finally agreed upon by Basque linguists) and raising their nationalist consciousness.

(MacClancy, 1996: 213)

This conflict can also be represented – once again – as that between individuals and the social collectivity, between small groups and institutions. Defenders of HABE, the government organisation, argue that this is a more legitimate, democratic organisation than the somewhat abitrary AEK cooperatives. Tejerina (1996) discusses what he sees as a shift from 'individual responsibility' and 'personal awareness' to 'public institutions'. He rightly links this shift in language and language teaching policies with the wider shift in politics in post-Franco Spain:

> The process of political rationalisation through the *Estado de las Autonomías* . . . entitled the Basque Government to find solutions to social demands. . . . The presence of a resourceful government shifted the centre of gravity of the linguistic recovery from the sphere of social movements to the sphere of institutions. The control of different resources along with the power to plan and carry out linguistic policies created a subsidiary relationship . . . between the government and the initiatives that arose in the civil society.
>
> (Tejerina, 1996: 235)

Conclusion

The degree of institutionalisation and potential removal of responsibility from the people is an issue that we have observed in the attempts to promote language rights in many parts of the world. It is a complex and sometimes paradoxical situation which on the one hand requires popular involvement and empowerment, and on the other hand political control and resources. In both the Basque Country and Catalonia at present an impartial observer might wonder if the institutionalised power of the politicians and language planners is not directing the agenda to the exclusion of more grassroots level popular support. It is a delicate balance, which appears still to be holding, and holding well in Catalonia in particular. But unexpected or unwelcoming factors may shake this balance, be they the arrival of significant non-European immigrants with new language needs, or the pressure to learn English that increasingly challenges the language curricula in both regions (see e.g. Cenoz, 1998).

Meanwhile judged by the criterion of increased speakers of the two minority languages, both regions should claim success for their language education policies. As we noted earlier (Chapter 5) 94 per cent of Catalonia's population understand Catalan, and 75 per cent speak it. In the Basque Country the figures for understanding and speaking Basque are considerably lower – approximately 27 per cent (Cenoz, 1998) – the significant data as far as language educators are concerned is the increase in young people speaking Basque (Garmendía, 1994). To many watching the post-Franco language policies in Spain, the learning of Catalan and Basque are encouraging success stories.

Part IV

Language politics in the new millennium: the outlook for Spanish

9   Spanish as minority language

In this last section of the book we will discuss the relationship of politics and language in today's world and speculate on the future. A postmodern world, a place of globalisation, poses challenges to the conventional role of language politics as it does also to the status of the nation and of nationalism. Within this context we want to examine the likely future for the Spanish language in particular. Questions arise as to whether Spanish can be categorised as a world language and what that means. What will its relationship be with English? To what extent is Spanish still expanding its numbers of mother tongue speakers and is it competing in the global market? And in which parts of the world will the presence of Spanish be more marked and significant?

In this chapter we will look at an area where Spanish has indeed increased its presence and its influence in recent years and where all figures point to this as a continuing trend, that is, in the United States. Here, however, for the first time in our discussions, Spanish is not the language of the majority group, neither in numerical terms, nor in terms of power and prestige. On the contrary, Spanish-speakers in the US are in their vast majority marginalised, poor and perceived as inferior to their white 'Anglo' fellow-citizens. Despite being a minoritised community displaying many of the characteristics we have previously observed with indigenous minority groups in other parts of Spanish-speaking America, this group is already the fourth largest Spanish-speaking community in the world, and set to rise higher still. It is predicted that by the middle of the next century, US *Latinos* could number more than the entire population of Spain (*ABC*, 15.6.1998; Fishman, 1991).

In this chapter we will trace the recent history of this Spanish-speaking US population and discuss some of its specific features. In particular we will examine the legislation underpinning language policies which have affected these Spanish-speakers. Nation-building, language rights, language legislation and language education all come together in this discussion of US identity and its uneasy relationship with this large immigrant community. In the second part of the chapter we will also investigate the particular situation of the Puerto Ricans, whose special status in relation to the US is highlighted in the symbolic role of language in the politics of the island. If the proximity of the less-privileged regions of Latin America to their wealthy and powerful neighbour has been responsible for the contemporary waves of Spanish-speaking immigrants, the unique situation of Puerto Rico has developed this phenomenon into a circular 'returning migrant' syndrome. The implications for language are obvious and important.

The *Latinos* in the US

Spanish-speakers now make up the largest immigrant community in the US. Estimates of the numbers vary widely depending how the significant groups of illegal migrant workers who come and go across the Mexican-US border are counted. However, the 1996 US census reports 32 million of Hispanic origin, which is about 12 per cent of the total US population. It is also a notable increase on earlier census figures, reflecting continued immigration and, importantly, a high birth rate amongst this community. It is reported that the growth rate in the past decade amongst those of Hispanic origin is 38 per cent as opposed to the US national average of 9 per cent. The forecasts for the next half century or so embrace this continuing increase overtaking American blacks as the second ethnic group after whites. In cities such as Los Angeles, San Francisco, New York, Houston and Miami they will be (if they are not already) the largest ethnic group. By 2020 it is predicted that the two largest states in the US, California and Texas, will have more of Hispanic origin than any other ethnic group amongst their large populations. This trend of Hispanic dominance will, it is forecast, be followed by the next most populated states, which will by then be Florida, New York and Illinois, in that order.[1] However, it is important to note that of this Hispanic, Spanish-speaking population it is estimated that at the most, only a mere 3 per cent do not speak some English (Zentella, 1997b), and that the inter-generational transmission of Spanish to second and third generation immigrants is very low (Fishman, 1991).

A constant misconception is to assume that all Spanish-speaking Americans can be lumped together as a homogenous group. On the contrary they come from many varying backgrounds, with the Mexican community the largest, followed by Puerto Ricans and Cubans. In 1996 the respective percentage of the overall Hispanic-origin population for these three groups was 63 per cent, 12 per cent and 8 per cent. There are immigrants from other parts of Latin America (a growing group being Dominicans) and from Spain. There are also important communities living in the Southwest, particularly in New Mexico, Arizona and Colorado, who are of Spanish origin pre-dating Anglo-Americans (Dicker, 1996: Chapter 2). This part of the US was colonised by Spain and then formed part of Mexico until the middle of the nineteenth century. Some of the older members of this Spanish-speaking community still tend to think of themselves as 'Spanish' rather than *Latino* or even Mexican.

Inevitably the immigrant groups tend to concentrate in particular areas, and where others from their place of origin live. California, Texas and the Southwest in general are therefore host to the Mexican Americans, and the Mexican-US border sees a steady stream of migrants, often illegal. Puerto Ricans are found principally in New York and surrounding areas, whilst Florida is home to most Cuban Americans.

As we have seen many of these have migrated to the US in search of work and better living conditions. They are poor, undereducated, frequently of black or Indian race, and live on the edges of society. Many Cubans, on the other hand, are refugees from Castro's Cuba and tend instead to be white and middle class. This latter group has often resented being linked with the image of the illiterate, impoverished 'black' Hispanic.

The rise of Hispanophobia

The discrimination and antagonism that these groups have suffered, particularly in recent decades, however, have led them to recognise their similarities and common cause (Zentella, 1997b). They have come to accept the need to unite in a common struggle for their basic rights — including linguistic ones — and to accept the general label of '*Latino*' to identify them. Nonetheless, their cultural, historical and social differences remain, and are often reflected too in linguistic differences.[2]

The creation of the United States is of course a prime example of conscious nation-building as a result of its history of a 'melting pot' of diverse immigration. From its early days of independence much of both its legislation and its cultural traditions have revolved round the aim of creating national identity, bringing together the different communities and races to forge one sense of American-ness. This is achieved through assimilation and integration into the dominant norm whilst discarding previous cultural and historical baggage. Language has been one such piece of baggage which is usually abandoned as immigrants have eagerly learnt, or have their children learn, English. Language policies as such were few or non-existent; nowhere in the Constitution is mention made of an official or national language. Only recently in fact has legislation affecting language begun to emerge. But, nonetheless, the role of language in American identity-construction is significant.[3] In three areas in particular language policies and language legislation have been important: the language of the education system, the language of government, and the language of employment.

Large waves of immigrants not speaking English, combined with the needs of industrialisation and urbanisation, at the end of the nineteenth and the beginning of the twentieth century had led to some quite radical — and restrictive — legislation being introduced at state level, although this was frequently subsequently overturned by the Supreme Court. Language at this point was indeed symbolic of many people's view of national unity. As Trueba writes:

> Between 1919 and 1925, in states that managed to pass laws against the use of languages other than English in school, at the ballot box, and in the employment office, the state courts sentenced over 1,000 individuals to jail for subversive speech, which was presumed to make individuals suspicious and dangerous. Thousands of cases were litigated between 1920 and 1950 on the grounds that the use of languages other than English was indicative of 'clear and present danger'. Thus, the power of the state to restrain free speech was justified on the basis of the state's right to prevent potential disorder and crimes, as well as to prevent national anarchy fostered by language diversity . . .
>
> (Trueba, 1989: 85)

The latter part of this period also coincided with the McCarthy era in US history, and it is perhaps no surprise that the end of this period followed by the Civil Rights era saw a liberalising of attitudes and laws concerning the use of languages other than English. It is also at this time – the sixties onwards – that the start of the heavy influx of Hispanic immigration began. Much of the language legislation from this point on, both in favour of linguistic diversity and, more recently, to curb it, has been above all aimed at the Spanish-speaking community.

In 1967 Congress introduced a major bilingual education bill which sought to authorise bilingual education in public schools, and the need for mother tongue teaching to linguistic minority children. The original impetus for this law had come from an awareness of the neglect of Spanish-speaking immigrant children by the Texan senator who proposed the bill, Ralph Yarborough:

> The failure of our schools to educate Spanish speaking students is reflected in comparative dropout rates. In the five Southwestern states . . . Anglos 14 years of age and over have completed an average of 12 years of school compared with 8.1 years for Spanish surnamed students.
>
> (cited by Lyons, 1990, in García and Baker, 1995: 1)

The original intention, then, was aimed at improving specifically the position of Spanish-speaking children by offering bilingual education programmes and teaching Spanish and some awareness of their cultural backgrounds. Attempts too were to be made to recruit teachers of Mexican and Puerto Rican origin. During the debates of the bill, however, the legislation was widened to address all linguistic minority children with mother-tongues other than English, which had the effect of diluting some of the specifically Spanish-speaking community measures (Lyons, 1990). The passing of the 1967 law is an important milestone in the US's attitude to linguistic diversity and has had a high-profiled and chequered path ever since, with many amendments and 'reauthorisations' in the years since then, reflecting closely the ideological leaning of the governments of the day (Dicker, 1996; Lyons, 1990; Trueba, 1989).

The arguments concerning bilingual education have, in particular, revolved around the debate regarding *maintenance* and *transitional* objectives. The majority of those involved in the debate, including many keen to have bilingual education programmes, favour the *transitional* method on the grounds that linguistic minority children must be offered the path to participation in mainstream society as quickly and effectively as possible by having competence in the language of power, English. These educators and politicians acknowledge that to achieve such participation some bilingual provision at an early age will make the transition gentler, but that mother-tongue provision should be limited. More radical proponents of this view question whether submersion schemes from the start are not the obvious (and cheaper) option. There has been acrimonious and lengthy debate over the decades regarding this right to mother-tongue provision and the effectiveness of bilingual education. In the vast majority of the cases it is the children of the Spanish-speaking community who are the object of these programmes. In an historic and no doubt precedent-setting vote, however, the electorate of California in June 1998 voted to abolish bilingual education in their state. This Proposition 227 was passed by a majority of 61 per cent of 'yes' votes to 39 per cent of 'no' votes, but with an apparent majority of *Latinos* (63 per cent) opposing the measure.

This backlash and rejection of bilingual education – and in one of the states with the highest population of Spanish-speakers – is not an unexpected culmination of the reaction against a certain liberalising of language legislation in the previous three decades, combined with an increasing 'hispanophobia' (Tatalovich, 1995; Zentella, 1997b). This reaction and response has been spearheaded by the English Only movement which we will discuss below.

The English Only movement

This movement which is also referred to as the 'Official English' movement emerged in the 1980s and had as its aim the establishment of English as the official national language of the US to be enshrined in legislation and thereby removing the offer of bilingual services, particularly in education.[4] The argument was that English was for all actual purposes the public language of the US and that this should be recognised officially and encouraged. It was claimed that immigrants had always learnt English and adopted this as their language, and that American identity was based on this concept of assimilation and integration into the dominant norm.

To some extent the movement was a reaction against the increase in bilingual education since the sixties and, in general, to some increase in bilingual services and circumstances, such as the Court Interpreter's Act of 1978 and the Voting Rights Act (1965) and the 1975 amendments to this.

However, this particular reaction also reflected a more general mood of the 1980s, the Reagan years. So-called 'middle America' was increasingly conservative and feeling threatened by such factors as unemployment, a loss of international status, and a post-Vietnam insularism. Those perceived as different and outsiders were unwelcome, and should adapt to the American way of life as quickly as possible. A further contributing factor to this sense of insecurity and retrenchment was the fact that the kind of immigration that the US was now experiencing had changed. Until now the vast majority of immigrants to the US had come from Europe, but more recently significant waves of immigrants have come from non-European, developing countries in Asia and, especially, Latin America.

As Dicker (1996) explains, this change in perception is underlined by a new and different way of conceiving of non-Anglo ethnic groups. In the past the concept of 'immigrant' had presumed the immediate willingness to adopt American norms and relinquish cultural and linguistic differences. Now these groups were more likely to define themselves as 'minorities' which brought with it a new relationship with the dominant, majority group. Dicker quotes Imhoff as, signficantly, attributing this change in conception to Hispanic group leaders:

> In the 1960s and 70s, according to Imhoff, Hispanic leaders reconfigured the Hispanic experience from the immigrant paradigm to the minority paradigm. . . . In this paradigm, 'the problems that arise between a minority and his or her society are presumed to be caused by – to be the fault of – the society. The responsibility for solving those problems, therefore, lies with the society . . . If Hispanics are a minority and not an immigrant group, then the responsibility for learning a new language lies with the general society and not with the Hispanics.'
>
> (Dicker, 1996: 147, referring to Imhoff)

This combination of factors attributed to the Hispanic community has led to it being seen as the focus of antagonism and reaction on the part of such people as the proponents of the English Only movement.

> Hispanics have largely become the symbol of American immigration and all the ills it has purportedly brought with it . . . Racism is certainly involved, European immigrants share a common heritage with many Americans, Asians are currently thought of as the 'model minority'. In contrast, Hispanics, representing immigrants from all Spanish-speaking countries in the developing world, comprise the largest immigrant group and have a significant contingent of dark-skinned people. Although they possess a hereditary link with European Americans, this link is rarely ackowledged . . .
>
> (Dicker, 1996: 149–50)

It is against this backdrop, then, that the English Only movement gained impetus. It was particularly active in those areas where a concentration of immigration had led Anglo-Americans to feel that they were being pushed out. This sense of invasion was particularly acute in parts of Florida such as Dade Country where the first attempt (in 1980) to produce a so-called 'anti-bilingual' law was unsuccessful. Here, as Dicker points out, the added threat was that the large Hispanic community, mainly consisting of anti-Castro Cubans, was middle class, articulate and successful.

> A consequence of the Latinization of Miami and a major source of annoyance for the monolingual-English speakers was the need for workers who spoke both Spanish and English. This was a telling sign for mainstream Americans that they no longer had the upper hand; for the first time for many of them, being a monolingual, native English-speaker carried no presumption of advantage in the labor market. In addition it defied the proverbial melting-pot fantasy; Hispanics in Miami did not have to give up their native identity in order to make it in America.
>
> (Dicker, 1996: 158)

It is important to stress that poor Mexican or Puerto Rican Americans do not have this sort of social and economic clout, but nonetheless the fear of Hispanic-origin people is generalised across all communities.

In 1981 the then Senator for California (a state with a large Hispanic population) Hayakawa presented to Congress a proposed English Language Amendment (ELA) which would seek to make English the only official language of the US (Donahue, 1995). At a federal level this proposition has been hard-fought but considered by the majority to be unconstitutional. Not only would it imply no bilingual education, nor bilingual services, but also even the possibility that learning foreign languages is unlawful. For many congressmen and women it was seen as a blatant denial of the human rights upheld in the US constitution. Although the ELA proposals have also had substantial support, this has never amounted to the necessary two thirds majority needed to enact an amendment. In August 1996 the House of Representatives passed an English-Only bill, but with less than a two thirds majority, which would have been necessary in the Senate for the bill to become law. In May 1998, as part of a debate concerning the future status of Puerto Rico, once again a group of Republicans attempted in the House of Representatives to attach a proviso that incorporation of the island as fifty-first state should include the introduction of English as national official language as a precondition. The House approved the bill's proposal to hold a plebiscite on the island's future (see below) but not this English-only requirement.

However, at individual state level, the notion of English as the only official language, supported amongst others by the large private group, the 'US

English Initiative', has been far more successful and has in fact been endorsed by seventeen states, who have made English their official state language. In California not only was such an amendment passed in 1986 (Proposition 63), but later in 1994, Proposition 187 was passed to refuse medical and educational services to illegal immigrants (Zentella, 1997b: 71).[5] As we have already noted, this has since been followed by Proposition 227 in 1998, banning all bilingual education in California.

As we have seen on so many occasions politics and language are impossible to untangle. And the scenario where they meet is again above all the education system. As Trueba writes,

> It is unfortunate that bilingual education and other educational programs for minority students have become part of a political struggle between opposing groups. Educators and parents have been forced into political camps and have campaigned for or against these programs, without a thorough understanding of their instructional attributes and characteristics.
>
> (Trueba, 1989: 104)

The image of the Latino:[6] solidarity versus homogenisation

With the passing of the English-only laws in many states, not only has education been affected, but so too has the situation in the workplace. Legitimate uses of Spanish to communicate with fellow Spanish-speaking employees have resulted in fines or even sackings. Many anecdotal examples of discrimination – almost always directed at Spanish-speakers – can be given to illustrate this effect (Zentella, 1997b). However, a consequence also of the aggressive attitudes to *Latinos* is that it has helped create a feeling of solidarity amongst them which was largely absent before:

> Unwittingly the movement to make English the official language has heightened Latino awareness of Hispanophobia, and promoted the defence of the Spanish language. Experiencing similar incidents of language discrimination has served to unite diverse groups of Latinos, who ordinarily reject a pan-ethnic label like Latino or Hispanic in favor of labels that proclaim their national origin. . . .
>
> (Zentella, 1997b: 78)

At the same time Zentella does warn against what she calls a 'process of *chiquitafication*', whereby the lumping together of all Hispanic-origin peoples 'diminishes the complexity of Latino cultures and linguistic codes' (Zentella, 1997b: 82). This view that there is a danger of oversimplification and homogenisation as regards the *Latino* world is one shared by many commentators. For example, the media are an important point at which this generalised image is often confirmed, through Spanish language television programming (which is now quite a booming industry), film-casting of the stereotypical Hispanic, and newspaper coverage which tends to pigeon-hole the Hispanic community, or ignore it altogether (see Aguirre and Bustamante, 1993; Rodriguez, 1997).

One important phenomenon characterising the whole Hispanic community is that of codeswitching which is now a vibrant and highly-skilled linguistic repetoire shared across this community (see e.g. Fernández, 1990; Zentella, 1985, 1990, and 1997a). It serves to create an important sense of 'them' and 'us', as outsiders cannot easily share in this linguistic code. To outsiders such combinations of English and Spanish, which may be at the level of sentence or word, or even within the word, are described (or even caricatured) as 'Spanglish' or 'TexMex'. To insiders this is a legitimate form of communication with its own unconscious rules and forms. It serves as an important identity marker for the Spanish-speaking community, and like any linguistic code, is a dynamic, evolving symbol of solidarity.

This increasing awareness of being *Latino* (as well as, for example, Mexican or Puerto Rican) produces an identifiable cultural and artistic output, where the use of, for example, codeswitching has a natural role. It helps to give the communities pride and support, but, from the outside, it also serves to blur the important lines of difference within the Hispanic world.

The struggle against the English Only movement and the discrimination and 'chiquitafication' of *Latinos* is being mounted increasingly from the Hispanic community. In 1994 a legal ruling declared unconstitutional the 1988 law passed by referendum in Arizona to prohibit the use of Spanish by public employees. This was a major victory for the anti English-only supporters in a state where the movement was particularly active. But *Latino* involvement in national politics is still limited,[7] and therefore their voices are not powerful. They do, however, command support from other parts of the Spanish-speaking world,[8] and it is no coincidence that the (right-wing) Madrid daily *ABC* reported on a manifesto produced by Chicano (*Latinos* of Mexican origin) writers to counter the withdrawal of bilingual education in California. Part of this manifesto stated:

> Los abajo firmantes creen que las lenguas nativas de las minorías representan no sólo un patrimonio nacional, sino también una muestra de valioso talento que enriquece las capacidades y potencialidades de cualquier nación. La xenofobia en forma de política 'English Only' constituye un elemento de quiebra, división y destrucción dentro de una nación que continúa teniendo una fértil historia de tradiciones lingüísticas y culturales y reivindican la libertad democrática de practicarlas.
> (*Manifiesto en Defensa del Idioma,* quoted in *ABC* 4.4.98)[9]

Here, once again, as we have seen so often in this book, is the tension and conflict between monocultural hegemony of a dominant (usually European) group and the claims for the rights and benefits of pluralist diversity.

Amongst the *Latino* groups the Puerto Ricans are especially perceived as inferior and are denied normal rights for reasons of linguistic insecurity and lack of education. They too are beginning to be more aware of their unequal status within the US, and also, as Zentella puts it because 'heightened Puerto Rican consciousness is due to the colonial experience of their home-land' (1997b: 83). It is, therefore, to a study of this unique community that we turn in the second half of the chapter.

The language issue and Puerto Ricans

Because of Puerto Rico's particular relationship with the US the issue of language – the use of Spanish and English – has been at the forefront for a century. The large waves of Puerto Rican immigration that have arrived in the US have also had to face the linguistic challenges that other Hispanic groups there face. What is special, however, about this group is the fact that many of these immigrants later return to Puerto Rico, and are then faced with a reverse linguistic and cultural identity crisis. The 'returning migrant' is a more common phenomenon amongst the Puerto Rican com-munity in the US precisely because of the special civic status of Puerto Ricans who have citizenship rights in both countries.

Below, therefore, we will first outline what this special relationship is and what its implications for language are, and then look at the experience of the 'returning migrant'.

Puerto Rico and the US: a privileged or subordinate relationship?

Puerto Rico was one of the first places to be occupied by the Spaniards in 1493. The indigenous population was completely eradicated, with the result that Spanish was the only language of the island for many hundreds of years. In 1898, however, the Spaniards lost their last colonies, including Puerto Rico, in a war with the US, and the United States effectively took control of the island. For the first half of the twentieth century, then, the US sought to 'Americanise' the island (Morris, 1996; Pousada, 1996; Vélez and Schweers, 1993), and, in particular, to impose English as the principal public language through control of the political system and, above all, by its compulsory use in the education system.

During this period, up until the end of the 1940s, the struggle for political autonomy was symbolised also by the struggle to prevent English dominance and to promote Spanish as Puerto Rico's national language. As Morris notes:

> . . . Puerto Rico's principal political demands were for self-government and for a return to Spanish as the school language. These two issues inter-twined in many ways, the education system becoming a symbolic arena in which larger struggles were played out.
>
> (Morris, 1996: 18)

In 1947 the US Congress passed a bill allowing a significant degree of self-government for Puerto Rico in internal matters, and the right to elect its own governor (who had previously been appointed by the US). The governor was elected in 1949, and one of his earliest acts was to appoint an education commissioner who decreed that Spanish should be the language of Puerto Rico's education system, thereby replacing English. In 1952 a new Puerto Rican constitution was drafted which defined the US–Puerto Rico relationship as somewhere between total independence and US statehood. It allowed for a fair amount of internal political autonomy but with close political and economic links with the US. It also maintained the right to US citizenship for Puerto Ricans. This special status is known as 'commonwealth' in English, but '*Estado libre asociado*' in Spanish.

In the ensuing years there have been endless debates over Puerto Rico's political status, represented by the three ultimate objectives of complete independence, the 'commonwealth' *status quo*, or becoming a US state. Frequently, too, the language issue has been a marker of these debates.[10]

Alongside the demand for complete independence goes also that for Spanish as sole official language of Puerto Rico. The latter is advocated principally for two reasons: firstly, 'for Puerto Rico to reaffirm its Hispanic heritage as a way to develop ethnic pride' (Vélez and Schweers, 1993: 118), and secondly, to protect and maintain the language which is perceived as threatened by the dominance of American English and is considered by many as inferior because of the interference from English and higher literacy skills of English-speakers (Pousada, 1996; Vélez and Schweers, 1993). Spanish is identified, then, by its supporters with the twin roles of symbol of Puerto Rican identity, and also means of effective and efficient communication which is, however, in need of protection.

In 1991 an alliance of pro-independence and pro-commonwealth parties resulted in the passing of a law to introduce Spanish as the sole official language in Puerto Rico (with English as a compulsory school subject). This law was widely acclaimed in the Spanish-speaking world as a victory for Spanish over the dominance of English (Mar-Molinero, 1997: 165–7). Its life was short, however, as the pro-statehood party won elections in 1992 and immediately repealed the Spanish-only law and reinstated the right for English to be used as well as or instead of Spanish in Puerto Rican public life.

Those Puerto Ricans who do not support the Spanish-only campaigns argue that Spanish is manifestly safe as the language of the island demonstrated by the fact that it is so widely spoken, with as much as 52 per cent of the population in the 1990 census claiming monolingualism in Spanish, and 28 per cent as speaking English 'with difficulty' (Morris, 1997). It is also pointed out that English is perceived as a threat in many other parts of the world because of its widespread use, and that Puerto Rico is not in this sense different. Such opinions are generally held by those who would like to see Puerto

Rico incorporated into the US as a fully-fledged state, or who believe close association via the present status is essential.

Plebiscites on the political status of Puerto Rico have been held on three occasions since the 1952 constitution. The latest was held in December 1998 and showed that support for total independence from the US is low (only 2.4 per cent), a larger 46 per cent voted in favour of US statehood, but the majority percentage of 50.3 per cent opted for the strange category of *'ninguna de las anteriores'* ('none of the others') which only serves to underline the uncertainty felt about Puerto Rico's political future.[11]

Whatever the political objectives of different Puerto Rican groups, that Spanish is viewed as an integral part of their national identity is not in doubt (see e.g. Zentella, 1990, 1997a). In a survey carried out in August 1998 more than 90 per cent of Puerto Ricans questioned said they preferred to use Spanish rather than English, and that if Puerto Rico should ever become a US state that Spanish should be an official US language (Ateneo Puertorriqueño, quoted in *El País*, 26.8.96). In fact a campaign of 'Spanish Also' in opposition to 'English Only' legislation has been mounted to protect Puerto Rico's use of Spanish as well as Puerto Rican Spanish-speakers living in the US (*El País* 26.8.96).

The significance of language in the political debates over Puerto Rico's future is recognised by those we have called 'Hispanophobics' in the US, as well as by the Puerto Ricans themselves. When Congress in March 1998 debated the bill which eventually led to the latest plebiscite, it agreed that the US would commit itself to respecting whatever result emerged. Attempts were made during the debate to insist that if Puerto Rico opted for US statehood, English should become the official language of the island. This proposal, put forward by defenders of the English-only campaigns, was ultimately defeated, but the bill was passed by only one vote. It was claimed during the debate that the annexation of a fifty-first state where Spanish was an official language would be the red light for the downgrading of the status of English that the English-only campaigners so fear. According to the Spanish daily *El País* (8.3.98): *'Congresistas republicanos afirman que la llegada de un estado hispano será un Caballo de Troya de la lengua y cultura de raíz española'* ('Republican Congressmen claimed that the arrival of a Hispanic state will be the Trojan Horse of language and culture of Spanish origin').

The importance of language to Puerto Rican identity is highlighted too by the dilemma it presents to Puerto Rican writers, and, in particular, those who have emigrated to the States. The role of language in the work of two leading writers, Julia Alvarez and Esmeralda Santiago, is discussed in an article by John Perivolaris (1997). In this Perivolaris emphasises the ambiguities and ambivalences which such writers experience towards their language and towards their sense of identity because of their condition of immigrant, but in particular because of their experience of returning to their homelands. Alvarez is a Dominican writer settled in the US and who has returned to visit her Dominican roots, whilst Santiago is a Puerto Rican.

The experiences and reactions of such writers as Santiago can be seen as representative of the identity confusions of Puerto Rican immigrants in general, and is expressed in her attitudes to her language. Santiago's best-seller *When I was Puerto Rican* (the best-selling Spanish edition *Cuando era puertorriqueña* was translated by the author herself) is an autobiographical account of her life in Puerto Rico and the move to the US. Perivolaris (1997: 121) quotes from Santiago's introduction to the Spanish edition,

> The life lived in this book was lived in Spanish, but was initially written in English. Often, as I wrote, it surprised me to hear myself speaking in Spanish whilst my fingers typed the same phrase in English. It was then that I would be tongue-tied and lose all sense of what I was saying and writing, as if observing that I was translating from one language to another were making me lose both.
>
> (Perivolaris, 1997: 121)

This identity confusion so strongly symbolised by the doubts over what language to use is a common experience for immigrants settling in a new country, but it is particularly poignantly felt by those Puerto Ricans who live this experience twice over when returning to Puerto Rico.

The experience of the returning migrant

One of the consequences of the 'Americanisation' process in the earlier part of this century in Puerto Rico was the high level of immigration to the US, partly because the new economic order created high unemployment, partly because of the perceived advantages of the special status of Puerto Ricans in the US. However, this trend stopped in the early seventies as a result of the recession in the northeastern region of the US, precisely the part to which most Puerto Ricans had gone (Clachar, 1997). It has been estimated that since the mid-seventies approximately 35,000 Puerto Ricans per year have returned to the island (Clachar, 1997; Zentella, 1990). For the adults this has represented a second adjustment and settlement experience and the majority of the children of these returning migrants having been born and originally educated in the US speak very little, if any, Spanish on arrival in Puerto Rico. This has been a particularly difficult challenge for the island's education system where, since 1949, the language of instruction has been Spanish.

With such large groups of returning migrants, the awareness of separate identities between those born and raised on the island and those who have lived in the US has emerged, challenging the definition of 'Puerto Rican-ness'. This is most clearly manifested in use and competence in the Spanish language. It has created a particularly complex and uncomfortable situation for the returned migrant:

> On the United States mainland, many Puerto Ricans often assert ethnic identification by expressing their 'Puerto Rican-ness', thereby manifesting an allegiance to the Spanish language, the ingroup language, even if it is not spoken fluently. However, when they return to the island to live, they are stigmatised and made to feel separate and subordinate partly because of their low proficiency in Spanish.
>
> (Clachar, 1997: 109–10)

Clachar argues that this means that the returned migrants begin to emphasise their US-related characteristic, that is their knowledge of English, as a way of marking their group identity and thereby reversing their situation. She goes on:

> The paradox which, therefore, surfaces is that in the former interethnic situation (on the United States mainland), Spanish represented the ingroup language (the symbol of unity) while in the latter (on the island of Puerto Rico), it is the outgroup language (the symbol of divisiveness). Spanish, as the outgroup language, is not acquired to optimal levels of proficiency. . . .
>
> (Clachar, 1997)

These so-called returnees find themselves in the midst of the dilemma over the significance of Spanish to Puerto Rican identity. As we have already noted, the protection and promotion of Spanish is linked with the notion of the survival of Puerto Rico's separate identity. As Zentella (1990: 84) claims 'the survival of Spanish has become inextricably linked for many with the survival of Puerto Rican identity and that of the Puerto Rican nation itself.' And, as she explains, '[The] issue is, does language change/loss necessarily spell cultural loss? More pointedly, are returnees who cannot speak Spanish Puerto Ricans?'

Various studies (including Zentella's own, reported in Zentella, 1990) are inconclusive as to the answer to this question. Certainly those she interviewed in the US did not feel that proficiency in the Spanish language was the essential characteristic to define 'Puerto Rican-ness'. Also, amongst some of the younger generation in the island itself there appears to be more tolerance towards the notion that not every Puerto Rican must speak fluent Spanish. However, amongst the older generation, and in particular amongst intellectuals and radical politicians, the protection of Spanish remains paramount in defending Puerto Rico's identity. Once again, as we have noted so often in this book, language issues constitute a political football, and the education system is an important forum for influencing outcomes. Bilingual Spanish–English programmes have now been introduced into Puerto Rico's education system for some of the children of returnees – somewhat ironically precisely at a time when bilingual education programmes in the US are being reduced.

The cyclic migration between the US and Puerto Rico is likely to continue given the uncertainties of the political relationship on the one hand and of the economic markets on the other. This sets challenges as much for the US as it does for Puerto Rico. As Zentella points out:

> The revolving door migration of Puerto Ricans, which represents a distinct departure from the usual immigration pattern, challenges the prevalent model of assimilation and demands a reevaluation of the objectives and impact of many governmental policies, such as the proposed English language amendment [discussed in the earlier part of the chapter], and of some educational approaches, particularly transitional bilingual education.
>
> (Zentella, 1990: 82)

Conclusion

As we have seen throughout this chapter Spanish-speaking immigrants will continue to arrive in the US, and the special situations of the *Latinos* there will continue to be of interest. Whilst it is easy to argue that their presence is not the threat perceived and claimed by some Americans, nonetheless, that an apparent challenge to the hegemony of English is so strongly resisted in a part of the world where it can really not be in any danger has lessons for how the dominance of English might be defended in many other parts of the world.

In the following and concluding chapter we will examine Spanish as a world language and its contact with the dominance of English. We will also be observing the changes taking place in terms of some of the issues of national sovereignty as trends of globalisation and internationalisation challenge this accepted order. One such challenge is, indeed, that of cyclic migration of the type already seen in Puerto Rico. As world economies fluctuate on the one hand, and as technology such as better transportation and good communication systems keep communities in touch, even when finding themselves in a state of diaspora on the other, we might expect more revolving movements as described by Zentella and others – movements which will indeed present challenges to language planning and policies.

10 Spanish in a global era

It has been the contention throughout this book that language use and language practices are inextricably bound up with politics. As we enter the twenty-first century, then, our expectations and predictions about language politics, and in particular, about the Spanish language, should reflect current political and ideological trends in general. Commentators describe us as living in a postmodern world which is above all characterised by globalisation and internationalisation.[1] For many this is seen as the ultimate threat to the past two centuries' stable order of the nation-state. It is argued that with the enormous technological advances in such things as transportation and modes of communication frontiers are now easily crossed and re-crossed. Territorial uniqueness and discreteness are no longer guaranteed. Television networks, satellite telephone connections, the world wide web, all such phenomena remove the distinctiveness of the relatively small areas occupied by nation-states and challenge separate national identity and culture.

Of equal significance in this wider mapping of the world is the spread and control of economies by large multinational businesses. Linked also to these multinational companies are international economic and monetary organisations, as well as political and military alliances which transcend national borders. Political, economic and social decision-making can rarely be made today by reference only to national issues and constraints. Smith (1995, 1998) explores the claims that as a result of this increasing political and economic dependency of nation-states on wider supra-national and international organisations that the nation-state is therefore close to its demise, and as a result new global identities and cultures are replacing national ones. This is of course of importance to any discussion of the politics of language as it raises questions regarding the future of so many of the issues we have explored in this book: who will now decide language policies and implement language planning; where will the core be located that determines the dominant, hegemonic group and what its consequent periphery and minoritised groups are? Will the concept of 'national' language become less significant? Will multiculturalism, and therefore multilingualism, become the recognised and supported global norm, or will a homogenisation of cultures and languages reduce communication channels essentially to the use of English, and possibly one or two other 'world' languages? Might the latter include Spanish?

Smith (1998) however is not entirely convinced that the nation-state and nationalism can be so easily written off, not least in the sphere of cultural and social identity. Whilst he does not dismiss the claims of the emergence of 'supra-nationalism' and 'global culture', he argues that some forms of localised identity remain strong. In particular he points out that although increasing political and economic dependency beyond the nation-state is clearly happening (and, in fact, questions the extent to which many such states were ever truly autonomous), he also reminds us that in recent years important social and cultural trends have been firmly advocated, directed and resourced internally by many states:

> In the post-1945 era, the political and economic dependence of most states has been accompanied by a huge expansion of internal state power and penetration in the social and cultural spheres, notably in such fields as mass education, the cultural media, health and social welfare. This expansion has been legitimated by nationalist ideologies and has done much to offer and 'compensate' the 'nation-state' for its external dependance . . .
>
> (Smith, 1998: 214)

Smith also argues that even transnational firms must have headquarters, where they are 'vulnerable to the regulations and policies of that state' (Smith, 1995: 118) and adds:

> The politicians whom the transnational elites [e.g. financiers, bankers, directors] must in the end influence and persuade remain answerable to other groups within each national state, and, through the ballot box, to the general population.
>
> (Smith, 1995: 118)

He contends that 'the national state remains the core unit of military technology and violence, and the main supplier and procurer of armaments', although conceding the 'internationalization of command structures' (Smith, 1995: 118).

In an analysis such as this, we would expect the role of dominant national groups in determining such things as language and education policies to remain supreme. In fact, this is indeed the interpretation we gave the new (arguably, postmodern) Spanish constitution. However, as with the Spanish *estado de autonomías*, Smith recognises an increasing awareness of and power to substate communities. He describes this new condition as the 'regional-continental network' (Smith, 1995). It is this model that we will discuss in greater detail later in this chapter in terms of future trends in Europe and Latin America.

Billig (1995) is less certain of a continuing role for the nation-state, and also identifies a dual pull of localised and global trends. He argues that:

> The forces of globalization are not producing cultural homogeneity in an absolute manner. They may be eroding differences between national cultures, but they are also multiplying differences within nations.
>
> (Billig, 1995: 132)

Billig argues that new (non-national) 'life-styles' are emerging as a result of the globalising trends we have already mentioned, such as television, targeted comsumer groups, etc. These are creating new 'imagined' communities which are no longer linked by national identity. He writes that 'the processes of globalization, which are diminishing differences and spaces between nations, are also fragmenting the imagined unity within these nations' (Billig, 1995: 132). The social, cultural and linguistic implications of this argument are very different from those concluded from Smith's analyses. We might expect education policy and language practices to be linked to these separate 'life-styles' rather than to the national community.

Billig continues:

> The state, declining in its powers, is no longer able to impose a uniform sense of identity. With the pressure for national uniformity removed, a variety of other forces is released. Within the national territory, multiple narratives and new identities are emerging. Local, ethnic and gender identities have become the site for postmodern politics . . .
>
> (Billig, 1995: 133)

These identities (with the exception of gender identities) have been the focus of much of this book, and therefore we will discuss to what extent the argument that they are taking on centre-stage in place of national identities is actually the case in the contemporary Spanish-speaking world.

In the case of Spain some of the issues outlined above can be seen when analysing Spain's relationship with Europe and the European Union, on the one hand, and with its '*autonomías*' on the other. If, as we alleged in earlier chapters, nation-building in Spain has been considerably less successful than state-building, then the supra-national pulls of the EU will be very significant. At a time when confidence in their own separate cultural and linguistic identities is rising amongst some of Spain's minority communities this pull can be expected to have repercussions not only in political and economic areas, but also in linguistic and cultural ones.

In Latin America we will be interested to observe how far the 'regional-continental' model is evident both in terms of greater local ethnic awareness amongst, for example, indigenous groups, and also across borders through any pan-continental associations. We will discuss the extent of any pan-indigenous movements, as well as pan-Hispanic associations. How far does the existence of the latter indicate a reaction to the neighbouring US dominance, and how far might we detect alliances between Latin American Spanish-speakers and those across the globe?

Spain and Europe

Throughout our discussions the concept of 'Spain', whilst often not convincing as a single unit 'nation', has certainly represented the ultimate political unit as 'state' in terms of its power over the regions within its territory, and, during a lengthy period, over its empire. Today, as with many other European nation-states, this concept is challenged by the presence and role of the European Union, as well as by the more general globalising tendencies we outlined above.

Ironically this challenge comes at precisely the moment in Spain's history when the central government has accorded a significantly high level of regional control to the so-called '*comunidades autónomas*'. As we noted in Chapter 5, the post-Franco *estado de las autonomías* as enshrined in the 1978 Constitution, is a marvel of compromise and an attempt to satisfy the perceived need to maintain strong central 'Spanish' unity with the persistent desires for greater regional control and development of local identities.

A 'Spain of the Regions', however, is now being challenged by a 'Europe of the Regions', as the EU both removes some power from its member states' governments as well as supporting and promoting certain aspects of the substate regions' identities. Whitehead (1996) suggests that this challenge could have a series of outcomes, all of which might threaten the delicate compromise underlying the 1978 Constitution and indicative of the Spanish nation-region debates over the centuries. He sees these as being, firstly, the increasing importance of regions in the 'institutional structures [of the EU] in which Spanish regions will be invited to play a leading role' (Whitehead, 1996: 258). He also suggests that what he calls the 'desire for administrative uniformity in European structures' (ibid.) might threaten the delicate and special balance created with Spain's particular *comunidades autónomas* system. Thirdly, he wonders about the effect on Spain's political structures from the developing and promoting of the EU's regional network system. And, finally, he explores the possibilities for a future parallel network system which he calls 'Europe of the Cities'. He emphasises that in all these EU initiatives Spain, by virtue of her special *estado de las autonomías* model, is considered a principal actor. All the scenarios imply possible (further) lessening of the power and control of the central government in Madrid. Given the analysis we offered in Chapter 5 that Madrid does still ultimately control the national agenda in terms of cultural and linguistic dominance and authority, any weakening of Madrid's political and legal powers could have a significant impact on regional linguistic and cultural policy making.

Language policies at EU level, however, are also ambiguous and, arguably, in flux, making predictions regarding language politics in Spain in the immediate future difficult. To understand this current situation it is necessary to give a brief summary of what the language policies in the EU are and how, therefore, Spanish and Spain's languages fit these policies.

Languages and the European Union[2]

The Treaty of Rome in 1958 outlined the status of equal official language for the languages of the then member states for all working purposes of the Community. As further members joined, the treaty was amended to include more languages. Only Irish and Luxemburgish were exceptions, being termed 'national' languages rather than 'official', and thereby not requiring the full translating and interpreting services and documentation normally expected for official languages. Another category, 'working language', has also been used to describe certain bilateral arrangements, as with Catalan, which we will comment on below.

At the time of writing there are fifteen member states of the (now) Union, with eleven official languages (some states share the same official national language). The principle clearly observed by the EU with the concept of official languages is that of national sovereignty. All national languages are considered equal, and – particularly significantly – *which* those 'national' languages should be is decided by the national (central) government of the member state. Where only certain languages of a member state are considered official, that government will limit the proposed EU official language to these. As a result – not surprisingly – the linguistic battles that may be fought within the nation-states are replicated at European level. Welsh, Catalan, Breton, Frisian, etc., remain non-official languages. That even the official languages should be treated as totally equal is an increasingly unrealistic and burdensome principle. The matrix of translation/interpreting pairs that this now generates is extremely expensive, slow (and therefore inefficient) and with potential for an enormous range of misunderstanding, mistakes and inaccuracies.

In practice two or three languages only are used for the majority of the time. French is mainly used for administrative purposes, whilst English is, above all, the language of oral communication and, without doubt, the most known and spoken. German retains importance in that it is the language with, at present, the largest number of mother-tongue speakers in the EU. There are, therefore, inevitably debates about the future language policy to be followed, made more urgent by the imminent addition of further members from Eastern Europe. The debate, of course, ranges between the need to make communications quick, cheaper and efficient by using only one or two languages, and the desire to retain what in many countries are seen as important symbols of national identity. As we have constantly noted, these two aspects of language are in conflict. It is not only in political and economic matters that the tension between national sovereignty and wider European ideals exists; language politics also reflect this.

However, it is not only at the level of national sovereignty versus supranational policies that tensions arise. As we have noted, the role of the regions in the EU is in many senses heightened, but their linguistic rights are still importantly determined by their national governments. The Catalans – arguably the most powerful of the EU's minority linguistic groups – fought a long hard campaign on the part of the local governments of the Catalan-speaking *comunidades autónomas* (Catalonia, Balearic Islands, and Valencia) to convince the Union that Catalan should be an official language too. Their arguments included the points that Catalan was the '*llengua pròpia*' of their communities, and widely spoken there. It also emphasised the size of the population speaking Catalan (estimated by some as high as ten million), and contrasted this with some of the other official EU languages with fewer speakers, such as Danish. The Catalans achieved only partial victory: the right to use Catalan as a 'working language' in bilateral communications with the Commission (Generalitat de Catalunya, 1991). For the language to be accepted as a full official language of the EU, it would have to be proposed as such by the national government in Madrid – an entirely improbable proposition!

In terms of official status the EU does not offer much to encourage minority linguistic communities within its borders. However, in other ways the status of these communities is enhanced, which may indirectly help increase the prestige of certain languages. We have already touched on the fact that the EU structures are supporting regional networking which may in the future serve both to improve the economic and social prestige of certain areas[3] as well as the wider use and recognition for their cultural and linguistic practices. Moreover, the *Charter of Regional Languages and Cultures and Rights of Ethnic Minorities* produced in 1981 has helped underpin efforts to raise the profile of minority linguistic communities and protect their rights. An increased awareness of their existence also helps create networks between groups and offers a larger base in terms of solidarity and pressure. The EU itself has promoted linguistic rights through such things as the European Bureau for Lesser-Used Languages and the MERCATOR network. These institutions and projects offer some actual resources for research and data collection on lesser-used languages in the Union, as well as producing publications, organising conferences and collating data bases.

Other activities support language awareness in general as well as the lesser-used languages in particular, such as the student and teacher exchange programmes like LINGUA, ERASMUS and SOCRATES, as well as the European Language Council with its various Thematic Networks examining language issues in Europe's Higher Education Institutions.[4] In fact, language education is another important area where the European Union (and the Community before that) have attempted to influence attitudes and policies regarding language. Not only have exchange programmes been created to further the learning of the Union's languages, but various directives have been issued with the intention of supporting language education in the EU (and, formerly, EC).

Significant amongst these directives has been that issued in 1977 recommending the teaching of mother-tongue languages to the children of immigrants. The recognition of the linguistic needs of non-European origin mother tongue speakers is an important new component in Europe's linguistic map. It adds a further element to the discussion of a European-wide language policy, but needs also to be considered in the context of individual member states. Whilst the number of non-Spanish speaking immigrants in Spain is small, it has been increasing in recent years, with immigrants arriving from North Africa. A significant proportion of these arrive looking for work in the prosperous region of Catalonia, particularly around Barcelona. This is inevitably putting a strain on the language policies there insofar as they have dealt until recently only with the concept of bilingualism between the indigenous languages of Castilian and Catalan, and not with wider concepts of multiculturalism and immigrant languages.

Spanish and EU language policies

It is not yet clear what the future of Spanish within the European framework will be. Whilst we have argued in earlier chapters that it remains ultimately the dominant language in Spain, an increasingly separate and assertive role for some of the Spanish regions within the EU and bypassing Madrid might indicate some weakening of this. On the other hand, we noted in Chapter 5 that the language policies protecting Spain's minority languages are largely predicated on a territoriality principle. It could be argued that this principle is greatly weakened by the over-riding European ideal of open borders and freedom of movement. The latter encourages member state residents to move within and across national territories, making it very difficult, if not impossible, to protect community language rights by linking them only to particular areas. In fact it could be argued that true freedom of movement for EU citizens can only be a realistic possiblity if the necessary linguistic (and cultural) rights can be guaranteed. Exactly what these rights should be is a difficult question. It will depend eventually on whether the argument for one or two widely-spoken languages becomes the accepted norm, or whether the EU continues to protect (and expand) its concept of multilingualism and diversity. The parallels with a single common currency and the upgrading of the role of the European Parliament are obvious. Equally obvious is that resolution of this is a long way off.

If one main language does eventually emerge as the common linguistic currency in regulations as well as simply in practice – and such a language is certain to be English, it is possible that Spain may consider that Spanish has in some sense been downgraded. At present Spanish as an equal official EU language can build on this base by further enhancing its prestige through its role in other parts of the world. If it is only a national language of the EU and consequently considerably less used in terms of documentation published in Spanish, the fact that in those other parts of the world where it is spoken a high proportion of the population is under-educated, may reduce its prestige vis-à-vis other (admittedly less widely spoken) European languages. Such scenarios might encourage less tolerant attitudes to the promotion of minority languages and even the role of Castilian itself in Spain.

Pan-continental movements in Latin America

In the discussion above of language and the EU, and a possible future frame-work for political, social and cultural structures in Europe, the counter-structure to the classic nation-state can be described in Smith's terms as regional-continental. This model is also of potential application in the case of Latin America, and we will explore that possibility below.

Smith (1995) discusses how his view of regional-continental associations may involve 'associations founded upon cultural affinities and embracing an ideology of "Pan" nationalism' (1995: 119), in which he includes Pan-Latin-Americanism. Despite their name, he argues that their nature and objectives are ambiguous.

> The functions of such 'Pan' nationalisms are ambivalent. On the one hand, they seem to be suggesting a supersession of existing national states in the interests of much larger super-states and super-nations. On the other hand, they underpin the national state by linking it to a wider category of 'protected' states and strengthening its cultural profile and historic identity through opposition to culturally different neighbours and enemies. They provide another set of 'border guards', a new panoply of symbols and myths, memories and values, that set the included national states apart from others.
>
> (Smith, 1995: 120)

Smith believes, then, that at least until now, associations between nation-states far from collapsing borders and creating supra-nations, largely serve to consolidate existing nation-states. But he accepts that late twentieth century trends have started to question this assumption and that the regional-continental model, expressed by 'Pan' nationalism might change this.

> Undoubtedly the rapid growth of telecommunications and the mass media have encouraged the creation of wider regional-continental net-works. What needs to be explored is the degree to which regional-continental associations based on 'Pan' nationalism can generate overarching cultures and identities that compete with, or even replace, national state and ethnic identities.
>
> (Smith, 1995: 121)

We have already seen that this phenomenon is taking place in Europe between the creation and development of the European Union and the resistance and maintenance of the sovereign nation-states. Here we will examine how far such movements are operating in Latin America and what implications they have for language.

Certainly in terms of economic collaboration the varied continental networking that has taken place in Latin America has tended to be of the kind that does indeed help to consolidate nation-state bases. As Barton (1997: 93) explains 'Regional pacts have, on the whole, provided Latin American nation-states with the opportunities to redress the overbearing commercial ties that the majority of them have established with the USA.' Examples of these economic, trade associations include CACM, the Central American Common Market (Guatemala, El Salvador, Honduras, Nicaragua and Costa Rica); the Andean Group (Venezuela, Colombia, Ecuador, Peru and Bolivia); and MERCOSUR, the Southern Cone Common Market (Argentina, Paraguay, Uruguay, Brazil and Chile) (Barton, 1997). These associations, however, are more strictly limited to their economic objectives than the similar 'common market' association that developed in Europe. Whilst it is obviously the existence (in most cases) of a shared language, colonial history and geography helps bring them together, cultural goals are not part of their overt agenda. However, a major reason for their association is the recognition that in today's world international blocs are more successful than single nation-states, and these Latin American groupings react to the pressure and dominance of the US (and increasingly to other global blocs, such as the EU) in a way which is both economic and political as well as social and cultural.

Against this we should note the powerful association of NAFTA which includes the US, Canada and Mexico in a free trade zone, and is certainly having an impact on Mexico's society and cultural life. We have already noted that the pressure to learn English there is now greater than ever and likely to clash with any efforts to teach more native Mexican languages.

As we have seen in earlier chapters, nation-building in Latin America has been a constructed, and often minority endeavour. As a result these nation-states still feel insecure of their identity and vulnerable. This is partly why the economic pressures from the global economy are seen as a threat, and one that is better confronted by association with other nation-states in the region.

Few Latin American states have really solved the problem of the cleavages presented by their multiethnic, multicultural societies. As Barton remarks:

> Late twentieth century Latin American citizens are likely to be noted more by racial and ethnic origins than by their national identity. There are more commonalities among Amerindian groups, wherever located within the continent, and between citizens of European descent, than there is sense of national identity between them.
>
> (Barton, 1997: 167)

Barton discusses how the constant ignoring of the different cultural, linguistic, social and spatial practices of the indigenous groups by the European-origin elites and the consequent attempts at assimilation and acculturation are unlikely to succeed. This is a view we examined in earlier chapters where we showed how in a few areas the realisation of this has led to greater attempts at intercultural education and to the granting of a certain degree of local autonomy. Barton believes that it is also important to recognise the links across indigenous groups and, therefore, across national boundaries. He argues:

> What is required in contemporary Latin American nation-states is to establish recognition of Amerindian groups as an integral part of the American nature of Latin American nationalism. A recognition of diversity, rather than the pursuit of uniformity, . . . is the only way that a mobilisation of national conscience can lead to recognition of and rights (particularly human rights) for these groups, rather than in their integration and absorption into an alien structuring of national space based on traditional European elite conceptualisations of spatial organisation.
>
> (Barton, 1997: 171)

In fact in recent years there are signs of indigenous groups becoming aware of the need to organise themselves in like communities and to challenge the divisions and loss of identity created by nation-states. As Delgado-P writes:

> The vigour of ethnic identity is forging transnational, transregional, inter-gender and inter-ethnic alliances amidst groups of Indigenous Peoples living both in Mexico and the United States. The *International Frente Mixteco-Zapoteco*, formed by migrant rural workers in the US, criss-crosses the 'border' (between the US and Mexico) as they reconstitute their diasporic Indigenous nation rooted in Oaxaca, Mexico.
>
> (Delgado-P, 1995: 15)

Other such indigenous associations include COICA, the Co-ordinating Body of Indigenous Organisations of the Amazonian Basin (Barton, 1997; Delgado-P, 1995), and the Mayan-based Committee for *Unidad Campesina* which in October 1990 issued a declaration to 'all Mayan peoples, indigenous groups, trade unions, popular organisations, all Guatemalans, indigenous people throughout the world, and the international community' (cited in Barton, 1997) calling for unity and popular resistance amongst indigenous peoples against colonial and neocolonial repression.

In 1991 a meeting in Quito, Ecuador, set up the Confederation of Indigenous Peoples of Ecuador and in the 'Quito Declaration' this organisation called for a 'continental alliance' of America's indigenous peoples and aimed to challenge 'the notion of a homogenous nation-state in Latin America' (Delgado-P, 1995: 16).

In recent decades other trans-border groupings as well as indigenous ones have emerged in Latin America. Known as 'new social movements' or NSMs (Barton, 1997) these reflect other marginalised groups who are resisting state bureaucracies and exclusive politics (Radcliffe, 1999). These groups (which are often formed by women) 'have redefined power relations which, in turn, have been reflected spatially' (Barton, 1997: 174). These movements seek empowerment and to defend their human rights. They have much in common with (or in fact include) those groups we examined in Chapter 7 who through new understandings of the power of language, literacy and education also aim to change their marginalised condition and to participate in society.

An important aspect of these new social movements is their increasing access to technological support that can broaden their contact and influence. Radcliffe describes how this has helped break down the traditional national borders that enclosed them:

> Within a globalizing world, spaces of flow (Castells, 1997) extend across Latin America, giving wider reception to social demands from diverse audiences . . . and to the nature of political and social strategies adopted by the social movements themselves.
>
> (Radcliffe, 1999: 218–19)

The implications for language use and language policies of these various intra-continental associations and networks are clear. On the one hand, national differences may be diminished (as with a pan-continental use of Spanish and Quechua); on the other greater awareness of solidarity and commonality can help revive and protect minority languages. The latter is particularly true in the case of indigenous languages with little history of standardisation and literacy, as a wider geographical use of their language may help create the imagined community of this linguistic group, giving it higher prestige and certain necessary accepted norms. As Von Gleich comments when writing about the spread of Quechua in parts of Latin America today:

> I argue that the degree of pervasiveness among Quechua speakers can be improved through participation. Once awareness exists that Quechua is still creative and useful in various social functions outside the home, in most cases the positive evaluation as ethnic group identifier is reinforced, and this ultimately increases the wish for better proficiency and more usage of Quechua.
>
> (Von Gleich, 1994: 89)

Von Gleich also refers to what she calls 'an excellent example of promising supraregional and international cooperation' in the form of the 1989 workshop held in Bolivia on the Normalization of Pedagogical Language for Andean Languages.

As well as social movements of the sort referred to above and indigenous associations in Latin America, more specifically political radical movements have also emerged in the latter part of the twentieth century. Whilst these are initially at least limited to fighting the political systems of particular nation-states, such as the Shining Path Maoist movement in Peru, or the Zapatista movement in Chiapas in Mexico, these movements reflect a more general heightening of awareness of indigenous issues, including linguistic ones. Gutiérres comments specifically on the Chiapas revolt:

> The 'Indianist' theme has become associated with current forms of global interest, ecological and environmental issues . . . , awareness of multiculturalism and protection of human rights. . . .
> The word 'Indian' (the generic word for Amerindian people) is gradually losing its 16th century colonial meaning (i.e. status of racial and cultural inferiority) and is today gaining a wider meaning that includes the 'underprivileged' generally speaking.
>
> (Gutiérres, 1995: 19)

She furthers suggests that 'the merit of the Zapatista revolt is that it has awoken interest in the future of autochthonous peoples within large and semi-modernised states' (1995: 21).

Certainly one of the most important characteristics of Latin American language politics in the next decades is likely to be that relating to the linguistic rights of indigenous groups who are increasingly identifying themselves by their socio-cultural rather than any national borders.

Conclusions: Spanish as pluricentric world language

It is, however, finally to the future of the Spanish language that we will look in this concluding part. On many occasions we have referred to the role, or even the threat, of English in future global linguistic politics. The dominance of English is largely a result of it being the language, first, of the British Empire in the nineteenth century, and, secondly, of the US, the most powerful nation in the world since the Second World War. The dominance of Britian and then the US in world politics has assured English a position and role that pervades all linguistic practices in the modern world. This all-pervasiveness may be seen by some as making the members of the world community more able to communicate with one another and therefore potentially more successful and efficient in social, political and cultural exchanges. By many, however, it is viewed as a form of 'linguistic imperialism', a term championed in particular by Robert Phillipson (1992).

While the Spanish-speaking world has not, perhaps, reacted as strongly as its French counterpart to the encroachment of English in many domains previously dominated by Spanish, there is undoubtedly an awareness of the presence of English affecting Spanish in such areas as the adoption of English words and phrases, directly or by direct translation. In the media, in particular, where global trends are transmitted with such speed and urgency through advanced technological means, the dominance of English is held responsible also for new grammatical forms. Spanish competes with English, too, not only as far as its internal form is concerned but also in terms of use. While both languages are often the official languages of international organisations, it is well known that English will in the vast majority of places be the one chosen for communication. As a result most international fora expect (and require) their participants to know English. Spanish or Latin American business people must master some English; academics publish books and give papers in English. Equally significantly, much popular cultural activity which expects to cross national boundaries is in English, such as pop music, sports events and cinema. Despite the large numbers globally of speakers of Spanish, in all these scenarios Spanish takes a back seat to English. Ironically, too, this situation may even be used to the advantage of those speakers of minority languages who share their territorial space with Spanish. For example, Catalan business people and academics will prefer to use Catalan amongst themselves in daily work and to give talks, send electronic mail, publish documents, etc., in English, thereby bypassing the equal bilingual partner language of Castilian within their community. 'Comandante Marcos' the self-styled spokesperson for the Zapatista movement in Chiapas is well-known for his use of the internet and electronic media in general, frequently in English, to publicise the Zapatista cause (Radcliffe, 1999: 219). Such examples point again to the fragility of national frontiers and national identity when language is a marker of conflicting identity.

Nonetheless, we can also see that the vitality of Spanish is still healthy today. In fact, in terms of language spread (Cooper, 1982), Spanish can still be judged to be benefiting. For a language to spread and expand its speakers, not only does it need a demographic base of increasing numbers (which Spanish has in many parts of the world), but it must also have such characteristics as favourable attitudes, easy accessibility, efficient forms of (re)production and political support.

As far as favourable attitudes are concerned, we have demonstrated clearly throughout the book, that, with the possible exception of *Latinos* in the US and some of the speakers of minority languages in Spain, Spanish has an overwhelmingly superior status as perceived by the citizens of the countries where it is spoken.

As with other European or Western languages, Spanish can be considered easily accessible insofar as it has a long cultural and literate tradition with a highly developed corpus of standardised norms. Whilst we have sought to question some of the assumptions and beliefs underlying traditional literacy in Part III, it is hard to escape from the conclusion that the global economy and global politics are heavily reliant on Anderson's concept of print capitalism. A language, such as Spanish, with a huge range of publishing outputs is able to be an important player on this world stage.

Not only does a language need to be produced orally, as well as through print (and electronic media), and reproduced with the regeneration of its mother tongue speakers, it must also be taught and learnt through the education system. Here again, Spanish finds itself in a strong position. As we have already seen, it is the principal (and often only) language of the national education systems throughout the Spanish-speaking world where it is the, or one of the, national language(s). Moreover, it is experiencing a considerable increase in where it is being offered and learnt as a main foreign language in the curriculum. This is particularly true in parts of the Far East, as well, of course, as with its overwhelming domination of the school curriculum in the US. Notable in this drive to teach more Spanish as a foreign language is the establishment of the Institutes named in each of their locations as the *Instituto Cervantes* following the death of Franco and the 'opening up' of a democratic Spain. For all Franco's rhetoric about the grand concept of '*Hispanidad*' – a family of Spanish-speaking countries – it has been after his death that the structures and resources have been made available to set up the Institutes across the world. Besides offering classes in Spanish, the Institutes act as focal points for Spanish cultural activities, venues for lectures and conferences, and offer qualifications and courses for the training of teachers as teachers of Spanish as a second/foreign language. This network has clearly been inspired to some extent by models in other parts of the world, such as the British Council and the Goethe Institutes, and it raises the important questions and issues so heavily challenged by Phillipson (1992) amongst others about the underlying ideology and political goals of such an organisation. It is also important to note that there is a certain degree of ambivalence in the agenda of the Institutes as regards their role in promoting pan-Hispanic culture and language, incorporating Latin American varieties, in their programmes. This is hardly surprising given that they are financed and supported by the Spanish government.

Finally, political support for Spanish is also clearly available. This is true both at national level, as we have seen in our discussions of the various constitutions and education systems, and also at international level. In this area the language academies have a role to play. The existence of association of the RAE in Madrid and of the Latin American language academies who collaborate with it, allows supporters of Spanish to bring pressure in certain international fora where language is an issue. An example of this was the campaign to resist the EU's attempt to eliminate the Spanish letter 'ñ' from the alphabet (on the grounds that this created problems for computer use). Apart from any linguistic justification for its retention, Spanish speakers certainly felt it performed a role of marking their identity. In fact, the 'ñ' has been chosen as the logo for the *Instituto Cervantes*.

There is, of course, the argument that such pan-Hispanic associations might break down the distinctiveness of individual national varieties. As we argued in the earlier part of this chapter that is not necessarily the outcome of supranational organisations. Instead they may rather give confidence to individual members whilst offering them support. To a large extent that seems to be the case with the relatively loose association amongst speakers of Spanish.

A useful model to refer to here is that of 'pluricentric' language. Clyne defines this concept as:

> A term . . . to describe languages with several interacting centres, each providing a national variety with at least some of its own (codified) norms. Pluricentric languages are both unifiers and dividers of people. They unify people through the use of the language and separate them through the development of national norms and indices and linguistic variables with which the speakers identify.
>
> (Clyne, 1992: 1)

This model inevitably necessitates 'multiple group membership' (Clyne, 1992). In the case of Spanish-speakers, for example, people would relate to both the idea of being, say, a Peruvian, as well as part of the Spanish-speaking world. Clyne points out that there may be differing attitudes between the various 'centres' to language cooperation, and that in particular the traditional ultimate centre (in the case of Spanish, Madrid) does not always easily accept the pluricentric model.

Ultimately whether the continuing vitality and spread of Spanish results from a cooperative sense of pan-Hispanic community, or from a more hierarchical unity led by Madrid in the face of challenges from minority groups or from English, will depend on the kind of global and local politics we have examined in this chapter. What is certain is that the future of Spanish, as with all questions of language, will be determined by issues of politics and power.

Notes

Introduction

1 The geographical spread and extension of this use of Spanish will be discussed and plotted in Chapter 2.
2 The issues surrounding this choice of terms is examined further in Chapter 1.

1 Language and nationalism

1 Amongst the very extensive bibliography on nationalism, see for example, Alter, 1985, English translation 1991; Anderson, 1983, 2nd edn 1992; Billig, 1995; Connor, 1978; Eriksen, 1993; Gellner, 1983, 1994; Hobsbawm, 1990; Hutchinson and Smith, 1994; Kedourie, 3rd edn 1993; Llobera, 1994; Nairn, 1997; Seton-Watson, 1977, Smith, 1991, and Smith, 1995.
2 For more detailed discussion of this debate amongst the so-called 'primordialists' and the instrumentalists', see Smith, 1991, 1996, and 1998: Chapter 7.
3 See, for example, the debate between Dominique Schnapper and Anthony Smith in the *Bulletin of the Association for the Study of Ethnicity and Nationalism* (Schnapper, 1996) and discussions in Smith, 1996, 1998.
4 For a useful summary of Rousseau's thinking on the nation and nationalism and his contribution to political nationalism, see Llobera, 1994: 157–64.
5 For more detailed discussion of Herder's writings and enduring influence, see Barnard, 1969 and Llobera, 1994: 164–70.
6 See Chapter 4 for discussion and definition of this term.
7 For a far fuller discussion of the role of national education systems in the creation of collective and individual identity, and its link with language, see the conclusion to this chapter, and particularly Chapter 6.
8 This very European emphasis on the written word as the legitimiser of history and a shared past will be discussed and challenged in the later sections on literacy where oral and visual traditions are also defined as forms of literacy.

2 The 'Castilianisation' process

1 This chapter will examine the historical processes leading to the present day position of Spanish in Spain and in Latin America. There is not space here to give a full outline of Spanish and Spanish American history, and I have therefore to assume some prior knowledge. Useful reading in these areas include: Carr, 1982; Vicens Vives, 1972; Vilar, 1967, on Spain; and Bethell, 1995; Lynch, 1973, on Latin America.
2 For a good general survey of Spanish across the world in terms of location, variety, population, history, etc., see Thompson, 1992.

3 This will be touched on further in the discussions on the future of Spanish in Chapter 10.

4 For far fuller accounts of the history of the Spanish language see, e.g. Diez, Morales and Sabin, 1977; Lapesa, 1980, Penny, 1991.

5 For useful and thought-provoking syntheses of the debates on Spanish nation-building, see, e.g. Alvarez Junco, 1996; Barton, 1993; Linz, 1973. For more general discussions on Spanish nationalism, see Hernández and Mercadé, 1986; Herr and Polt, 1989; Mar-Molinero and Smith, 1996.

6 The Leonese dialect was only used in rural speech. The Aragonese dialect, highly influenced by Castilian, soon disappeared from literature. The importance of the great writers of Castilian coincided with the decline and displacement of Catalan literature. Even writers from other different linguistic regions were using Castilian as the means of literary expression . . . We can now legitimately talk of the Spanish language.

7 'Cleanse, fix and make splendid.'

8 For a very interesting discussion of the intellectual agenda of this period and its analysis of Spanish national identity and reaction to the growing awareness amongst the non-Castilian communities, see Serrano, 1998.

9 Language is the receptacle of a people's experience and the sediment of its thinking, in the deep folds of its metaphors it has left its footprints of the collective spirit of the people.

10 Another highly significant fact is that the official language of Spain is Castilian. Because from Latin there sprouted many Romance languages in Spain, but one amongst them, Castilian, has become the national and even international language, and is moving towards becoming the true Spanish language which is being formed on the nucleus of Castilian.

11 Castile made Spain and Castile was Spain's undoing. As the original nucleus for the Iberian enterprise, Castile was successful in overcoming her own individuality and invited the rest of the peoples of the Peninsula to collaborate in a vast project of a shared life.

12 Castile is hegemonic amongst her sister peoples of the Peninsula, because in the individualistic Spain, Castile shelters in her popular masses a more efficient individualism.

13 For good comprehensive descriptions of the history of Spanish and the distinct Spanish dialects in Latin America, see Lipski, 1994 and Solé, 1990.

14 For a country by country breakdown, see Lipski, 1994.

15 It must be remembered that in this era there was still a common belief that languages could be placed hierarchically in terms of their efficiency, usefulness, richness and beauty. Needless-to-say, to the Spanish colonisers, European languages were considered far superior to any native American varieties.

16 The independent Latin American republics certainly fit the definition of 'state' (as opposed to 'nation') outlined in Chapter 1, as these were arbitrarily mapped out as the result of wars and alliances.

17 I have preferred throughout this book to use the term 'indigenous' rather than 'Indian' to describe the pre-conquest Amerindian communities. However, it is true that recently there has been a swing back to favouring the use of this term by the communities themselves after many centuries of associating 'Indians' with racism and discrimination. Hamel (1994a: 284) comments on this changing attitude and says 'No doubt the word "indio" had and still has a discriminating connotation in a number of contexts and has therefore been replaced by the less specific "indígena" . . . Over the past decades, however, the Indian population themselves have increasingly vindicated the term "indio" and its derivatives . . .'

18 We will look in greater detail at the role of constitutions in the development of Latin American language policies in the post-colonial period in Chapter 5.

19 The man who does not know his rights and who is not free to exercise them finds himself in a sad situation in which civil rights will be for him like an unexpected piece of charity falling on him, political rights are prohibited and he cannot achieve social rights, because with difficulty he would reach the minimum economic level which would permit him to live with the dignity that every man should insist on.

20 In one way or another, almost without exception, all the governments have been faced with the same problems and have tried to find solutions to them. In such cases it is necessary to come down from the grandiose heights to the poor reality of daily life, and the poor reality is about national budgets, teachers and the fight against illiteracy.

21 We will look in much greater detail at the issues of education, particularly bilingual education and literacy programmes in Chapter 7.

22 Language has been witness to oppression and imperialism: what at the end of the fifteenth century was a historical reality, however much we might abhor this, in the twentieth century continues to be an instrument of intervention and troubling consciences.

23 For fuller discussions of this debate, see, e.g. Alonso, 1943; Alvar, 1986; González Ollé, 1978; López García, 1985; Menéndez Pidal, 1947; Mondéjar Camplán, 1981; Salvador, 1987, 1992; Williams, 1995. A more detailed examination of this issue in the context of the 1978 Constitution will be given in Chapter 5.

24 We could say that the community concept 'Spanish' did not arise in a territory which gave its name to the language – as with French – nor around an ethnic group which likewise baptised it – as with German – but that in the Peninsula it is the language which creates the community and precisely the language as an acquired instrument of communication and therefore freely adopted.

25 I feel myself to be a citizen of the Spanish language and not a Mexican citizen; for this reason it annoys me a great deal that people talk about the Castilian language, because Castilian belongs to the Castilians and I am not one, I am Mexican and as a Mexican I speak Spanish and not Castilian.

3 Counter-nationalism and the other languages

1 The intention here is to trace these examples up to the present century. Most will then be further elaborated in the chapters on the current situation in Parts II and III.

2 From a relatively large bibliography on the Catalan language, and, in particular, its relationship with Catalan nationalism, see the following: Conversi, 1997; Ferrer i Gironés, 1985; Hernández, 1983: Nicolás, 1998; Siguan, 1993; Valverdú, 1984; Woolard, 1989.

3 Federation is a system by which different human groups without losing their autonomy in those areas that are special and particular to them, can come together in a joint endeavour in all things that they have in common. It is applicable to all groups and to all forms of government. It establishes unity without destroying variety, and can manage to unite everyone without lessening their independence nor altering the character of a nation, or province or people.

4 I have taken the quotations from Prat's seminal book from the Spanish translation of his original Catalan, which is a fascinating text in its own right as a result of the prologue by the translator Antonio Royo Villanova who is a staunch opponent of Prat's thesis concerning the existence and relationship of the Catalan nation to the rest of Spain.

5 If to be a homeland, if to be a nation was to have a language, a conception of the judicial, a sense of one's own art, if it was to have a national spirit, a national character and thought, the existence of a nation or of a homeland was a natural thing, like the existence of man, independent in fact from the rights that he might be granted.

We arrive at a clear and neat idea of nationality, at the conception of this primary, fundamental, social unity destined to be world society, in humanity, what man is for civil society.

6   In order to know a people it is necessary to share their language; to appreciate their literature it is necessary to know the language in which it is written. Every nation thinks as it speaks and speaks as it thinks.

7   The mother tongue is not a dying *patois*. On the re-awakening of old popular ways of speaking, the Catalan language rose up sincere and strong, full of renewed life and began the long reconquering of Catalan culture. The Catalan language had a glorious history; it had been spoken and written by kings and conquistadores, by wise men and apostles, by poets and legislators.

8   For more detailed accounts of the Basque language, Basque history, and Basque nationalism, see, Conversi, 1997; Heiberg, 1989; Linz, 1986; MacClancy, 1996; Nuñez Astrain, 1995.

9   Arana's created word for 'Basque' which is commonly used today rather than 'Vasco' even amongst Castilian-speakers.

10   Derogatory term for non-Basques.

11   Inhabitants of Vizcaya.

12   Less is available on Galician nationalism and the Galician language than is written on Catalan and Basque, reflecting many of the differences between the regions that we note. In particular there is very little in English. See: Diez, Morales and Sabin, 1977; Henderson, 1996; Hernández and Mercadé, 1986; Siguan, 1993.

13   This is based largely on Lipski, 1994: 5–7. For a useful overview summary of the broad classifications and numbers of language families in the Americas, see Crystal, 1987: 320–23.

14   See, for example, Key, 1991; Klein and Stark, 1985; Lozano, 1990.

15   For an excellent and authoritative account of language policy in Mexico and its relationship to nation-building, see, Brice Heath, 1972; for good overviews of linguistic issues in Mexico, including discussion of the history and role of the indigenous languages, see, *International Journal of the Sociology of Language*, 1992; and *Language Problems and Language Planning*, 1994.

16   According to the ideas of the Enlightenment, which Clavijero and his contemporaries followed, a coherence had to exist between the level of culture and the specific characteristics of the language: to a great civilisation there should correspond a greater lexicon, a rich numerical system, and the capacity of expressing the necessary metaphysical concepts for the development of thought. At the same time, a symptom of civilisation was the unity of the language, a unity which came about as a result of control and attention to the form of the language by its speakers, and specifically by its government. In the judgement of the specialists, the Mexican language – one of the varieties of Nahuatl – satisfied the prerequisites to be considered a language of civilisation.

17   For a good overview on the history of Quechua and its role in the lives of Quechua-speakers, see Brice Heath and Laprade, 1982; and Von Gleich, 1994; for a comprehensive analysis of Quechua, see Cerrón-Palomino, 1987. Specifically on Quechua in Peru, see Cerrón-Palomino, 1989; and in Ecuador, Abrám, 1992.

18   This statistic refers to the 1920s. Today there are estimated to be nearly four and a half million Quechua speakers in Peru (Cerrón-Palomino, 1989) and around eight and a half million throughout South America (Von Gleich, 1994).

19   The Indians lack national attachments. Their protests have always been regional. This has contributed to a large extent to their defeat. A people of four million men, conscious of their size, never despair of their future. The same four million people whilst they are only an organic mass, a dispersed crowd, are not capable of deciding the direction of their history.

20 For more detailed discussion of the Guarani and Paraguayan case, see Corvalán and Granda, 1982; Granda, 1988. There is little available in English, but see Fasold, 1984: 13–20; Lipski, 1994: Chapter 21.

4 Rights, policies and Language Planning

1 Amongst the many books on this subject, two useful texts are Galtung, 1994 and Vincent, 1986. Pennycook, 1998: 74–7, gives a very concise summary of some of the major lines of debate, basing his framework on Galtung.

2 For a list and selected extracts of the major relevant documents produced by the international community regarding human rights, see Skutnabb-Kangas and Phillipson, 1994a: 371–412.

3 And see also the 'Guidelines' agreed for a 'Literacy and Language Policy' particularly for Third World countries summarised in Barton, 1994b: 101–3 where it is stated that *'there should be a constitutional guarantee for the rights of all languages and literacies where they are valued by their communities'* (1994b: 101, original's italics).

4 In a footnote to their chapter (1994b: 107–8) Skutnabb-Kangas and Phillipson offer an excellent typology for the concept of 'minorities'.

5 For detailed discussion of this debate see Laponce, 1984a, 1984b; Patanayak and Bayer, 1987; and for a discussion of the polarised positions of these two, see Mar-Molinero and Stevenson, 1991.

6 See Coulmas, 1998, and O'Riagáin, 1997, for interesting discussions of the issues of language rights and language policy in what O'Riagáin calls a 'postmodern' world where the classic divisions of the nation-state have been broken down.

7 In a recent article, Lambert (1999) offers what he calls a 'scaffolding' for analysing language policy, and in particular 'ethnic language policy'. He identifies six domains, which include Language Planning as one of these. His six categories are: official language selection, the setting of national language norms, the 'projection of linguistic hegemony across national boundaries', the organisation of language teaching (including, he stresses, foreign language teaching), the direction of language learning outside the formal systems, and Language Planning.

8 Since its emergence as an academic discipline in the 1960s, publications on Language Planning have boomed. Many major journals now are primarily or significantly concerned with work in this field, such as *Language Problems and Language Planning* and many of the articles in *the International Journal of the Sociology of Language*. For a selection of some of the major work published on general Language Planning theory during this period see, Blommaert, 1996; Cobarrubias and Fishman, 1983; Cooper, 1989; Eastman, 1983; Fishman, 1974; Fishman, Ferguson and Das Gupta, 1968; Haugen, 1966; Kaplan and Baldauf, 1997; Kennedy, 1984; Rubin and Hernudd, 1971; Tollefson, 1991; Williams, 1992.

9 However, see Baldauf (1994) for a discussion of what he calls 'unplanned' policy and planning.

5 The state and language policies

1 Amongst the many texts written about the Franco regime, see, for example, Preston (1993) for the most comprehensive history of this period. See Almira Picazo (1998) for an interesting discussion of the nature of Francoist nationalism.

2 For the full text of the 1978 Constitution and an article-by-article commentary on this by a well-known Spanish political economist, see Tamames (1980, 6th edn 1992).

3 The Constitution is based on the indissoluble unity of the Spanish Nation, a common and indivisible fatherland of all Spaniards, and it recognises and guarantees the right

to autonomy of the nationalities and regions which are contained in it and the solidarity between them.

4 1 Castilian is the official Spanish language of the State. All Spaniards have the duty to know it and the right to use it.

2 The other Spanish languages will also be official in their respective Autonomous Communities in accordance with their Statutes.

3 The wealth of Spain's distinctive linguistic varieties is its cultural patrimony which will be the object of special respect and protection.

5 See, for example, Bastardas and Boix, 1994b; Linz, 1981; Mar-Molinero, 1997; Salvador, 1987, 1992; Siguan, 1993; Vernet i Llobet, 1994.

6 It is very important to note that the use of 'duty' is not found in the statements about the status of the non-Castilian languages. Mirambell i Abancó (1989: 52) in fact argues that it is the 'duty' to know the language which gives it its official status, and that, therefore, if the minority languages have official status within their territories, the 'duty' to know them must also apply there. The Constitutional Tribunal (the guardian of the constitution) however does not agree with this.

7 Spaniards are equal before the law, without there being any discrimination for reasons of birth, race, sex, religion, opinion or any other condition or personal or social circumstance.

8 For examples of some of this work see, Martínez Ferrer, 1995, on Aragonese; Novo Mier, 1980, on Asturian; Sanchis Guarner, 1972, 19th edn 1996, on Valencian; Narbona Jiménez and Morillo-Velarde Pérez, 1987; and Payán Sotomayor, 1983, 6th edn. 1993, on Andalusia.

9 The political repercussions of multilingualism have always been and continue to be, if not extremely serious, certainly fairly serious. . . . Spain is a country with bilingual zones and bilingualism is always problematic.

10 Limitations of space mean that the following discussion is both very brief and rather general. For more detailed discussion of LP in the three regions under examination with critical evaluations of their success, see, e.g. Cobarrubias, 1988; Garmendía, 1994; Tejerina, 1992, on the Basque Country; García Sendón and Monteagudo Romero, 1983; Radio, 1980, 3rd edn. 1989; Santamaría Conde, 1985 on Galicia; and many of the articles in Generalitat de Catalunya, 1989; Reniu i Tresseres, 1994, on Catalonia; and Hoffmann, 1996b; Mar-Molinero, 1997: Chapter 10; Siguan, 1993 for all three.

11 See Mirambell i Abancó, 1989, for a useful discussion of the definition of 'official' language, and in particular, how the Constitutional Tribunal has tried to deal with clarification of this, and the various relevant articles in *Llengua i Dret*, 29, 1998.

12 For good discussions of legislation and the rights of the indigenous communities see, Alvar, 1986; Hamel, 1994b, 1997b; and Stavenhagen, 1988.

13 The terms 'multiculturalism' and 'pluriculturalism' are used differently in different parts of the world and in different academic disciplines. For example, most European commentators would consider 'multiculturalism' much closer to Hamel's definition of 'pluriculturalism'. In fact when discussing these phenomena in Spain it is usually considered that 'multiculturalism' translates the Spanish word 'pluriculturalismo'. It is important, then, to stress that I am using the terms here exactly according to Hamel's interpretation. Recently in discussions of these issues in Latin America – and increasingly in Europe – the term 'intercultural' is used to refer to what he here calls 'pluricultural'.

14 It is necessary to distinguish between national and official: the first concept affects all the languages of a nation, while the second is a much more restricted concept in that it only gives a special privilege to one out of all the national languages.

15 What was considered *national language* was encompassed in the new concept of *official*, and therefore the indigenous languages are elements of *national culture*. When in 1946

they turned to officiality, they recognised that of Castilian, because, silencing the other languages, they could not consider themselves alien from the idea of national.
16 For a brief period in fact between 1975 and 1979 Quechua was declared co-official with Spanish throughout Peru, but this position was retreated from in the 1979 Peruvian constitution.
17 See discussion on LP below.
18 By far the majority of literature in this area is specifically aimed at examining LP and bi/multilingual education in Latin America. For writing on LP in a more general sense, see Hornberger, 1994, on South America; Richards, 1989, on Guatemala; Cerrón-Palomino, 1989, Hornberger, 1995, on Peru; Plaza and Albó, 1989, on Bolivia; Hidalgo, 1994; Lara, 1992; Patthey-Chavez, 1994, on Mexico.
19 The role of the SIL in Latin America (and others parts of the developing world) is often highly controversial, as its motivation and alliances have often made it the object of suspicion and mistrust amongst educators and language planners from indigenous communities (see, Barros, 1995; Patthey-Chavez, 1994; Richards, 1989).

6 Literacy and language in education systems

1 Amongst the vast amount of literature in this field, see, for example, Appel and Muysken, 1987; Baker and Prys Jones, 1998; Skutnabb-Kangas, 1984; Skutnabb-Kangas and Cummins, 1988, and, on multilingual education, as opposed to specifically bilingual, Cenoz and Genesee, 1998.
2 In this discussion of bilingual education I shall be concentrating only on the school sector, i.e. compulsory education as it is now in most countries. This is not to deny that adult education can also play an important role in the provision of language teaching, as we will see with the later examination of literacy classes. It is also the case that much good mother-tongue instruction to, for example, immigrants and their children takes place in non-formal classes, often completely outside the state system.
3 In many of the contexts discussed below more than one minority language may be in existence. Very often the multilingual nature of a state will actually entail education programmes which teach a third or even a fourth language. For the purposes of the discussions in this chapter the issues and arguments are broadly the same whether we examine bilingual or multilingual education. However, for analyses of some of the differences and further challenges that multilingual acquisition presents the education systems, see the edited volume by Cenoz and Genesee, 1998.
4 Exceptions to this assertion are such ventures as the European Bilingual schools (see, e.g. Hoffmann, 1998) where various EU languages are offered equally as part of the school curriculum and day-to-day operations. Some of the examples of immersion education, which we will discuss later, also are aimed at students who are majority language speakers but living in areas where a minority language is in fact dominant.
5 As we shall see in Chapter 8 the extent to which learning Catalan in immersion programmes in Catalonia today is considered by all mother-tongue Castilian-speakers as being entirely voluntary is a controversial and widely-debated issue.
6 See, for example, Barton, 1994a, b; Baynham, 1995; Gee, 1990; Hamilton *et al.*, 1994; Lankshear, 1997; Maybin, 1994, and Street, 1993.
7 For a recent evaluation and critique of Freire's work, see McLaren and Lankshear, 1994.
8 The learner in all of Freire's work is always referred to as 'man' and 'he', etc., which is somewhat ironic given that some of the most successful Freirean projects have been undertaken with women's groups.
9 Some of the actual methods that Freire uses to achieve literacy will be described and evaluated further in the Latin American contexts examined in the following chapter.

7 Latin American educational policies

1 For an interesting assessment of educational policies in various Latin American countries in the period we are discussing, see Morales-Gómez and Torres, 1992.

2 For a brief country by country summary, see Lastra (1992), and for a good bibliographical overview of the topic, see Hornberger, 1992.

3 For fuller discussions of bilingual education in Mexico, particularly from an historical perspective, see Brice Heath, 1972, and Hidalgo, 1994.

4 Bilingual education entails knowing how and being able to read and write in both languages as well as being familiar with their structure, that is in the mother tongue and in Castilian. The bicultural aspect implies taking into account the native culture (its philosophy, values and indigenous objectives) of those being educated in educational planning both in the content and in the psychopedagogic methods.

5 The mastery that teachers might have in both languages does not guarantee, however, that they have the technical knowledge that allows them to confront the problems of teaching the languages both at the oral and written levels.

6 For a full account of these events see, for example, Tello Diaz, 1995. Further discussion of Chiapas is also found in Chapter 10.

7 To claim that in Mexico there exist bilingual education programmes for the indigenous population is to talk of good intentions and scant reality. It is true that education for the ethnic groups has been changing towards the recognition of the languages and cultures as legitimate and important parts of the cultural patrimony of the nation, and today it is recognised as necessary to set off from the linguistic and cultural reality of each group, as the fundamental basis for the education processes aimed at these sectors, in the framework of their economic and political insertion into the Mexican capitalist system. The actual practice however, shows that the history of domination represented by Castilianisation has left a profound mark in society and the ideological effect of linguistic imposition has many peoples demanding access to education in many ways.

8 For a useful historical overview of Peruvian education, focusing less on the current situation which we are examining, see Portocarrero, 1992.

9 An exception to this was the legacy of the indigenist thinker Luis Varcárcel's two months as minister of education in 1945. His project of *Núcleos Escolares Campesinos* was an interesting experiment in alternative education based in the heart of indigenous communities (Devine, 1999).

10 Besides the three case studies offered here, Guatemala and Ecuador are the two other countries with the closest kind of bicultural education programmes sharing similar experiences of success and failure to those outlined here. Constraints of space make it impossible to discuss them here, but the Ecuadorian one in particular offers us an interesting experiment in intercultural education for Ecuador's Quechua speakers (see Yáñez Cossio, 1992). For fuller details of both countries, see Chiodi (1990).

11 For reasons of space I have chosen only to discuss those literacy programmes here which can be described as radical. During the sixties onwards, in fact there was an increasing awareness (by international bodies like UNESCO and by the US) of the need for literacy drives in Latin America. Many of these state-backed programmes, however, were designed to offer functional literacy, and used relatively traditional methods and institutions for their work. The result was either limited success or the further confirmation by the learners of their subordinate role in society.

12 Official Nicaraguan government figures talk of around 13 per cent, but this is because they exclude a sector they describe as 'unteachable' or 'learning impaired' (Torres, 1990).

13 For fuller accounts of women and education, in general, and literacy programmes in particular, see Archer and Costello, 1990, on Bolivia, Schirmer, 1993 [in Radcliffe and Westwood], on Guatemala, and Stromquist, 1992, on Latin America in general.

14 For an overview of Guatemala's sociolinguistic situation, see Richards, 1989.

8 Politics, language and Spanish education

1 For a good overview of how the different autonomous communities have responded to the invitation in the 1978 Constitution to introduce their local languages in the education system, see Siguan, 1988.

2 For the recent growth in the provision of Catalan in the Balearic Islands see Sbert and Vives, 1994.

3 For a more detailed overview of the post-Franco Catalan language education policies and the early implementation of these, see Arnau and Boada, 1986; and Mar-Molinero, 1989.

4 I shall use throughout this term in its Catalan form.

5 'Lengua habitual' or 'normal/usual language' is preferred in this legislation, for example, 'mother tongue'. The language of the home may well be dictated by the language of the child's immediate environment which is, of course, not necessarily that of the mother.

6 For an interesting and persuasive discussion and analysis of this debate, see Branchadell, 1997, and also Woolard's (1998) somewhat critical review of Branchadell's book.

7 Sadly at this advanced stage of Spanish democracy murky ink still flows from certain press. The imagination of these anticatalanists does not limit itself to filling its ink up with a supposed mercantilistic conspiracy in Catalanism. Anything will do. A paradigmatic example is the harsh attack launched in yesterday's edition of *ABC* against language normalisation in Catalonia.

8 The most serious aspect to this affair is that such irresponsible demonstrations as these only contribute to putting more wood on the fire. They ignore the excellent social coexistence that prevails and fuel incomprehension towards Catalonia and the autonomous state.

9 For an extremely detailed and scholarly examination of this long and complicated legal challenge which has been very sketchily summarised here, see Institut d'Estudis Autonòmics, 1994.

10 The Catalan language is a fundamental element in the national personality and formation of Catalonia, a basic instrument of communication, of integration and of social cohesion amongst its citizens. Furthermore, it has been witness to the loyalty of the Catalan people to their land and their particular culture.

11 Catalan and Castilian as official languages can be used without distinction by all citizens in any public or private activities without discrimination.

12 As far as education is concerned, this law guarantees all the population the full recognition of both languages and, moreover, guarantees that the students should not be discriminated against and separated into different groups for reasons of language.

13 Clause 6 of Article 21, which establishes the requirement of the accreditation of knowledge of the two official languages in order to obtain the title of graduate in secondary education, is probably the key to the concept of the linguistic model of double officiality. On the one hand, it guarantees all citizens recognition of the two languages and, on the other, it guarantees all citizens their right to choose between the two without any subordination.

14 For a detailed discussion and evaluation of the earlier years of the *Ikastolas*, see Garagorri and Eguilior, 1988.

15 For further details about these different models of bilingual education in the Basque Country, see, e.g. Artigal, 1994; Cernoz, 1998; Gobierno Vasco, 1990; and Sierra, 1994. For specific case studies of some of the immersion projects within these models, see Artigal, 1993; and Olaziregi, 1994.

16 • understand Basque well,
 • equip the students to be able to express themselves in Basque on the most simple daily topics,
 • foster a favourable attitude towards Basque,

- equip the students so that they might integrate into a Basque-speaking environment.
17 • help the students to have, besides a good level of comprehension in Basque, an adequate competence to develop the use of that language,
- equip them to continue their studies in Basque.
18 • foster competence in Basque, enriching their knowledge of this language, and making it their colloquial language as well as the school language of instruction,
- reinforce the community of Basque-speaking students, in order to counteract the predominant linguistic pressure of the environment and promote its crucial role in the achievement of a generalised bilingualism,
- guarantee an adequate knowledge of Castilian.

9 Spanish as minority language

1 These demographic trends are extrapolated from the 1996 US census.
2 For discussions of the characteristics of US Spanish varieties, see for example Torres, 1991.
3 For useful histories of language policy-making in the US and its close link with nation-building see, e.g. Dicker, 1996; Donahue, 1995; Ruiz, 1994; Trueba, 1989.
4 For good in-depth discussions of the underlying issues of this movement, see, e.g. Crawford, 1992; Dicker, 1996; and Donahue, 1995.
5 However, it is significant that the backlash by the Hispanic community to this last piece of legislation has been enormous, and has – perhaps for the first time – served to mobilise and politicise a range of people from this community. By 1999 the new Governor of California, Gray Davis, recognising this opposition, quietly shelved the law as unconstitutional.
6 For a very interesting and important discussion of the terms 'Hispanic' versus 'Latino' and the concept of such a community in global (as well as US) terms, see Gracia (2000).
7 President Clinton did appoint two Hispanic-origin members to his government, but they both later resigned. In 1999 there were twenty-one *Latino* members of Congress.
8 For example, in February 1997, the Spanish *Casa de América* co-organised with a US foundation a conference entitled *'Presencia hispana en los Estados Unidos'* to study the Hispanic influence on history, art, literature and language in the US. The conference, which took place in New Mexico was opened by the Spanish king's son.
9 The signatories below believe that minority native languages represent not only a national patrimony, but also an example of valuable talent which enriches the capabilities and potential of any nation. The xenophobia in the form of the 'English only' policy constitutes an element of upheaval, division and destruction within a nation which continues to have a fertile history of linguistic and cultural traditions and they demand the democratic freedom to practise them.
10 For a useful table outlining the dates and major language-related events in Puerto Rico from 1902 to 1990, see Vélez and Schweers, 1993: 119.
11 Election results reported in *El País* 14.12.98.

10 Spanish in a global era

1 Amongst the growing volume of literature in this field, e.g. Held *et al.*, 1999, and Hirst and Thompson, 1999.
2 For more detailed discussions of language policies and language issues in Europe, see the collection of papers edited by Coulmas, 1991; Pool, 1996; Ramón i Mimó, 1994; Siguan, 1996; Truchot, 1991.

3 Such as the so-called 'Four Motors' grouping which includes Barcelona, Baden-Württemberg, Lombardy and Rhône Alpes, or the 'Atlantic Arch' which includes regions in Spain, France and the UK bordering the Atlantic coast.

4 The European Language Council (ELC) was officially launched in 1997. Its main aim is 'the quantitative and qualitative improvement of knowledge of the languages and cultures of the European Union and beyond. . . . The objective of the ELC is, therefore, to create the framework and conditions necessary for common policy development and provide a platform for the launching of joint projects specifically designed to bring about real improvement' (quoted from ELC homepage, http://www.fu-berlin.de/elc/).

Bibliography

Abrám, M. (1992) *Lengua, cultura e identidad: El proyecto EBI 1985–1990*, Quito: Ediciones Abya-Yala.

Aguire, A. and Bustamante, D. (1993) 'Critical notes regarding the dislocation of Chicanos by the Spanish-language television industry in the United States', *Ethnic and Racial Studies*, 16.1, pp. 121–32.

Ajuntaments de Catalunya (1986) *Padrons municipals d'habitants de 1986*, Catalunya: Ajuntaments de Catalunya i Consorci d'Informació i Documentació de Catalunya.

Almira Picazo, C. (1998) *¡Viva España! El nacionalismo fundacional del régimen de Franco 1939–1943*, Granada: Comares.

Alonso, A. (1943, 2nd edn.) *Castellano, español. Idioma nacional*, Buenos Aires.

Alter, P. (1985, English translation, 1990, 1991) *Nationalism*, London/New York: Edward Arnold.

Alvar, M. (1986) *Hombre, etnia, estado: actitudes lingüísticas en Hispanoamérica*, Madrid: Gredos.

Alvarez Junco, J. (1996) 'The nation-building process in nineteenth century Spain', in Mar-Molinero and Smith (eds) (1996), pp. 89–107.

Amadio, M. and López, L.E. (1991) *La educación bilingüe intercultural en América Latina. Una guía bibliográfica*, La Paz: Ministerio de Educación y Cultura and UNICEF.

Anderson, B (1983, 2nd edn 1992) *Imagined Communities: Reflections on the Origins and Spread of Nationalism*, London/New York: Verso.

Appel, R. and Muysken, P. (1987) *Language Contact and Bilingualism*, London: Edward Arnold.

Archer, D. and Costello, P. (1990) *Literacy and Power: the Latin American Battleground*, London: Earthscan.

Arenas, J. (1986) *La immersió lingüística*, Barcelona: Llar de Llibre.

Arnau, J. and Boada, H. (1986) 'Languages and school in Catalonia', *Journal of Multilingual and Multicultural Development*, 7, pp. 107–22.

Artigal, J.M. (1993) 'Catalan and Basque immersion programmes', in Baetens Beardsmore (ed.) (1993), pp. 30–54.

Badiola Astiagarriaga, A. (1989) 'El decreto sobre uso y normalización del euskera en las administraciones públicas de la comunidad autónoma del País Vasco', in Generalitat de Catalunya (ed.) (1989), pp. 207–15.

Baetens Beardsmore, H. (ed.) (1993) *European Models of Bilingual Education*, Clevedon/Philadelphia/Adelaide: Multilingual Matters.

Baker, C. and Prys Jones, S. (1998) *Encyclopedia of Bilingualism and Bilingual Education*, Clevedon: Multilingual Matters.

Baldauf, R.B. (1994) 'Unplanned Language Planning', *Annual Review of Applied Linguistics*, 14, pp. 82–9.

Barnard, F. (1969) *Herder on Social and Political Culture*, Cambridge: Cambridge University Press.

Banton, (1996) 'International norms and Latin American states' policies on indigenous peoples', *Nations and Nationalism*, 2, 1, pp. 89–105.

Barros, M.C. (1995) 'The missionary presence in literacy campaigns in the indigenous languages of Latin America', *International Journal of Educational Development*, 15, 3, pp. 277–89.

Barton, D. (1994a) *An Introduction to the Ecology of the Written Language*, Oxford: Blackwell.

—— (ed.) (1994b) *Sustaining Local Literacies*, Clevedon/Reading: Multilingual Matters/ Education for Development.

Barton, J. (1997) *A Political Geography of Latin America*, London/New York: Routledge.

Barton, S. (1993) 'The roots of the national question in Spain', in Teich, M. and Porter, R. (eds) *The National Question in Europe in Historical Context*, Cambridge: Cambridge University Press, pp. 116–28.

Bastardas, A. and Boix, E (eds) (1994a) *¿Un estado. Una lengua? La organización política de la diversidad lingüística*, Barcelona: Octaedro.

—— (1994b) 'Introducción', in Bastardas and Boix (eds) (1994a), pp. 9–25.

Baynham, M. (1995) *Literacy Practices: Investigating Literacy in Social Contexts*, London/New York: Longman.

Bergen, J.J. (ed.) (1990) *Spanish in the United States: Sociolinguistic Issues*, Washington DC: Georgetown University Press.

Bethell, L. (ed.) (1995) *The Cambridge History of Latin America*, Cambridge: Cambridge University Press.

Bhola, H. (1984) *Campaigning for Literacy*, UNESCO.

Billig, M. (1995) *Banal Nationalism*, London: Sage.

Blommaert, J. (1996) 'Language Planning as a discourse on language and society: the Linguistic Ideology of a scholarly tradition', *Language Problems and Language Planning*, 20, 3, pp. 199–23.

Boogerman Castejón, A. (1997) 'Educational policy, mixed discourses: responses to minority learners in Catalonia', *Language Problems and Language Planning*, 21, 1, pp. 20–35.

Branchadell, A. (1997) *Liberalisme i Normalització Lingüística*, Barcelona: Empúries.

Brassloff, A. (1996) 'Centre–periphery communication in Spain: the politics of language and the Language of Politics', in Hoffmann, C. (ed.) (1996), pp. 111–24.

Bravo Ahuja, G.R. de (1992) 'The process of bilingualism in a multiethnic context', *International Journal of the Sociology of Language*, 96, pp. 45–53.

Breton, R. (1996) 'The dynamics of Ethnolinguistic Communities as the central factor in Language Policy and Planning', *International Journal of the Sociology of Language*, 118, pp. 163–81.

Brice Heath, S. (1972) *Telling Tongues: Language Policy in Mexico. Colony to Nation*, New York/London: Teachers College Press, Colombia University.

Brice Heath, S. and Laprade, R. (1982) 'Castilian colonization and indigenous languages: the cases of Quechua and Aymara', in Cooper (ed.), pp. 119–34.

Brookes, H. and Brice Heath, S. (1997) Book review of Skutnabb-Kangas and Phillipson (1994), *International Journal of the Sociology of Language*, 127, pp. 197–207.

Bugarski, R. (1992) 'Language education and general policy', in Bugarski, R. and Hawkesworth, C. (eds) *Language Planning in Yugoslavia*, Columbus, OH: Slavica, pp. 10–26.

Campos Carr, I. (1990) 'The politics of literacy in Latin America', *Convergence* XXIII(2), pp. 50–65.

Carr, R. (1982 2nd edn.) *Spain 1808–1975*, Oxford: Oxford University Press.

Casanova, U. (1991) 'Bilingual education: politics or pedagogy?' Reprinted in García and Baker (eds) (1995) *Policy and Practice in Bilingual Education: Extending the Foundations*, Clevedon/Philadelphia/Adelaide: Multilingual Matters, pp. 15–25.

Cebrián Abellán, A. (1992) *Marginalidad de la población gitana española*, Murcia: Universidad de Murcia.

Cenoz, J. (1998) 'Multilingual education in the Basque Country', in Cenoz and Genesee (eds) (1998), pp. 175–92.

Cenoz, J. and Genesee, F. (eds) (1998) *Beyond Bilingualism: Multilingualism and Multilingual Education*, Clevedon: Multilingual Matters.

Cenoz, J. and Perales, J. (1997) 'Minority language learning in the administration: data from the Basque Country', *Journal of Multilingual and Multicultural Development*, 18, 4, pp. 261–71.

Centro de Investigaciones Sociológicas (CIS) (1994) *Conocimiento y uso de las lenguas de España*, Madrid: CIS.

Cerrón-Palomino, R. (1987) *Lingüística Quechua*, Cuzco: Centro de Estudios Rurales Andinos 'Bartolomé de las Casas'

—— (1989) 'Language policy in Peru: a historical overview', *International Journal of the Sociology of Language*, 77, pp. 12–33.

Chen, A. (1998) 'The philosophy of language rights', *Language Sciences*, 20, 1, pp. 45–55.

Chiodi, F. (ed.) (1990) *La Educación indígena en América Latina*, Vols I and II, Quito: P.EBI(MEC-GTZ) and ABYA-YALA/Santiago, Chile: UNESCO/OREALC.

Cifuentes, B. (1994) 'Las lenguas amerindias y la conformación de la lengua nacional en México en el Siglo XIX', *Language Problems and Language Planning*, 18, 3, pp. 208–23.

Clachar, A. (1997) 'Ethnolinguistic identity and Spanish proficiency in a paradoxical situation. The case of Puerto Rican returned migrants', *Journal of Multilingual and Multicultural Development*, 18.1, pp. 107–24.

Clyne, M. (ed.) (1992) *Pluricentric Languages: Differing Norms in Differing Nations*, Berlin: Mouton de Gruyter.

Cobarrubias, J. (1987) 'Models of language planning for minority languages', *Bulletin of the CAAL*, 9, pp. 47–70.

—— (1988) 'Normalización y planificanción lingüística en el País Vasco', in II Congreso Mundial Vasco (co-ordinator) *Conference on the Basque Language*, Vitoria: Gobierno Vasco, pp. 145–73.

—— and Fishman, J. (eds) (1983) *Progress in Language Planning*, Berlin: Mouton.

Cobreros Mendazona, E. (1989) 'Situación actual del régimen jurídico lingüístico en el País Vasco y Navarra', in Generalitat de Catalunya (ed.) (1989), pp. 195–207.

Connor, W. (1978) 'A nation is a nation, is a state, is an ethnic group . . .', *Ethnic and Racial Studies*, Vol. 1, 4, pp. 377–400.

Conversi, D. (1990) 'Language or race? The choice of core values in the development of Catalan and Basque nationalisms', *Ethnic and Racial Studies*, 13, 1, pp. 50–70.

—— (1997) *The Basques, the Catalans, and Spain: Alternative Routes to Nationalist Mobilisation*, London: Hurst.

Cooper, R. (ed.) (1982) *Language Spread Studies in Diffusion and Social Change*, Washington: CAP.

—— (1989) *Language Planning and Social Change*, Cambridge: Cambridge University Press.

Coronado, G. (1992) 'Educación bilingüe en México: propósitos y realidades', *International Journal of the Sociology of Language*, 96, pp. 53–71.

Corvalán, G. and de Granda, G. (eds) (1982) *Sociedad y lengua: Bilingüismo en el Paraguay*, Asunción: Centro Paraguayo de Estudios Sociológicos.

Coulmas, F. (issue ed.) (1990) 'Spanish in the USA: New quandraries and prospects', *International Journal of the Sociology of Language*, 84.

—— (ed.) (1991) *A Language Policy for the European Community: Prospects and Quandaries*, Berlin/New York: Mouton de Gruyter.

—— (1998) 'Language rights – interests of state, language groups and the individual', *Language Sciences*, 20, 1, pp. 63–73.

Crawford, J. (1992) *Hold your Tongue. Bilingualism and the Politics of 'English-Only'*, Reading MA: Addison Wesley.

Crystal, D. (1987) *The Cambridge Encyclopedia of Language*, Cambridge: Cambridge University Press.

Delgado-P, G. (1995) 'Indigenous movements of the Americas: reflections on nationalism and ethnicity', *ASEN Bulletin*, 9, pp. 13–17.

Devine, T.L. (1999) 'Indigenous Identity and Identification in Peru: 'indigenismo, education and contradictions in state discourses', *Journal of Latin American Cultural Studies*, Vol. 8, 1, pp. 63–75.

De Witte, B. (1985) 'Linguistic equality: a study in comparative constitutional law', *Revista de Llengua i Dret*, pp. 43–126.

—— (1993) 'Conclusion: a legal perspective', in Vilfan, S. (ed.) *Ethnic Groups and Language Rights*, Dartmouth: New York University Press, pp. 303–14.

Díaz-Polanco, H. (1987) *Etnia, Nación y Política*, Mexico: JP.

—— (2nd edn 1988) *La cuestión étnico-nacional*, Mexico: Fontamara.

Dicker, S. (1996) *Languages in America: A Pluralist View*, Clevedon: Multilingual Matters.

Díez, M., Morales, F. and Sabín, A. (1977) *Las lenguas de España*, Madrid: Ministerio de Educación.

Donahue, T. (1995) 'American language policy and compensatory opinion', in Tollefson (ed.) (1995), pp. 112–41.

Eastman, C. (1983) *Language Planning: An Introduction*, San Francisco: Chandler and Sharp.

Edwards, J. (1985) *Language, Society and Identity*, Oxford: Blackwell.

Eriksen, T. (1993) *Ethnicity and Nationalism: Anthropological Perspectives*, London: Pluto.

Fairclough, N. (1989) *Language and Power*, London/New York: Longman.

Fasold, R. (1984) *The Sociolinguistics of Society*, Oxford: Blackwell.

Fernández, R. (1990) 'Actitudes hacia los cambios de códigos en Nuevo México: reacciones de un sujeto a ejemplos de su habla', in Bergen (ed.) (1990), pp. 49–59.

Ferrer i Girones (1985) *La persecució politica de la llengua Catalana*, Barcelona: Edicions 62.

Fishman, J. (1972) *Language and Nationalism*, Rowley, Mass.: Newbury House (reprinted in Fishman, 1989, pp. 105–77; pp. 269–368).

—— (ed.) (1974) *Advances in Language Planning*, The Hague: Mouton.

—— (1989) *Language and Ethnicity in Minority Sociolinguistic Perspective*, Clevedon: Multilingual Matters.

—— (1991) *Reversing Language Shift*, Clevedon: Multilingual Matters.

—— (1994) 'On the limits of ethnolinguistic democracy', in Skutnabb-Kangas and Phillipson (eds) (1994a), pp. 49–63.

Fishman, J., Ferguson, C. and Das Gupta, J. (eds) (1968) *Language Problems of Developing Nations*, New York: John Wiley and Sons.

Freeland, J. (1993) 'I am Creole, so I speak English. Cultural ambiguity and the "English"/Spanish bilingual-bicultural programme of Nicaragua's Atlantic coast', in Graddol, D., Thompson, L. and Byram, M. (eds) *Language and Culture*, British Studies in Applied Linguistics, 7, Clevedon: BAAL and Multilingual Matters.

—— (1995) '"Why go to school to learn Miskitu?" Changing constructs of bilingualism, education and literacy amongst the Miskitu of Nicaragua's Atlantic Coast', *International Journal of Educational Development*, 15, 3, pp. 245–63.

—— (1998) 'An interesting absence: the gendered study of language and linguistic diversity in Latin America', *International Journal of Educational Development*, 18, 3, pp. 161–79.

Freire, P. (1972, English edn) *Pedagogy of the Oppressed*, Harmondsworth: Penguin.

Galtung, J. (1994) *Human Rights in Another Key*, Cambridge: Polity.

Garagorri, X. and Eguilior, E. (1988) 'Desarrollo y situación actual de la enseñanza en las ikastolas', in Siguan (coord./ed.) (1988), pp. 35–83.

García Sendón, M. and Monteagudo Romero, E. (1983) 'La oficialidad del gallego: historia y actualidad', *Revista de Llengua i Dret*, 2, pp. 89–95.

Garmendía, C. (1994) 'El proceso de normalización lingüística en el País Vasco: datos de una década', *International Journal of the Sociology of Language*, 109, pp. 97–109.

Gee, J. (1990) *Social Linguistics and Literacies: Ideology in Discourses*, London/New York/Philadelphia: Falmer.

Gellner, E. (1983) *Nations and Nationalism*, Oxford: Blackwell.

—— (1994) *Encounters with Nationalism*, Oxford: Blackwell.

Generalitat de Catalunya (co-ordinator/ed.) (1989) *Dret lingüístic*, Barcelona: Generalitat de Catalunya.

Generalitat de Catalunya (1991) *El català recongut pel parlament europea*, Barcelona: Generalitat de Catalunya.

Gobierno Vasco (1990) *10 años de enseñanza bilingüe*, Vitoria/Gasteiz: Gobierno Vasco.

González Ollé, (1978) 'El establecimiento del castellano como lengua oficial', *Boletín de la Real Academia Española*, LXV, pp. 231–80.

Gracia, J. (2000) *Hispanic/Latino Identity: A Philosophical Perspective*, Oxford/Massachusetts: Blackwell.

Graham-Brown, S. (1991) *Education in the Developing World*, WUS (Germany).

Granda, G. de (1988) *Sociedad, historia y lengua en el Paraguay*, Bogotá: Instituto Caro y Cuervo.

Grillo, R. (ed.) (1989) *Social Anthropology and the Politics of Language*, London/New York: Routledge.

Guibernau, M. (1997) 'Nations without states: Catalonia, a case study', in Guibernau, M. and Rex, J. (eds) *The Ethnicity Reader: Nationalism, Multiculturalism and Migration*, Oxford: Polity, pp. 133–54.

Gutiérres, N. (1995) 'Indians without "patria", the claims for autonomy of the Zapatista revolt in Mexico', *Asen Bulletin*, 9, pp. 18–21.

Gwynne, R. and Kay, C. (eds) (1999) *Latin America Transformed: Globalization and Modernity*, London/Sydney/Auckland: Arnold.

Hamel, R.E. (1994a) 'Indigenous education in Latin America: policies and legal frameworks', in Skutnabb-Kangas, T. and Phillipson, R. (eds) (1994), pp. 271–89.

—— (1994b) 'Linguistic rights for Amerindian peoples in Latin America', in Skutnabb-Kangas and Phillipson (eds) (1994), pp. 289–305.

—— (1997a) 'Introduction: linguistic human rights in a sociolinguistic perspective', *International Journal of the Sociology of Language*, 127, pp. 1–25.

—— (1997b) 'Language conflict and language shift: a sociolinguistic framework for linguistic human rights', *International Journal of the Sociology of Language*, 127, pp. 105–35.

Hamilton, M., Barton, D. and Ivanic, R. (eds) (1994) *Worlds of Literacy*, Clevedon: Multilingual Matters/Toronto: Ontario Institute for Studies in Education.

Haugen, E. (1966) *Language Planning and Language Conflict: The Case of Modern Norwegian*, Cambridge: Harvard University Press.

Heiberg, M. (1980) 'Basques, anti-Basques and the moral community', in Grillo, R. (ed.) *'Nation' and 'State' in Europe: Anthropological Perspectives*, London: Academic Press, pp. 45–59.

—— (1989) *The Making of the Basque Nation*, Cambridge: Cambridge University Press.

Held, D., McGrew, A., Goldblatt, D. and Perraton, J. (1999) *Global Transformations: Politics, Economics and Culture*, Oxford: Polity.

Henderson, T. (1996) 'Language and identity in Galicia: the current orthographic debate', in Mar-Molinero and Smith (eds), pp. 237–55.

Hernández, F. (1983) *La identidad nacional en Cataluña*, Barcelona: Vicens Vives.

Hernández, F. and Mercadé, F. (eds) (1986) *Estructuras sociales y cuestión nacional en España*, Barcelona: Ariel.

Herr, R. and Polt, J.H.R. (eds) (1989) *Iberian Identity: Essays on the Nature of Identity in Portugal and Spain*, Berkeley: IIS, University of California.

Hidalgo, M. (1994) 'Bilingual education, nationalism and ethnicity in Mexico', *Language Problems and Language Planning*, 18, pp. 185–208.

Hill, J. (1989) 'Ambivalent language attitudes in modern Nahuatl', in Hamel, R.E., Lastra de Suárez, Y., and Muñoz Cruz, H. (eds) *Sociolingüística latinoamericana*, Mexico: Instituto de Investigaciones Antropológicas de la UNAM.

Hill, J. and Hill, K. (1986) *Speaking Mexicano. Dynamics of Synchronic Language on Central Mexico*, Tucson: University of Arizona Press.

Hirst, P. and Thompson, G. (eds) (1999, revised edn) *Globalization in Question*, Oxford: Polity.

Hobsbawm, E.J. (1990) *Nations and Nationalism since 1980*, Cambridge: Cambridge University Press.

Hoffmann, C. (ed.) (1995a) *Language, Culture and Communication in Contemporary Europe*, Clevedon: Multilingual Matters.

—— (1995b) 'Language planning at the crossroads: the case of contemporary Spain', in Hoffmann, C. (ed.) (1995a), pp. 93–111.

—— (1998) 'Luxembourg and the European Schools', in Cenoz and Genesee (eds) (1998), pp. 143–75.

Hornberger, N. (1988) *Bilingual Education and Language Maintenance: A Southern Peruvian Quechua Case*, Berlin: Mouton.

—— (1992) 'Literacy in South America', *Annual Review of Applied Linguistics*, 12, pp. 190–215.

—— (1994) 'Language policy and planning in South America', *Annual Review of Applied Linguistics*, 14, pp. 220–40.

—— (1995) 'Five vowels or three? Linguistics and politics in Quechua Language Planning in Peru', in Tollefson, (ed.) (1995), pp. 187–205.

Hornberger, N. and López, L.E. (1998) 'Policy, possibility and paradox: indigenous multilingualism and education in Peru and Bolivia', in Cenoz and Genesee (eds) (1998), pp. 206–42.

Howard-Malverde, R. and Canessa, A. (1995) 'The school in the Quechua and Aymara communities of highland Bolivia', *International Journal of Educational Development*, 15, 3, pp. 231–45.

Hutchinson, J. and Smith, A. (eds) (1994) *Nationalism*, Oxford: Oxford University Press.

Institut d'Estudis Autonòmics (1994) *La lengua de enseñanza en la legislación de Cataluña*, Barcelona: Generalitat de Catalunya.

International Journal of Sociology of Language (1992) 'Sociolinguistics in Mexico', 96.

Jou i Mirabent, L. (1998) 'Els principis de llengua pròpia i llengües oficials en l'articulat de la Llei 1/1998, de 7 de gener, de política lingüística', *Revista de Llengua i Dret*, 29, pp. 7–23.

Kaplan, R.B. and Baldauf, R.A. (1997) *Language Planning: From Practice to Theory*, Clevedon: Multilingual Matters.

Kedourie, E. (revised 3rd edn 1993) *Nationalism*, Oxford: Blackwell.

Kennedy, C. (ed.) (1984) *Language Planning and Language Education*, London: George Allen and Unwin.

Key, M.R. (1991) *Language Change in South American Indian Languages*, Philadelphia: University of Pennsylvania Press.

Klein, H. and Stark, L. (eds) (1985) *South American Indian Languages: Retrospect and Prospect*, Austin: University of Texas Press.

Kloss, H. (1969) 'Research possibilities in group bilingualism: a report', Quebec: International Center for Research on Bilingualism.

Lambert, R. (1999) 'A scaffolding for language policy', *International Journal of the Sociology of Language*, 137, pp. 3–27.

Language Problems and Language Planning, (1994) Special Issue: 'Mexico's language policy and diversity', 18, 3.

Lankshear, C. (1997) *Changing Literacies*, Buckingham/Philadelphia: Open University Press.

Lapesa, R. (1980, 8th edn) *Historia de la lengua española*, Madrid: Escelicer.

Laponce, J. (1984a) 'The French language in Canada: tensions between geography and politics', *Political Geography Quarterly*, 3, 2, pp. 91–104.

—— (1984b) *Langue et Territoire*, Quebec: Université de Laval.

Lara, L. (1992) 'Sociolingüística del diccionario del español de México', *International Journal of the Sociology of Language*, 96, pp. 19–35.

Lastra, Y. (1992) *Sociolingüística para hispanoamericanos. Una introducción*, Mexico: El Colegio de México.

Linz, J. (1973) 'Early state-building and late peripheral nationalism against the state: the case of Spain', in Eisentadt, S.N. and Rokkan, S. (eds) *Building States and Nations*, Vol II, London/Beverly Hills: Sage, pp. 32–116.

—— (1981) 'La crisis de un estado unitario; nacionalismos periféricos y regionalismo', in Acosta España, R. *et al.* (eds) *La España de las autonomías*, Madrid: Espasa-Calpe, Vol. II, pp. 651–752.

—— (1986) *Conflicto en Euskadi*, Madrid: Espasa Calpe.

Lipski, J.M. (1991) 'Clandestine Radio Broadcasting as a Sociolinguistic Microcosm', in Klee, C.A. (ed.) and Ramón-García, L.A. (assoc. ed.) *Sociolinguistics of the Spanish-Speaking World: Iberia, Latin America, United States*, Tempe, Arizona: Bilingual Press/ Prensa Bilingüe.

—— (1994) *Latin American Spanish*, London: Longman.

Llobera, J. (1994) *The God of Modernity: the Development of Nationalism in Western Europe*, London/Washington DC: Berg.

López García, A. (1985) *El rumor de los desarraigados*, Barcelona: Anagrama.

López, L.E. (1988) 'Balance y perspectivas de la educación bilingüe en Puno', in López, L.E. (ed.) *Pesquisas en lingüística andina*, Lima and Puno: Universidad Nacional del Altiplano/GTZ, pp. 79–106.

Lozano, E. (1990) 'Bibliography: Latin American Indian languages', *Latin American Indian Literatures Journal*, 6, 2, pp. 180–93.

Lynch, J. (1973) *The Spanish American Revolutions 1808–1826*, London: Weidenfeld and Nicolson.

Lyons, J. (1990) 'The past and future directions of federal bilingual education policy', in García and Baker (eds) (1995), pp. 1–15.

MacClancy, J. (1996) 'Bilingualism and multinationalism in the Basque Country', in Mar-Molinero and Smith (eds), pp. 207–21.

Mariátegui, J.C. (1973 edn) *Siete ensayos de interpretación de la realidad peruana*, Lima: Biblioteca Peruana.

Mar-Molinero, C. (1989) 'The teaching of Catalan in Catalonia', *Journal of Multilingual and Multicultural Development*, 10, 4, pp. 307–27.

—— (1990) 'Language policies in post-Franco Spain', in R. Clark *et al.* (eds) *Language and Power*, London: BAAL/CILT, pp. 52–64.

—— (1995) 'Catalan education policies: are Castilian-speakers persecuted?', *ACIS*, 8.1, pp. 49–56.

—— (1997) *The Spanish-Speaking World: A Practical Introduction to Sociolinguistic Issues*, London/New York: Routledge.

—— (in press) 'The Iberian peninsula: conflicting linguistic nationalisms', in Barbour, S. and Carmichael, C. (eds) *Language and Nationalism in Europe*, Oxford: Oxford University Press.

Mar-Molinero, C. and Stevenson, P. (1991) 'Language, geography and politics: the "territorial imperative" debate in the European context', *Language Problems and Language Planning*, 15, 2, pp. 162–77.

Mar-Molinero, C. and Smith, A. (eds) (1996) *Nationalism and the Nation in the Iberian Peninsula*, London/New York: Berg.

Marshall, D. (ed.) (1991) *Language Planning*, Amsterdam/Philadelphia: John Benjamins.

Martínez Ferrer, J. (1995) *Bilingüismo y enseñanza en Aragón*, Zaragoza: Edizions de l'Astral.

Maybin, J. (ed.) (1994) *Language and Literacy in Social Practice*, Clevedon: Multilingual Matters in association with The Open University.

McLaren, P. and Lankshear, C. (eds) (1994) *Politics of Liberation: Paths from Freire*, London/New York: Routledge.

Menéndez Pidal, R. (1947, 3rd edn) *la Lengua de Cristóbal Colón*, Madrid: Espasa-Calpe.

Milian i Massana, A. (1992) *Drets lingüístics i dret fonamental a l'educació*, Barcelona: Generalitat de Catalunya.

Mirambell i Abancó, A (1989) 'La desfiguració jurídica del concepte d'oficialitat lingüística: sentència del tribunal constitucional 74/1987', in Generalitat de Catalunya, pp. 51–9.

Mondéjar Camplán, J. (1981) *'Castellano' y 'Español': dos nombres para una lengua*, Granada: Ed Don Quijote.

Morales-González, D. and Torres, C. (eds) (1992) *Education Policy and Social Change: Experiences from Latin America*, Westport/London: Praeger.

Morren, R.C. (1988) 'Bilingual education: curriculum development in Guatemala', *Journal of Multilingual and Multicultural Development*, 9, 4, pp. 353–71.

Morris, N. (1996) 'Language and identity in twentieth century Puerto Rico', *Journal of Multilingual and Multicultural Development*, 17.1, pp. 17–32.

Mühlhäusler, P. (1990) '"Reducing" Pacific languages to writings', in Joseph, J.E. and Taylor, T.J. (eds) (1990) *Ideologies of Language*, London/New York: Routledge, pp. 189–206.

—— (1996) *Linguistic Ecology: Language Change and Linguistic Imperialism in the Pacific Region*, London/New York: Routledge.

Myhill, J. (1999) 'Identity, territoriality and minority language survival', *Journal of Multilingual and Multicultural Development*, 20, 1, pp. 34–51.

Nahmad, S. (1998) 'Derechos lingüísticos de los pueblos indígenas de México', *International Journal of the Sociology of Language*, 132, pp. 143–63.

Nairn, T. (1997) *Faces of Nationalism: Janus Revisited*, London/New York: Verso.

Narbona Jiménez, A. and Morillo-Velarde Pérez, R. (1987) *Las hablas andaluzas*, Cordoba: Cajasur.

Nelde, P. (1991) 'Language conflicts in multilingual Europe: prospects for 1993', in Coulmas (ed.), pp. 59–75.

Nelde, P., Labrie, N. and Williams, C.H. (1992) 'The principles of territoriality and personality in the solution of linguistic conflicts', *Journal of Multilingual and Multicultural Development*, 13, 5, pp. 387–407.

Nicolás i Amorós, M. (1998) *La història de la llengua catalana*, Valencia/Barcelona: Publicacions de L'Abadía de Montserrat.

Ninyoles, R. (1977) *Cuatro idiomas para un Estado*, Madrid: Cambio 16.

Niño-Murcia, M. (1997) 'Linguistic purism in Cuzco, Peru: a historical perspective', *Language Problems and Language Planning*, 21, 2, pp. 134–61.

Novo Mier, L. (1980) *El habla de Asturias*, Oviedo: Asturlibros.

Nunan, D. and Lam, A. (1998) 'Teacher education for multilingual contexts: models and issues', in Cenoz and Genesee (eds) (1998), pp. 117–43.

Nuñez Astrain, L. (1995) *La razón vasca*, Pais Vasco: Txalaparta.

Olaziregi, I. (1994) 'Evaluación de una experiencia de inmersión en el País Vasco', in Siguan (ed.) (1994), pp. 43–61.

O'Riagáin, P. (1997) 'Postmodernity and language policy: a need to refocus?', *Sociolinguistica*, 11, pp. 16–28.

Ozolins, U. (1996) 'Language policy and political reality', *International Journal of the Sociology of Language*, 118, pp. 181–201.

Patanayak, D.P. and Bayer, J.M. (1987) 'Laponce's "The French Language in Canada: Tensions between Politics and Geography" – a rejoinder', *Political Geography Quarterly*, 6, 3, pp. 251–63.

Patthey-Chavez, G.G. (1994) 'Language policy and planning in Mexico: indigenous language policy', *Annual Review of Applied Linguistics*, 14, pp. 200–20.

Paulston, C.B. (1972) 'Las escuelas bilingües in Peru: some comments on second language learning', *IRAL*, November 1972.

—— (1997) 'Epilogue: some concluding thoughts on linguistic human rights', *International Journal of the Sociology of Language*, 127, pp. 187–97.

Payán Sotomayor (1983) *El habla de Cadiz*, Cadiz: Quorum Libros Editores.

Penny, R. (1991) *A History of the Spanish Language*, Cambridge: Cambridge University Press.

Pennycook, A. (1998) 'The right to language: towards a situated ethics of language possibilities', *Language Sciences*, 20, 1, pp. 73–89.

Perivolaris, J. (1997) 'Travelling voices of Caribbean nationhood: bilingualism, translation and diaspora in the work of Julia Alvarez and Esmeralda Santiago', *Journal of Iberian and Latin American Studies*, 3.2, pp. 117–25.

Phillipson, R. (1992) *Linguistic Imperialism*, Oxford: Oxford University Press.

Pi i Margall, F. (1973 edn) *Las nacionalidades*, Madrid: Editorial Cuadernos para el Dialogo.

Plaza, P. and Albó, X. (1989) 'Educación bilingüe y planificación lingüística en Bolivia', *International Journal of the Sociology of Language*, 77, pp. 69–93.

Pool, J. (1996) 'Optimal language regimes for the European Union', *International Journal of the Sociology of Language*, 121, pp. 159–81.

Portocarrero, G. (1992) 'Peru: education for national identity ethnicity and Andean nationalism', in Morales-González and Torres (eds) (1992), pp. 69–82.

Pousada, A. (1996) 'Puerto Rico: on the horns of a Language Planning dilemma', *TESOL Quarterly*, 30.3, pp. 499–510.

Prat de la Riba, E. (1982 edn, Spanish translation) *La nacionalidad catalana*, Barcelona: Aymá.

Preston, P. (1993) *Franco: A Biography*, London: Harper Collins.

Puig i Pla, (1997) 'La declaració de drets lingüístics', *Llengua i Us*, 8, pp. 4–7.

Puiggrós, A. (1994) 'Politics, praxis and the personal: an Argentine assessment', in McLaren and Lankshear (eds) (1994), pp. 154–73.

Radcliffe, S. (1999) 'Civil society, social difference and political issues of identity and representation', in Gwynne and Kay (eds) (1999), pp. 203–25.

Radcliffe, S. and Westwood, S. (eds) (1993) *'Viva' Women and Popular Protest in Latin America*, London/New York: Routledge.

—— (1995) *Re-making the Nation: Identity and Politics in Latin America*, London/New York: Routledge.

Radio, S. (1980, 3rd edn 1989) 'Estudio sociolingüística sobre a normativización e normalización do galego' and 'Analise da Lei da Normalización Lingüística', in Aracil, L. *et al.*, *Problemática das linguas sen normalizar, situación do Galego e Alternativas*, Ourense: Galiza, pp. 129–70.

Ramón i Mimó, O. (1994) 'Plurilingüismo en las comunidades europeas', in Bastardas and Boix (eds) (1994), pp. 155–67.

Reniu i Tresserras, M. (1994) *Planificació lingüística: estructuras i legislació*, Barcelona: Generalitat de Catalunya.

Richards, J.B. (1989) 'Mayan Language Planning for bilingual education in Guatemala', *International Journal of the Sociology of Language*, 77, pp. 93–115.

Rivera, J. (1992) 'Bolivia: society, state and education in crisis', in Morales-Gómez and Torres (eds) (1992), pp. 23–35.

Rodríguez, C. (ed.) (1997) *Latin Looks: Images of Latinas and Latinos in the US Media*, Boulder: Westview.

Rona, J.P. (1975) 'The social and cultural status of Guaraní in Paraguay', in Bright, W. (ed.) *Sociolinguistics*, The Hague/Paris: Mouton, pp. 277–98.

Ros, M, Cano, H. and Huici, C. (1988) 'Language and intergroup perception in Spain', in W. Gudykanst (ed.) *Language and Ethnic Identity*, Clevedon: Multilingual Matters, pp. 87–103.

Rubin, J. (1977) 'Bilingual education and Language Planning', in Spolsky, B. and Cooper, R. (eds) *Frontiers of Bilingual Education*, Rowley, Mass: Newbury House, pp. 282–95.

Rubin, J. and Jernudd, B.H. (eds) (1971) *Can Language be Planned?*, Honolulu: East West Center and University of Hawaii Press.

Ruiz, R. (1994) 'Language policy and planning in the US', *Annual Review of Applied Linguistics*, 14, pp. 111–26.

Salvador, G. (1987) *Lengua española y lenguas de España*, Barcelona: Ariel.

—— (1992) *Política lingüística y sentido común*, Madrid: Istmo.

Sanchis Guarner, M. (1972) *La llengua dels valencians*, Valencia.

Santamaría Conde, X. (1985) 'A lei de normalización lingüística do idioma galego' *Revista de Llengua i Dret*, 5, pp. 205–17.

Sbert, M. and Vives, M. (1994) 'Las lenguas en el sistema educativo de las Iles Balears', in Siguan (coordinator/ed.) (1994), pp. 109–31.

Schiffman, H.F. (1996) *Linguistic Culture and Language Policy*, London: Routledge.

Schirmer, J. (1993) 'The seeking of truth and the gendering of consciousness. The comadres of El Salvador and the Conavigua widows of Guatemala', in Radcliffe and Westwood (eds) (1993), pp. 30–65.

Schnapper, D. (1996) 'Beyond the opposition: "civic" nation versus "ethnic" nation', *ASEN Bulletin*, 12, pp. 4–11.

Serrano, C. (1998) 'Conciencia de la crisis, conciencias en crisis', in Pan-Montojo, J. (ed.) *Más se perdió en Cuba: España 1898 y la crisis de fin de siglo*, Madrid: Alianza, pp. 335–405.

Seton-Watson, (1977) *Nations and States: An Enquiry into the Origins of and the Politics of Nationalism*, London: Methuen.

Sierra, J. (1994) 'Modelos de enseñanza bilingüe: su resultado y su futuro', in Siguan (ed.) (1994), pp. 61–79.

Siguan, M. (ed.) (1980) *La problemática del bilingüismo en el estado español*, Vizcaya: Universidad del País Vasco.

—— (ed.) (1982) *Lenguas y educación en el ámbito del estado español*, Barcelona: Universidad de Barcelona.

—— (1992) *España plurilingüe*, Barcelona: Ariel.

—— (English translation, 1993) *Multilingual Spain*, Amsterdam: Swets & Zeitlinger.

—— (coordinator/ed.) (1994) *Las lenguas de la escuela*, Barcelona: Horsori.

—— (1996) *La europa de las lenguas*, Madrid: Alianza.

Skutnabb-Kangas, T. (1984) *Bilingualism or not. The Education of Minorities*, Clevedon: Multilingual Matters.

Skutnabb-Kangas, T. and Cummins, J. (1988) *Minority Education: from Shame to Struggle*, Clevedon: Multilingual Matters.

Skutnabb-Kangas, T. and Phillipson, R. (eds) (1994a) *Linguistic Human Rights: Overcoming linguistic discrimination*, Berlin: Mouton de Gruyter.

Skutnabb-Kangas, T. and Phillipson, R. (1994b) 'Linguistic human rights past and present', in Skutnabb-Kangas and Phillipson (eds) (1994a), pp. 71–111.

Smith, A.D. (1991) *National Identity*, Harmondsworth: Penguin.

—— (1995) *Nations and Nationalism in a Global Era*, Oxford: Polity Press.

—— (1996) 'Memory and modernity: reflections on Ernest Gellner's theory of nationalism', *Nations and Nationalism*, 2, 3, pp. 389–407.

—— (1998) *Nationalism and Modernism: A Critical Survey of Recent Theories of Nations and Nationalism* London/New York: Routledge.

Solé, C. (1990) *Bibliografía sobre el español de América (1920–1986)*, Bogotá: Instituto Caro y Cuervo.

Solé, Y.R. (1995) 'Language, nationalism and ethnicity in the Americas', *International Journal of the Sociology of Language*, 116, pp. 111–137.

Stavenhagen, R. (1988) *Derechos indígenas y derechos humanos en América Latina*, Mexico: IIDH Colegio de México.

Street, B. (ed.) (1993) *Cross-cultural Approaches to Literacy*, Oxford: Oxford University Press.

Stromquist, N. (ed.) (1992) *Women and Education in Latin America*, Boulder/London: Lynne Rienner.

Strubell, M. and Romani, J. (1986) *Perspectives de la llengua catalana a l'àrea barcelonina (comentaris a una enquesta)*, Barcelona: Generalitat de Catalunya.

—— (1998) 'Les dades lingüístiques de 1996', *Llengua i Us*, 12, 2, pp. 4–8.

Tamames, R. and L. (1980, 6th edn, 1992) *Introducción a la constitución española*, Madrid: Alianza.

Tatalovich, R. (1995) 'Voting on official English language referenda in five states: what kind of backlash against Spanish-speakers?', *Language Problems and Language Planning*, 19.1, pp. 47–59.

Tejerina, B. (1992) *Nacionalismo y Lengua*, Madrid: CIS.

—— (1996) 'Language and Basque nationalism: collective identity, social conflict and institutionalisation', in Mar-Molinero and Smith (eds) (1996), pp. 221–37.

Tello Díaz, C. (1995) *Chiapas: la rebelión de las cañadas*, Madrid: Acento.

Thompson, R.W. (1992) 'Spanish as a pluricentric language', in Clyne (ed.) (1992), pp. 45–70.

Tollefson, J. (1991) *Planning Language; Planning Inequality*, London: Longman.

—— (ed.) (1995) *Power and Inequality in Language Education*, Cambridge: Cambridge University Press.

Torres, C.A. (1990) *The Politics of Non Formal Education in Latin America*, Westport/London: Praeger.

Torres, L. (1991) 'The study of US Spanish varieties: some theoretical and methodological issues', in Klee and Ramos García (eds) (1991), pp. 255–71.

Truchot, C. (1991) 'Towards a language policy for the European Community', in Marshall (ed.) (1991), pp. 87–105.

Trueba, H. (1989) *Raising Silent Voices*, Rowley, Mass.: Newbury House.

Turi, J-G. (1995) 'Typology of language legislation', in Skutnabb-Kangas and Phillipson (eds) (1995), pp. 111–21.

Unamuno, M de (1957 edn) *En torno al casticismo*, Madrid: Espasa Calpe.

Valverdú, F. (1984) 'A sociolinguistic history of catalan', *International Journal of the Sociology of Language*, 47, pp. 13–29.

Vélez, J.A. and Schweers, C.W. (1993) 'A US colony at a linguistic crossroads: the decision to make Spanish the official language of Puerto Rico', *Language Problems and Language Planning*, 17, pp. 117–39.

Vernet i Llobet, J. (1994) La regulación del plurilingüismo en la administración española', in Bastardas and Boix (eds), pp. 115–41.

Vicens Vives, (1972) *Aproximación a la historia de España*, Barcelona: Vicens Vives.

Vilar, P. (1967) *A Brief History of Spain*, Oxford: Pergamon.

Vincent, R.J. (1986) *Human Rights and International Relations*, Cambridge: Cambridge University Press.

Von Gleich, U. (1989) *Educación primaria bilingüe intercultural en América Latina*, Eschborn: GTZ.

—— (1994) 'Language spread policy: the case of Quechua in the Andean republics of Bolivia, Ecuador and Peru', *International Journal of the Sociology of Language*, 107, pp. 77–115.

Wardaugh, R. (1986, 2nd edn 1992) *An Introduction to Sociolinguistics*, Oxford: Blackwell.

—— (1987) *Languages in Competition*, Oxford: Blackwell.

Watts, R. (1991) 'Linguistic minorities and language conflict in Europe: learning from the Swiss experience', in Coulmas (ed.), pp. 75–103.

Whitehead, A. (1996) 'Spain, European regions and city state', in Mar-Molinero and Smith (eds) (1996), pp. 255–73.

Williams, C.H. (1984) 'Ideology and the interpretation of minority cultures', *Political Geography Quarterly*, 3/2, pp. 105–35.

—— (1991) 'Language planning and social change: ecological speculations', in Marshall (ed.) (1991), pp. 53–75.

Williams, G. (1992) *Sociolinguistics*, London: Routledge.

Williams, L. (1995) 'Percepciones de identidad: el problema de la denominación lingüística en España', *Tesserae*, Vol. 1, pp. 263–75.

Woolard, K. (1989) *Doubletalk: Bilingualism and the Politics of Ethnicity in Catalonia*, Stanford: University of Stanford Press.

—— (1991) 'Linkages of language and ethnic identity: changes in Barcelona 1980–1987', in Dow, J.R. (1991) *Language and Ethnicity*, Amsterdam/Philadelphia: John Benjamins, pp. 61–81.

—— (1998) Review of A. Branchadell's 'Liberalisme i normalització lingüística', in *Language Problems and Language Planning*, 22.3, pp. 286–88.

Yáñez Cossio, C. (1992) 'Ecuador: basic Quechua education', in Morales-Gómez and Torres (eds) (1992), pp. 47–57.

Zentella, A.C. (1985) 'The fate of Spanish in the United States: the Puerto Rican experience', in Manes, J. and Wolfson, N. (eds) (1985) *The Language of Inequality*, Berlin: Mouton, pp. 43–59.

—— (1990) 'Returned migration, language and identity: Puerto Rican bilingualism dos worlds/two mundos', *International Journal of the Sociology of Language*, 84, pp. 81–101.

—— (1997a) *Growing Up Bilingual*, Oxford: Blackwell.

—— (1997b) 'The hispanophobia of the Official English movement in the US', *International Journal of the Sociology of Language*, 127, pp. 71–86.

Index

Printed in the United States
100057LV00004B/25/A

9 780415 156554